GDPR: A Game of Snakes and Ladders

T0362086

For many small businesses, organisations, clubs, artists, faith groups, voluntary organisations/charities and sole traders, applying the General Data Protection Regulation (GDPR) has been like playing a game of "Snakes and Ladders". As soon as you move along the board and climb a ladder, a snake appears, which takes you right back to where you started. Conflicting advice abounds and there is nowhere for these individuals to go for simple answers all in one place. With the threat of fines seeming around every corner, now more than ever is the time for smaller organisations to get to grips with GDPR so that they can demonstrate their compliance.

GDPR: A Game of Snakes and Ladders is an easy to read reference tool, which uses simple language in bite size easily signposted chapters. Adopting a no-nonsense approach, the Regulation is explained so that organisations can comply with the minimum of fuss and deliver this compliance in the shortest timeframe without the need to resort to expensive consultants or additional staff. The book is supported by a variety of easy to follow case studies, example documents and fact sheets. The author signposts warnings and important requirements (snakes) and hints and suggestions (ladders) and also provides a section on staff training and a Game of Snakes and Ladders training slide pack. Additional resources are available on the companion website.

This user-friendly book, written by a Data Protection Officer and business management specialist will help you understand the Regulation, where it applies in your organisation and how to achieve compliance (and win at the compliance game).

Samantha Alford is an established technical author, instructor and business management specialist and Data Protection Officer. She has over 35 years of experience in compliance, governance and oversight in the public, private and charity sectors. She is a Director and Owner of PPP Management Ltd.

GDPR: A Game of Snakes and Ladders

How Small Businesses Can Win at the Compliance Game

Samantha Alford

Routledge
Taylor & Francis Group

LONDON AND NEW YORK

First published 2020 by Routledge

2 Park Square, Milton Park, Abingdon, Oxon OX14 4RN
605 Third Avenue, New York, NY 10017

Routledge is an imprint of the Taylor & Francis Group, an informa business

First issued in paperback 2022

Publisher's Note

The publisher has gone to great lengths to ensure the quality of this reprint
but points out that some imperfections in the original copies may be apparent.

British Library Cataloguing-in-Publication Data
A catalogue record for this book is available from the British
Library

Library of Congress Cataloging-in-Publication Data
A catalog record has been requested for this book

ISBN: 978-0-367-43545-5 (hbk)
ISBN: 978-1-03-233698-5 (pbk)
DOI: 10.4324/9781003004790

Typeset in Bembo
by Swales & Willis, Exeter, Devon, UK

To Tom, without your encouragement this would not have been possible, and Ken for providing much needed graphics support.

Contents

List of tables   xi
List of figures   xii
List of case studies   xiv
List of quotes   xvi
Preface   xvii

1 What is the General Data Protection Regulation (GDPR)?   1

Basic concept of GDPR 3
Key principles or GDPR 3
The link to previous legislation 5
The European Data Protection Board and national
  Supervisory Authorities 5
Who has to comply with GDPR? 6
What has GDPR changed? 7
The penalties for Data Breaches 8
GDPR compliance as an ongoing journey 11
What must you do? 11
Appendix 1 13

2 GDPR terminology   18

GDPR terms – people or entities 18
GDPR terms – types of personal data 19
Key terms – actions 20
GDPR terms – consent 22
GDPR terms – the principles of GDPR 23
GDPR terms – lawful basis 23
GDPR terms – subject rights 23
Appendix 2 26

3 **The GDPR Articles and Recitals**   31

The Recitals of GDPR 31
The GDPR Articles explained "in a nutshell" 34

4 **Applying GDPR to your organisation**   83

How does GDPR apply to my business? 83
Build awareness 87
Understand the data 88
Communication 98

5 **Data Controllers, Data Processors and the Data
   Protection Officer**   101

Definition of processing 102
Data Controllers 103
Data Processors 110
Security of processing 113
Data Protection Officer (DPO) 114

6 **Analysing what personal data you hold**   117

What is personal data? 117
Special categories of information 121
What is processing? 126
What does GDPR mean by identified? 126
Personal data in the case study organisation 130
Deciding what information can be used to identify a person 130
Fill in the personal data grid for your organisation 132

7 **Privacy Policies and Notices**   134

Why do I need a Privacy Policy? 134
What information should a privacy document contain? 134
How should privacy information be presented? 137
Deciding what your privacy document includes 138
Benefits of a Privacy Policy 140
The layered approach 140
Creating a Privacy Notice/statement 140
GDPR consent 143

8 Recording your processing activities   147

Why do I need to map the data? 150
Is a Data Flow Analysis or Data Audit compulsory? 151
How long will it take? 151
Understanding how data flows in an organisation 151
Data Audit 153
Data security 165
Data Protection Impact Assessment (DPIA) 167
Data Subjects' rights 169

9 Sharing information electronically   170

Email 171
Direct marketing 178
Physical security 183
WhatsApp and Messenger 184
Email security and the data governance policy 184

10 Data Breaches   185

What is a Data Breach? 185
Reporting a Data Breach 186
Planning how to deal with a breach 189
Staff training 192

11 Keeping data safe   193

The risks to your data 194
The GDPR data security requirement 195
What does data security mean? 195
Identify data security risks 195
Put in place data security measures 196
Physical security measures 197
Cybersecurity measures 197
Testing your security measures 199
ISO 27001/2:2013 199
Data security terms 200
Keeping yourself "cyber safe" 200

12 Retaining and deleting data   203

Retaining data 203
Anonymisation 205

Pseudonymisation 205
Deletion 206
The right of erasure 206
Retaining data from dashcams/helmet cams/CCTV 211

13 An individual's rights under GDPR   212

Providing information to individuals 212
Data Subjects' rights 212
Individual's data access options 214
Subject Access Request 215
Freedom of Information Act 224
Accessing educational and medical records 227
Individuals' rights – exemptions 229

14 GDPR training   231

The requirement 231
What should the training include? 232
Guidance on handling, retaining, sharing and deleting data 237
*Details of how the organisation uses marketing including
   direct under GDPR 238*
Data minimisation 238
Individuals' rights 238

GDPR resource links   240

Index   245

Tables

1.1	Supervisory Authority Contact Details	6
1.2	Fines Imposed for Data Breaches	10
3.1	Cross Reference of GDPR Articles and Recitals	31
4.1	Examples of Personal Data Held by Exemplar Holistics	89
4.2	Personal Data Movement Questions – Exemplar Holistics	90
6.1	Direct and Indirect Identification	129
7.1	Information That Should Always Be Provided to Data Subjects	135
7.2	Information That Is Only Required When It Is Applicable	136
8.1	Data Audit Database – Kidz United Football Club	158
8.2	Kidz United Football Club – Data Sources	158
8.3	Lawful Basis for Processing – Kidz United Football Club	160
8.4	Reason for Processing – Kidz United Football Club	160
8.5	Access to Personal Data – Kidz United Football Club	161
8.6	Role in Relation to Personal Data – Kidz United Football Club	161
8.7	Collection and Update of Data – Kidz United Football Club	163
8.8	Format and Storage of Data – Kidz United Football Club	164
8.9	Data Retention Database – Kidz United Football Club	165
8.10	Complete Data Audit – Kidz United Football Club	166
10.1	High-profile Data Breach Examples	186
10.2	Supervisory Authority Fines and Sanctions Imposed	187
11.1	Common Cybersecurity Terms	201
14.1	GDPR Key Terms	234

Figures

1.1	Where GDPR Applies	2
2.1	People/Entities Identified in GDPR	18
2.2	Types of Personal Data	21
2.3	Choosing a Lawful Basis for Processing	24
4.1	GDPR Building Blocks	83
4.2	Simple Date Flow Diagram – Exemplar Holistics	91
4.3	High Level Data Map Diagram – Exemplar Holistics	92
4.4	Extract from Exemplar Holistics Data Audit Table	95
5.1	Data Processing Terms	102
5.2	Data Controller Decisions	103
5.3	Data Processor Decisions	111
6.1	Types of Personal Data	118
6.2	Exemplar Holistics Personal Data Analysis	131
6.3	Personal Data in Your Organisation	132
7.1	Simple Privacy Sign	139
7.2	Consent Boxes Must Not Be Pre-Filled	144
8.1	Exemplar Holistics Personal Data Analysis	152
8.2	Personal Data Flow Questionnaire for Exemplar Holistics	153
8.3	Exemplar Holistics Data Flow Chart	154
8.4	Detailed Data Flow – Exemplar Holistics	155
8.5	Lawful Basis for Processing	159
9.1	Email Addresses	172
9.2	Using "To" in Emails	173
9.3	Using "CC" in Emails	174
9.4	Using "BCC" in Emails	174
9.5	Simple Document Protection	176
9.6	Email Tracking	177
9.7	Pre-Filled "Opt In"	181
9.8	Informed and Specific "Opt In"	181
9.9	Example of a Clear Re-Permissioning Email	183
10.1	Simple Data Breach Reporting Flow Chart	189

10.2   Simple Example Data Breach Log Entry   191
11.1   Small Business Cybersecurity Statistics   194
12.1   Retaining Data in an Organisation   204
12.2   Request for Erasure Checklist   209
13.1   Individual Data Access Options   214
13.2   SAR Flow Chart   219
13.3   Flow Chart for Responding to a FOI Request   228
14.1   Our Organisation's Personal Data Honeycomb   235
14.2   Data Flows   237

Case studies

1.1	Selling Information On	7
4.1	Registration with the Supervisory Authority	85
4.2	Exemplar Holistics	88
4.3	CCTV Risk Analysis	94
4.4	Sharing Information Incorrectly	97
5.1	Controllers and Processors	101
5.2	Joint Controllers	108
6.1a	Considering Information in Relation to an Individual – Use of the Data Has an Impact on the Individual	119
6.1b	Considering Information in Relation to an Individual – Data Does Not Relate to the Individual	119
6.1c	Considering Information in Relation to an Individual – the Purpose for Which the Data Is Being Processed Makes the Information Personal Data	119
6.1d	Considering Information in Relation to an Individual – the Content Is About or Linked to an Individual	120
6.1e	Considering Information in Relation to an Individual – the Purpose of Processing the Information Changes in the Hands of a Second Organisation	120
6.2	Identifying an Individual by Name	127
6.3	Identifying an Individual by an Online Identifier	128
6.4	Indirect Identification Using Physical Characteristics	128
6.5	Identification Using Information Held Elsewhere in the Organisation	130
8.1	SME Organisations' Requirement to Document Processing Activities	148
8.2	Kidz United Football Club Data Audit	157
9.1	Email Forwarding	172
9.2	Sharing Information Incorrectly	173

11.1   Data Security of References   196
12.1   Individual Exercising the Right to Be Forgotten   208
13.1a Identifying the Individual Making a SAR   221
13.1b Identifying the Individual Making a SAR   221

Quotes

1.1   Article 5 of GDPR – Principles   4
2.1   Article 4(11) of GDPR – Consent   22
4.1   Article 4(1) of GDPR – Personal Data   87
5.1   Article 4(7) of GDPR – Data Controller   103
5.2   Article 24 of GDPR – Data Controller Responsibilities   104
5.3   Article 40 of GDPR – Codes of Conduct   106
5.4   Article 4(8) of GDPR – Data Processor   110
5.5   Article 28(3) of GDPR – General Responsibilities
of Processors   112
5.6   Article 37(1) of GDPR – Designation of a DPO   114
6.1   Article 4(1) of GDPR – Personal Data   117
6.2   Article 6 of GDPR – Lawful Basis for Processing   121
6.3   Article 9 of GDPR – Processing of Special Categories of
Personal Data   123
6.4   Article 4(2) of GDPR – Processing   126
7.1   Article 4(11) of GDPR – Consent   143
8.1   Articles 5 and 30 of GDPR – Record of Processing
Activities   149
8.2   Article 35 of GDPR – DPIA   167
11.1   Article 5(1) of GDPR – Principles Relating to Processing of
Personal Data   193
14.1   Articles 39(1) and 47(2) of GDPR – GDPR Awareness
Training   232
14.2   Article 4(2) of GDPR – Processing Data   234

Preface

There is much that has been written on the subject of GDPR both in books and online. A lot of this information is focussed on large enterprises that process highly sensitive information about large numbers of people. These organisations are likely to have their own "in house" GDPR advice and in many cases their own Data Protection Officer (DPO) and a team to keep them compliant. Smaller organisations have had to seek help and guidance direct from their supervisory authority or from consultants, websites and books on the subject.

This book is written to address the needs of the smaller organisations, be they businesses, clubs, charities, artists, schools, faith groups or sole traders. Many know that the Regulation applies to them but have no idea where to start on their journey to compliance.

Based on my experience I have tried to make this book as user-friendly as possible. With the aim of helping the reader to understand the Regulation and how it applies in their setting so that they can formulate a plan to achieve compliance. The simple no-nonsense approach used is at odds to some of the more complex guidance on the topic of GDPR. I make no apology for this. I believe that smaller organisations want to comply with the Regulation as quickly as possible, with the minimum of fuss, and get back to their core business.

As I was writing the book and developing the accompanying training package it struck me that complying with the legislation is a bit like playing a game of "Snakes and Ladders" (hence the title of this book). As you move along the board of day to day life you encounter something that helps you move further more quickly (a ladder), but every so often something takes you backwards (a snake). To help with training, I therefore developed a game of "Snakes and Ladders", which is available on the companion website at www.pppmanagement.co.uk/resources.

Structure of the book

The book follows an easy to use format. It contains case studies, quotes from the legislation and is interspersed with hints and guidance from the author, which are signposted by Snakes or Ladders in the margins.

    warnings or important requirements

    hints and suggestions

The book is set out in 14 chapters, with each chapter concentrating on a different subject area.

Chapter 1 – A basic overview of the GDPR

Discusses where the legislation applies and who has to comply with it. The key concepts are outlined and the principles on which processing must be based are given.

Chapter 2 – The main terms used in GDPR and their application within a business context

Contains an easy to use alphabetised list of the main terms used in GDPR. The roles of Data Subject, Controller and Processor are all discussed and the rights of Data Subjects are outlined.

Chapter 3 – The 99 Articles of the GDPR "in a nutshell"

The main purpose of this chapter is to distil the complex legal terminology in the legislation into terms that the reader will be able to understand. At the beginning of the chapter is a cross reference table of the Articles and recitals of GDPR.

Chapter 4 – How to apply the GDPR in your organisation

Covers how the legislation applies and provides guidance on how to decide if you are a Data Controller or Processor. A case study is used to allow the reader to understand the application of the legislation in an easy to follow setting.

Chapter 5 – The roles and responsibilities of the Data Controller, Data Processor and Data Protection Officer

Explains the decisions that Controllers and Processors make in relation to data, their roles and who has ultimate responsibility for the data being processed. The need to record processing activities and penalties for non-compliance are highlighted. The chapter concludes with a discussion of the role and impartiality of the Data Protection Officer (DPO) and when you should appoint one.

Chapter 6 – Analysing the data an organisation holds

Discusses the various types of personal data and how it can be used to identify a person. A useful "honeycomb" is provided to aid understanding. Case study examples are used to highlight different areas where content may be about or linked to an individual.

Chapter 7 – Privacy documents

The chapter includes practical guidance on creating a Privacy Notice/Statement including the mandatory information that must be included. It covers why a policy is needed, the benefits of a layered approach, what a policy should contain and how it should be presented. There is also a section on GDPR Consent, its definition in GDPR and how to apply it.

Chapter 8 – Recording activities documentation

Keeping a record of the activities being carried is mandatory for most organisations. This will inevitably need to include a document that describes the process you have in place to protect personal data. The various tools of data maps, flow charts, questionnaires and databases are all discussed and detailed case studies are used to explain the process further (these are available on the book's companion website).

Chapter 9 – Sharing information electronically

Discusses the common pitfalls when sharing information and the potential changes that the new legislation has made to direct marketing. There is basic guidance on cybersecurity and ideas on how to keep your data and the personal data of others safe.

Chapter 10 – Data Breaches

Describes what Data Breaches are, examples and a summary of fines and sanctions that organisations have been subject to as a result of breaches. How to recognise a breach and what to do in the event of a breach including reporting it and investigating it and the role of the Supervisory Authority.

Chapter 11 – Keeping the data the organisation holds safe

GDPR places an obligation on organisations to protect the information that they hold about individuals. The chapter discusses the risks posed to data and then describes security measures that can be put in place to protect that data (both physical and cybersecurity measures are discussed. There is a useful table of Data Security Terms at the end of the chapter.

Chapter 12 – Retaining and deleting data

One of the key tenants of GDPR is the minimisation of data. The chapter discusses the best way to go about the process of managing how long you keep data. It discusses the individual's rights of erasure, advice on how to delete data, archiving and concludes with a section on Retaining Data from Dashcams/Helmet cams/CCTV.

Chapter 13 – Rights of individuals

The rights of individuals as Data Subjects have been greatly improved with GDPR. The chapter discusses the right of individuals to obtain a copy of the personal data that an organization collects about them by submitting a Subject Access Request. Other access requests such as Freedom of Information Requests and Requests for specialist (e.g. medical) records are also discussed.

Chapter 14 – Staff training

The chapter provides advice for large and small organisations. Describing the training available, be this classroom training courses (for DPOs, Risk and Compliance staff and senior management), self-service style courses or "in house" training. To assist the reader there are a series of PowerPoint slide packs and a game of "GDPR" Snakes and Ladders available via the companion website.

The legislation

The GDPR legislation is made up of 99 Articles and 173 Recitals.

At some points in the book it is necessary to quote directly from the legislation. When this happens, the relevant article is introduced before the text is provided. It will look like the following example.

Article 4 of GDPR defines consent (*Article 4(11), EU GDPR, "Definitions"*). The exact text is extracted below:

> *"consent" of the data subject means any freely given, specific, informed and*   Article 4
> *unambiguous indication of the data subject's wishes by which he or she, by*   (11)
> *a statement or by a clear affirmative action, signifies agreement to the*
> *processing of personal data relating to him or her.*

Because the legislation is complex, each of the 99 Articles are explained "in a nutshell" in Chapter 3. Not every part of each Article is included but the main point(s) are covered.

The Recitals explain the Articles in more depth and contain examples to clarify difficult points. A cross reference of which recitals relate to each of the Articles is provided.

National Supervisory Authorities

All the National Supervisory Authorities are listed in Appendix 1 of Chapter 1. Some are more advanced than others in their adoption of the legislation. Therefore, many of the examples given are UK related as the ICO in the UK has provided a greater body of guidance than many other nations have thus far.

Open Government material

Information from the UK ICO and the UK National Cyber Security Centre have been included under the Open Government Licence v2.0. Reference links are provided to these organisations in the Resources section of the book and at the appropriate position in the text.

Chapter 1

What is the General Data Protection Regulation (GDPR)?

 If you keep someone's name and contact details in any form of database (be these paper files or on the computer) and you use that information for business within the EU then the GDPR applies to you. There are only a few exceptions such as if the processing is for purely personal use or law enforcement.

General Data Protection Regulation (GDPR) is the 2018 European Union Regulation on data protection and privacy for individuals. It enshrines the necessity to keep personal information private.

This chapter provides and introduction to the Regulation outlining the key components and principles of GDPR. It provides the reader with an overview of where the legislation applies, what has changed from previous data protection legislation and what these changes mean for business. It is designed as an overview for those wishing to understand more about how it will affect them and their businesses. The chapter concludes with a section on actions that small and medium size businesses should take in order to ensure that they are complainant with this relatively "new" Regulation.

Although GDPR appears quite complex at first glance, it is based on the very simple concept that individuals have a right to keep their personal data private, and have the right to understand and decide what happens to this information.

The legislation applies throughout Europe and will apply in the UK irrespective of Brexit. This is because the UK Data Protection Act was updated in May 2018 to replicate GDPR. On exit from the EU the UK-GDPR will come into effect which mirrors the EU GDPR legislation.

Getting data protection wrong can have a significant impact both on the individuals about whom data is being processed and the business processing the data. The fines that can be imposed on a business or organisation by the regulatory bodies are significant. Therefore, whatever the size of the organisation, it is essential that you take GDPR seriously. No matter how much personal data you hold, you must ensure that you comply with GDPR.

GDPR consolidated all the previous data privacy laws from across Europe. It is also a vehicle to protect the privacy of the individual (be they an EU citizen, a person living or working in the EU or someone whose data is processed by an entity based in the EU). Figure 1.1 shows these three instances where the GDPR applies.

In the UK, the EU (Withdrawal) Act 2018 gives the government regulation-making powers to transitionally recognise all EEA countries as having "adequate" systems of data protection (from the UK). It is unclear at the time of writing if this will be reciprocated by the EU, so UK companies wishing to do business in Europe after Brexit have been recommended to put safeguards in place so that they can pass an "adequacy" test. In order to pass this "adequacy" test, organisations will have to comply with GDPR and have suitable contracts in place with their Processors.

Any information that relates to an **identifiable** person is referred to in GDPR as "personal data". It doesn't matter whether the individual could be directly or indirectly identified through this data.

This means that personal data can include names, contact details, CCTV, photographs, car registrations, as well as dates of birth, credit card details, etc. (Personal data is covered in more detail in Chapter 6 on p. 117.)

Personal data can be held in paper files, on a phone or in a computer database. But, irrespective of how you hold the data, **all** information that is held on file is covered by the legislation.

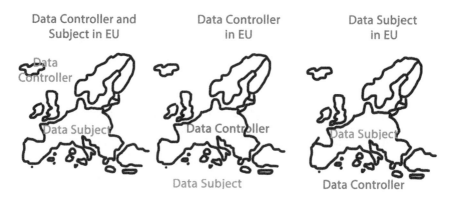

Figure 1.1 Where GDPR Applies

Basic concept of GDPR

The basic concept of GDPR is that processing should be **lawful, fair and transparent**.

- In order to collect and use personal data the organisation must have valid grounds under the GDPR (this is known as a "lawful basis").
- The data must only be processed in a way that is fair. Most especially data must not be processed in a way that is unduly detrimental, unexpected or misleading to the individuals concerned.
- The organisation must be clear, open and honest (transparent) with people from the start about how they plan to use an individual's personal data.

Key principles of GDPR

The six principles on which processing must be based are:

1. Processing must be lawful, fair and transparent.
2. Data may only be collected for specified, explicit and legitimate purposes. You may not process it subsequently in a way that is incompatible with the original purpose.
3. The data should be adequate, relevant and limited only that which is necessary to suit the purpose of your processing.
4. Data should be accurate (and kept up to date if necessary).
5. Data should be kept in a format that permits Data Subjects to be identified for no longer than is necessary to suit the purpose of the processing.
6. Data should be kept secure (this includes protecting it against unauthorised/unlawful processing as well as accidental loss, destruction or damage).

In addition to the six principles listed, the seventh principle of GDPR is the need for organisations to be able to **demonstrate** that they comply with the six principles listed.

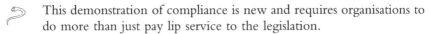 This demonstration of compliance is new and requires organisations to do more than just pay lip service to the legislation.

The key principles at the heart of the general data protection regime are set out in Article 5 of the GDPR (*Article 5, EU GDPR, "Principles relating to processing of personal data"*). The exact text is extracted in Quote 1.1.

QUOTE 1.1   ARTICLE 5 OF GDPR – PRINCIPLES

1. *Personal data shall be:*   Article 5.1

    *   processed lawfully, fairly and in a transparent manner in   Article 5.1(a)
        relation to the data subject ("lawfulness, fairness and
        transparency");

    *   collected for specified, explicit and legitimate purposes   Article 5.1(b)
        and not further processed in a manner that is incompa-
        tible with those purposes; further processing for archiving
        purposes in the public interest, scientific or historical
        research purposes or statistical purposes shall, in accor-
        dance with Article 89(1), not be considered to be incom-
        patible with the initial purposes ("purpose limitation");

    *   adequate, relevant and limited to what is necessary in   Article 5.1(c)
        relation to the purposes for which they are processed
        ("data minimisation");

    *   accurate and, where necessary, kept up to date; every   Article 5.1(d)
        reasonable step must be taken to ensure that personal
        data that are inaccurate, having regard to the purposes
        for which they are processed, are erased or rectified
        without delay ("accuracy");

    *   kept in a form which permits identification of data   Article 5.1(e)
        subjects for no longer than is necessary for the purposes
        for which the personal data are processed; personal data
        may be stored for longer periods insofar as the personal
        data will be processed solely for archiving purposes in the
        public interest, scientific or historical research purposes or
        statistical purposes in accordance with Article 89(1)
        subject to implementation of the appropriate technical
        and organisational measures required by this Regulation
        in order to safeguard the rights and freedoms of the data
        subject ("storage limitation").

    *   processed in a manner that ensures appropriate security   Article 5.1(f)
        of the personal data, including protection against
        unauthorised or unlawful processing and against acci-
        dental loss, destruction or damage, using appropriate
        technical or organisational measures ("integrity and con-
        fidentiality"). Article: 24, 32

2. *The controller shall be responsible for, and be able to*   Article 5.2
    demonstrate compliance with, paragraph 1 ("accountability").

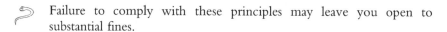 Failure to comply with these principles may leave you open to substantial fines.

These principles are set out at the start of the legislation, and inform everything that follows. They symbolise the spirit of the data protection regime but do not offer "hard and fast" rules. Compliance with the spirit of these key principles will be considered by the Supervisory Authorities as a building block for good data protection practice and a key to compliance.

The link to previous legislation

The good news is that if your business or organisation followed the previous data protection laws then there is no need for a complete change to what is already being done. Many of the new rules and themes build on the previous laws. GDPR is linked to National Data Protection Acts throughout Europe (e.g. the Data Protection Act 2018 in the UK), which were updated to coincide with the GDPR. Therefore, by complying with new national legislation you will also be complying with GDPR and vice versa.

Organisations who already complied with the previous data protection laws will be on the way to being GDPR compliant.

The European Data Protection Board and national Supervisory Authorities

The organisation tasked with ensuring that GDPR is applied in a consistent manner throughout the European Union is the European Data Protection Board, which is made up of representatives from the national data protection authorities of the Member States.

Each country within Europe has at least one public independent body set up to uphold information rights. These bodies are referred to as the Supervising Authority (SA).

The Supervisory Authorities publish a vast array of information on their websites and many provide advice and guidance by phone, live chat and email. In the UK, the Information Commissioner's Office (ICO) offer online questionnaires which organisations can use to use to assess the degree to which they comply with the GDPR legislation. A link to the ICO questionnaire (Resource 1.1) is available in the Resources section of this book.

National Supervisory Authorities are responsible for enforcing the Regulation on a national basis and are tasked with providing advice and guidance to businesses and individuals. Their responsibilities include:

- Dealing with concerns raised by members of the public.
- Imposing a monetary penalty.
- Maintaining a register of fee payers (where appropriate).
- Taking action to change the behaviour of organisations/individuals who collect, use and keep personal information (e.g. criminal prosecution, non-criminal enforcement and audit).

- Taking action to improve compliance with freedom of information, environmental information, INSPIRE and re-use laws.
- Upholding information rights in the public interest under national legislation (e.g. Data Protection, Freedom of Information, Privacy and Electronic Communications, Environmental Information).

Supervisory Authorities also play an international role, which includes working with other organisations in Europe and elsewhere to promote Data Protection compliance. Some nations offer a grants programme to support independent research and the development of privacy enhancing solutions.

Contact details for the most active European Supervisory Authorities (to date) can be found in Table 1.1. The complete list of Supervisory Authorities and their contact details are in Appendix 1 to this chapter (p. 13 and at Resource Link 1.2).

Who has to comply with GDPR?

GDPR is one of the most significant data protection laws in the world. It applies to any personal information that relates to an "identifiable person" and applies to **ALL** companies and organisations who process the personal data of individuals in the EU regardless of where the company is located (see Figure 1.1). GDPR also

Table 1.1 Supervisory Authority Contact Details

Country	Supervisory Authority	Tel	Email
France	Commission National de l'Informatique et des Libertés	+33 1 53 73 22 22	www.cnil.fr/
Germany	Die Bundesbeauftragte für den Datenschutz und die Informationsfreiheit	+49 228 997,799 0 +49 228 81,995 0	www.bfdi.bund.de/
Ireland	Data Protection Commissioner	+353 57 868 4800	www.dataprotection.ie/
Italy	Garante per la protezione dei dati personali	+39 06 69,677 1	www.garanteprivacy.it/
Netherlands	Autoriteit Persoonsgegevens	+31 70 888 8500	https://autoriteitper soonsgegevens.nl/nl
Spain	Agencia de Protección de Datos	+34 91,399 6200	www.agpd.es
United Kingdom	The Information Commissioner's Office	+44 1625 545 745	https://ico.org.uk
European Data Protection Supervisor		+32 2 283 19 00	www.edps.europa.eu/ EDPSWEB

applies to organisations inside the EU who process the personal data of individuals outside the EU.

What has GDPR changed?

GDPR has reshaped the way that businesses can collect, use and store an individual's personal information. The focus is now on the Data Subject's rights and freedoms rather than those of the organisation. It gives individuals the right to know how their information is used when, and with whom, it is shared and how and when it will be disposed of or deleted.

Organisations are now required to only gather the information that they require for a specific purpose. They are not permitted to collect information about an individual just in case it would be useful later. In addition to the specific purpose, organisations must also have a precise legal reason to process each item of information (referred to as a lawful basis for processing).

 You cannot sell personal information on or use it for another purpose without permission.

CASE STUDY 1.1   SELLING INFORMATION ON

The baby club "Emma's Diary" provided Experian with the records of 1,065,220 members in May 2017. Experian Marketing Services provided the records (including names, addresses and dates of birth) to the Labour Party for their direct marketing mail campaign for the 2017 general election. The UK ICO fined the club £140,000 for passing vulnerable groups' information on.

GDPR insists that companies use clear language to inform individuals what data they hold and how they plan to use it.

 Should this personal data be compromised then the individual must be informed within 72 hours.

These improved rights for individuals to learn how their data is going to be used and processed is complemented by rights to ask for their data to be erased or made more accurate. Individuals also have the right to obtain a copy of the personal data that organisations collect about them (via a Subject Access Request).

GDPR has introduced a new Data Minimisation rule, which for the first time require that businesses to do regular "housekeeping" of the data they hold. Where data is no longer needed, the Regulation requires that it should be anonymised or destroyed/deleted.

This does not mean you cannot keep something for archive reasons. You just need to document why you are doing this and how long the archive will be kept.

What the changes mean for you

All documents including emails that relate to the individual fall under GDPR. Because of the enhanced rights of individuals, organisations now need to have a detailed understanding of what personal data is and how they use it. In particular you will need:

- A clear privacy notice/policy, which you must abide by (this should be a living document that can be adapted when processes change).
- A documented record of your processes in order to DEMONSTRATE your compliance with GDPR.
- A mechanism for individuals to exercise their rights in respect of the data you hold about them (e.g. a Subject Access Request or a request for information to be erased or made more accurate).
- A mechanism to ask individuals for permission if you want to use their data for a purpose other than the original purpose.
- A process to ensure you keep all data up to date or delete what is no longer required.
- A process to inform individuals if you suffer a Data Breach.

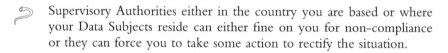 Supervisory Authorities either in the country you are based or where your Data Subjects reside can either fine on you for non-compliance or they can force you to take some action to rectify the situation.

The penalties for Data Breaches

Data Breaches are now quite a common occurrence, with one in four organisations likely to experience a breach of some sort. Managing your business in a way that mitigates the risks of any potential breach as much as possible is key to a successful GDPR strategy. You need to have a transparent process and a "plan" for how you will deal with any breach you do experience (e.g. a lost memory device, a phishing attempt or a more serious hacking or inadvertent disclosure situation).

Not every breach is "reportable" and not every reportable breach will result in a fine. The key is to be prepared.

Where a breach has been detected, reported and investigated it is likely that the Controller/Processor will receive a fine or be compelled to take some rectification action. Many factors will help determine the actual penalty, including the duration and gravity of the infringement as well as the type(s) of personal data affected. How well the organisation cooperated with authorities will also have a bearing.

The two tiers of fines available for non-compliance with the GDPR are dependent on the severity of the breach:

- The "higher maximum amount" (**up to €20 million or 4% of annual global turnover**) is usually applied to a failure to comply with one of the data protection principles, an infringement of an individual's rights or the transfer of data to third countries.
- The "standard maximum amount" (**up to €10 million or 2% of the total annual worldwide turnover**) is applied to an infringement of other provisions within the legislation (e.g. administrative matters).

Multiple Europe-wide investigations into "big tech" companies such as Microsoft, Google and Facebook are all ongoing. Some national organisations such as Ireland have yet to issue a fine as they have been focussed on getting their draft decisions completed. Others such as Germany have begun a programme of GDPR inspections. The UK have so far conducted numerous investigations and issued the largest number of fines to date.

Some recent examples of Data Breach fines in Europe can be found in Table 1.2.

Reducing the risk of a Data Breach

Every organisation should make sure they reduce the chances of a Data Breach happening. There are many reasons for this:

- Because of the risk of a fine.
- Because regulations demand it.
- Because it will have a negative impact on day to day operations.
- Because of the negative effect a Data Breach will have on consumer behaviour.

There are three ways to reduce the risk.

1. **Comply** with regulations such as GDPR. This way you will ensure that you recognise and reduce the risks and are able to respond effectively if you do suffer a breach.
2. **Train** your staff. The leading cause of Data Breaches is human error so a continuous training and awareness package is required.
3. **Be vigilant.** A 2018 survey revealed that the majority of SMEs are not prepared for a cyber attack. As the average cost to recover from a Data

Table 1.2 Fines Imposed for Data Breaches

Date	National Organisation	Reason for Fine	Amount
July 2019	UK	British Airways – for a breach of customer data in Sept 2018.	£183 million
July 2019	UK	Marriott – for failing to protect personal data contained in approximately 339 million guest records.	£99 million
July 2019	Netherlands	Haga Hospital – for not having proper measures in place to protect patients' information (staff members illicitly accessed the records of a TV star).	€460,000
June 2019	Italy	La Liga – for using the Spanish League's app to collect users' audio and location data in an attempt to combat piracy. Users were not aware of why their data was being collected because the consent they had given was not specific enough.	€250,000
April 2019	Poland	Bisnode (a Swedish Company) – for failure to tell six million of its Data Subjects that it has their data. The company processes data "scraped" from the internet and took the view that it would be too expensive to contact all the Data Subjects.	€220,000
March 2019	Denmark	Taxa 4x35 – for failing to delete customers' telephone numbers. The taxi firm claimed that they anonymise personal data after a two-year period. The regulator found that they did not anonymise the data adequately and had information about 8,873,333 customers from which the Data Subject could still be identified.	€180,000
Jan 2019	France	Google – for failing to be transparent about how it uses data and not having a legal basis for personalising ads.	€50 million
	UK	Uber – for paying hackers who stole the personal details of around 2.7 million UK customers without informing the victims.	£385,000
Jan 2019	Germany	Allowing health-related data to be seen publicly.	€80,000
Nov 2018	UK	CPS – for lost unencrypted DVDs containing recordings of police interviews that were to be used in a trial.	£325,000

Breach is £90,000 prudent businesses have begun to invest in measures that reduce their business's risks.

GDPR compliance as an ongoing journey

The Supervising Authorities have made it clear in all their literature that they do not intend to make early examples of organisations for minor breaches. Nor have they imposed large fines straightaway on organisations who already have GDPR preparations underway.

GDPR is seen as an evolutionary process for organisations and compliance is not focused on a fixed point in time. So, unlike the preparations for the "Y2K Millennium Bug" in 1999, there is no need to be fearful that an immature business will fall foul of the regulators.

GDPR preparation does require ongoing effort as businesses are expected to continue to identify and address emerging privacy and security risks in the weeks, months and years beyond May 2018. There is no "grace" period, because businesses already had two years to prepare. Supervising Authorities began regulating in May 2018 in a fair and proportionate manner. Experience so far has been if an organisation self-reports and engages with the Supervising Authority to resolve issues, demonstrating that they have effective accountability arrangements in place, they can expect this to be taken into account should regulatory action be considered. Many self-reported cases have ended with no further action required.

There are many "off the shelf" GDPR solutions that may help the organisation or it can choose to work through GDPR compliance at the organisation's own pace. No one solution will fit every business.

What must you do?

Irrespective of the size of your business or organisation, if you process personal information there are some things you **must** do. These are listed here.

Understand the information you hold and why you hold it

The easiest way to understand what information you hold is to talk about it in simple terms. Make a note of this analysis for future reference (even if you just send an email you will have a record). More complex organisations will want to complete a Data Audit. More information on how to complete a Data Audit can be found in Chapter 8 on p. 147.

Register with your Supervisory Authority (where this applies)

If you were previously registered with a Supervisory Authority, check when your registration expires. If you have not been registered before, check whether you need to now. In some countries the Supervisory Authority will fine you for not registering.

Work out what your lawful basis is

Work out what your most appropriate lawful basis is before you begin processing and make sure you document your decision. Review this decision regularly in case there is a more appropriate lawful basis. Remember that if you would still process the data in the absence of consent then consent is not the most appropriate lawful basis. More information on selecting the most appropriate "lawful basis" can be found in Chapter 7 on p. 134.

To help you decide on the lawful basis you will find online tools and guidance on the website of your Supervisory Authority.

Document your decisions and write a Privacy Notice/Policy

You should make sure that you document all your deliberations and the decisions you make. You should set out the information for Data Subjects in some form of Privacy Notice/Policy. This information should be made public. For more information on how to write a Privacy Notice and the layered approach to delivering privacy information, see Chapter 7.

Appendix 1

List of National Supervisory Authorities

Country	National Data Protection Authority	Contact Details	Website
Austria	Österreichische Datenschutzbehörde	Hohenstaufengasse 3 1010 Wien Tel. +43 1 531 15 202,525 Fax +43 1 531 15 202,690	dsb@dsb.gv.at www.dsb.gv.at/
Belgium	Commission de la protection de la vie privée	Commissie voor de bescherming van de persoonlijke levenssfeer Rue de la Presse 35/Drukpersstraat 35 1000 Bruxelles/1000 Brussels Tel. +32 2 274 48 00 Fax +32 2 274 48 35	commission@privacycommission.be www.privacycommission.be/
Bulgaria	Commission for Personal Data Protection	2, Prof. Tsvetan Lazarov blvd. Sofia 1592 Tel. +359 2 915 3580 Fax +359 2 915 3525	kzld@cpdp.bg www.cpdp.bg/
Croatia	Croatian Personal Data Protection Agency	Martićeva 14 10,000 Zagreb Tel. +385 1 4609 000 Fax +385 1 4609 099	azop@azop.hr or info@azop.hr www.azop.hr/
Cyprus	Commissioner for Personal Data Protection	1 Iasonos Street, 1082 Nicosia P.O. Box 23,378, CY-1682 Nicosia Tel. +357 22 818 456 Fax +357 22 304 565	commissioner@dataprotection.gov.cy www.dataprotection.gov.cy/
Czech Republic	The Office for Personal Data Protection	Urad pro ochranu osobnich udaju Pplk. Sochora 27 170 00 Prague 7	posta@uoou.cz www.uoou.cz/

(Continued)

(Cont.)

Country	National Data Protection Authority	Contact Details	Website
Denmark	Datatilsynet	Borgergade 28, 5 1300 Copenhagen K Tel. +45 33 1932 00 Fax +45 33 19 32 18	dt@datatilsynet.dk www.datatilsynet.dk/
Estonia	Estonian Data Protection Inspectorate (Andmekaitse Inspektsioon)	Väike-Ameerika 19 10,129 Tallinn Tel. +372 6274 135 Fax +372 6274 137	info@aki.ee www.aki.ee/en
Finland	Office of the Data Protection Ombudsman	P.O. Box 315 FIN-00181 Helsinki Tel. +358 10 3666 700 Fax +358 10 3666 735	tietosuoja@om.fi www.tietosuoja.fi/en/
France	Commission Nationale de l'Informatique et des Libertés – CNIL	8 rue Vivienne, CS 30,223 F-75,002 Paris, Cedex 02 Tel. +33 1 53 73 22 22 Fax +33 1 53 73 22 00	www.cnil.fr/
Germany*	Die Bundesbeauftragte für den Datenschutz und die Informationsfreiheit	Husarenstraße 30 53,117 Bonn Tel. +49 228 997,799 0; +49 228 81,995 0 Fax +49 228 997,799 550; +49 228 81,995 550	poststelle@bfdi.bund.de www.bfdi.bund.de/
Greece	Hellenic Data Protection Authority	Kifisias Av. 1–3, PC 11,523 Ampelokipi Athens Tel. +30 210 6475 600 Fax +30 210 6475 628	contact@dpa.gr www.dpa.gr/
Hungary	National Authority for Data Protection and Freedom of Information	Szilágyi Erzsébet fasor 22/C H-1125 Budapest Tel. +36 1 3911 400	peterfalvi.attila@naih.hu www.naih.hu/

Country	Authority	Address	Contact
Ireland	Data Protection Commissioner	Canal House Station Road Portarlington Co. Laois Lo-Call: 1890 25 22 31 Tel. +353 57 868 4800 Fax +353 57 868 4757	info@dataprotection.ie www.dataprotection.ie/
Italy	Garante per la protezione dei dati personali	Piazza di Monte Citorio, 121 00186 Roma Tel. +39 06 69,677 1 Fax +39 06 69,677 785	garante@garanteprivacy.it www.garanteprivacy.it/
Latvia	Data State Inspectorate	Director: Ms Daiga Avdejanova Blaumana str. 11/13-15 1011 Riga Tel. +371 6722 3131 Fax +371 6722 3556	info@dvi.gov.lv www.dvi.gov.lv/
Lithuania	State Data Protection	Žygimantų str. 11-6a 011042 Vilnius Tel. + 370 5 279 14 45 Fax +370 5 261 94 94	ada@ada.lt www.ada.lt/
Luxembourg	Commission Nationale pour la Protection des Données	1, Avenue du Rock'n'Roll L-4361 Esch-sur-Alzette Tel. +352 2610 60 1 Fax +352 2610 60 29	info@cnpd.lu www.cnpd.lu/
Malta	Office of the Data Protection Commissioner	Data Protection Commissioner: Mr Joseph Ebejer 2, Airways House High Street, Sliema SLM 1549 Tel. +356 2328 7100 Fax +356 2328 7198	commissioner.dataprotection@gov.mt http://www.dataprotection.gov.mt/
Netherlands	Autoriteit Persoonsgegevens	Prins Clauslaan 60	info@autoriteitpersoonsgegevens.nl

(Continued)

(Cont.)

Country	National Data Protection Authority	Contact Details	Website
		P.O. Box 93,374 2509 AJ Den Haag/The Hague Tel. +31 70 888 8500 Fax +31 70 888 8501	https://autoriteitpersoonsgegevens.nl/nl
Poland	The Bureau of the Inspector General for the Protection of Personal Data – GIODO	ul. Stawki 2 00–193 Warsaw Tel. +48 22 53 10 440 Fax +48 22 53 10 441	kancelaria@giodo.gov.pl; desiwm@giodo.gov.pl www.giodo.gov.pl/
Portugal	Comissão Nacional de Protecção de Dados – CNPD	R. de São. Bento, 148-3° 1200–821 Lisboa Tel. +351 21 392 84 00 Fax +351 21 397 68 32	geral@cnpd.pt http://www.cnpd.pt/
Romania	The National Supervisory Authority for Personal Data Processing	President: Mrs Ancuţa Gianina Opre B-dul Magheru 28–30 Sector 1, BUCUREŞTI Tel. +40 21 252 5599 Fax +40 21 252 5757	anspdcp@dataprotection.ro www.dataprotection.ro/
Slovakia	Office for Personal Data Protection of the Slovak Republic	Hraničná 12 820 07 Bratislava 27 Tel.: + 421 2 32 31 32 14 Fax: + 421 2 32 31 32 34	statny.dozor@pdp.gov.sk www.dataprotection.gov.sk/
Slovenia	Information Commissioner	Ms Mojca Prelesnik Zaloška 59 1000 Ljubljana Tel. +386 1 230 9730 Fax +386 1 230 9778	gp.ip@ip-rs.si www.ip-rs.si/
Spain	Agencia de Protección de Datos	C/Jorge Juan, 6 28.001 Madrid Tel. +34 91,399 6200 Fax +34 91,455 5699	internacional@agpd.es www.agpd.es/
Sweden	Datainspektionen	Drottninggatan 29 5th Floor Box 8114 104 20 Stockholm	datainspektionen@datainspektionen.se www.datainspektionen.se/

United Kingdom	The Information Commissioner's Office	Tel. +46 8 657 6100 Fax +46 8 652 8652 Water Lane, Wycliffe House Wilmslow – Cheshire SK9 5AF Tel. +44 1625 545 745	international.team@ico.org.uk https://ico.org.uk

EUROPEAN FREE TRADE AREA (EFTA)

Iceland	Icelandic Data Protection Agency	Rauðarárstíg 10 105 Reykjavik Tel. +354 510 9600; Fax +354 510 9606	postur@personuvernd.is
Liechtenstein	Data Protection Office	Kirchstrasse 8, P.O. Box 684 9490 Vaduz Principality of Liechtenstein Tel. +423 236 6090	info.dss@llv.li
Norway	Datatilsynet	The Data Inspectorate P.O. Box 8177 Dep 0034 Oslo Tel. +47 22 39 69 00; Fax +47 22 42 23 50	postkasse@datatilsynet.no
Switzerland	Data Protection and Information Commissioner of Switzerland	Eidgenössischer Datenschutz- und Öffentlichkeitsbeauftragter Mr Adrian Lobsiger Feldeggweg 1 3003 Bern Tel. +41 58 462 43 95; Fax +41 58 462 99 96	contact20@edoeb.admin.ch

* Germany divides complaints among a number of different agencies. To understand which one applies see www.bfdi.bund.de/bfdi_wiki/index.php/Aufsichtsbeh%C3%B6rden_und_Landesdatenschutzbeauftragte

Chapter 2

GDPR terminology

At the centre of GDPR is the simple concept that individuals have a right to keep their personal data private and the right to decide what happens to that information. GDPR places an obligation on organisations and businesses to put these rights at the heart of what they do so, ensuring that the rights and freedoms of the Data Subjects are protected.

This chapter discusses the terms used in GDPR and their application in a business context. An easy to use alphabetised list of these terms is provided in the Appendix at the end of this chapter (see p. 26).

GDPR terms – people or entities

GDPR describes a number of people or entities who can be involved with data processing. These are shown in Figure 2.1.

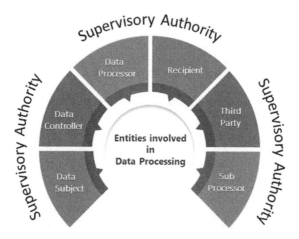

Figure 2.1 People/Entities Identified in GDPR

Data Subject

The Data Subject is the person whose data is being processed, collected or held. This data can directly or indirectly identify the person and may relate to their private, professional or public life.

Data Controller

The Data Controller is the person or organisation who decides what the purpose of processing is and how the processing will be done. A Data Controller can be a natural or legal person, a public authority an agency or any other body.

Data Processor

The Data Processor is anyone who processes the personal data on behalf of a Controller. The Data Controller and their staff, a sub-contractor or indeed outsourced platforms such as MS Office 365, are all Data Processors.

Third party

An organisation or person who has been authorised to process personal data by the Data Controller/Processor is known as a third party. The Data Subject, Controller and Processor cannot be a third party.

Recipient

A recipient is the person to whom the personal data are disclosed. They may or may not be a third party.

Supervisory Authority

Each Member State establishes at least one independent public authority to monitor the application of GDPR. This body is known as the Supervisory Authority.

Natural and legal person

GDPR differentiates between a natural person and legal person. A "natural" person is a living human being. A "legal" person can be a human being, a firm, or a government agency as long as it has a legal identity.

GDPR terms – types of personal data

"Personal data" is any information that relates to a living human being (referred to as the Data Subject); who can be identified, directly or indirectly by any part of that data. Personal data can include a name, identification number, location, an online identifier (such as a cookie or IP address) or one or more factors that are specific to the individual's identity (e.g. physical, genetic, economic, cultural features). Figure 2.2 shows the types of personal data that a health club may store about their clients.

Personal data is dealt with in more depth in Chapter 6 (p. 117).

Specific types of personal data are also defined because more stringent regulations relate to their processing. These are:

- **Biometric data** – data relating to physical, physiological or behavioural characteristics that allow or confirm the identification of a person (e.g. fingerprints, facial images or retina scans).
- **Genetic data** – data that relates to inherited or acquired genetic characteristics which give unique information about the physiology or the health of that individual.
- **Health data** – data that relates to a person's physical or mental health (this can include provision of health care services).
- **Special categories of data** – sensitive data is known as "special categories of personal data". This can include racial or ethnic origin, political opinions, religious or philosophical views, trade union membership, sexual orientation. It also includes health, genetic and biometric data if they are processed to uniquely identify an individual. It does not include data that relates to criminal convictions and offences.

Key terms – actions

There are a number of actions that personal data can be subjected to. These are described in this section.

Processing

Processing is an operation (or set of operations) which is performed on personal data. The operations can be both manual or automatic and include collection, recording, organisation, structuring, storage, adaptation or alteration, retrieval, consultation, use, disclosure, restriction, erasure and destruction.

Profiling

Profiling is any form of automated processing that involves the use of personal data to evaluate certain personal aspects. It is used to analyse or predict aspects of a person's life such as performance at work, health, personal preferences, location or movements.

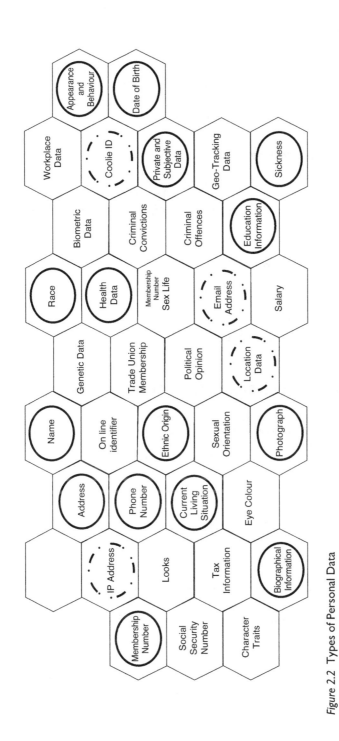

Figure 2.2 Types of Personal Data

(Circled elements indicate data that a health club may process)

Pseudonymisation

Pseudonymisation is the processing of personal data in a way that means it can no longer be attributed to a specific Data Subject without the use of additional information (a key). The additional information (key) should be kept separately and be kept safe so that it is not possible to once again attribute the information to an identifiable person.

Cross-border processing

Cross Border Processing is where personal data is processed by an organisation that is based in more than one Member State; or where the data processed by a single establishment will affect Data Subjects in more than one Member State.

GDPR terms – consent

At its simplest, consent means receiving a Data Subject's agreement to process their data.

Article 4 of GDPR defines consent (*Article 4(11), EU GDPR, "Definitions"*). The exact text is extracted in Quote 2.1.

QUOTE 2.1   ARTICLE 4(11) OF GDPR – CONSENT

"Consent" of the Data Subject means any freely given, specific, informed and unambiguous indication of the Data Subject's wishes   Article 4(11) *by which he or she, by a statement or by a clear affirmative action, signifies agreement to the processing of personal data relating to him or her.*

The process of gaining consent must be clear and unambiguous. The Data Subject must understand explicitly what they are providing their data for, how it will be processed, who will process it and how long it will be stored.

If you would continue to process the information in the absence of consent then consent is not the most appropriate lawful basis on which to process the information.

 The use of consent is a much–confused term and in their haste to achieve compliance with the GDPR legislation many organisations adopted the "consent model" with little thought as to whether it was actually the most appropriate basis on which to process personal data. To illustrate this point, in July 2019 the Greek Supervisory Authority fined PwriceaterhouseCoopers for processing employee data using "consent" as their lawful basis rather than "contract". With this in mind, it is recommended that all organisations who used consent as their lawful basis review this policy as soon as possible. More details on lawful basis to process can be found in Chapter 7 (p. 134).

GDPR terms – the principles of GDPR

There are six key principles to follow when processing personal data.

* Processing must be lawful, fair and transparent.
* Data may only be collected for specified, explicit and legitimate purposes. You may not process it subsequently in a way that is incompatible with the original purpose.
* The data should be adequate, relevant and limited only that which is necessary to suit the purpose of your processing.
* Data should be accurate (and kept up to date if necessary).
* Data should be kept in a format that permits Data Subjects to be identified for no longer than is necessary to suit the purpose of the processing.
* Data should be kept secure (this includes protecting it against unauthorised/unlawful processing as well as accidental loss, destruction or damage).

The Controller is accountable under GDPR to comply with these six principles and they should be able to demonstrate their compliance with the regulation should they be called upon to do so. This is often referred to as the seventh principle of GDPR.

GDPR terms – lawful basis

For personal data processed, the organisation must be able to state that it will be processed because they have one of the following six **Lawful Bases for processing**. These lawful bases (also known as legal basis/legal reason) are shown in Figure 2.3.

GDPR terms – subject rights

The GDPR 8 rights to individuals. These are summarised in this chapter and discussed in detail in Chapter 13 (p. 212).

Figure 2.3 Choosing a Lawful Basis for Processing

The right of access

Individuals have the right to access their personal data (subject access). They may ask for this access both verbally or in writing. The organisation has one month to respond to the request and cannot charge a fee to deal with it.

Right of erasure

Individuals have the right to ask for their personal data to be erased. There are some circumstances where the organisation does not have to comply with this request.

This is also known as the "Right to be Forgotten."

Right to be informed

Individuals have the right to be informed when their personal data is collected or uses their personal data. This is a key transparency requirement under the GDPR. The information you need to provide includes your purposes for processing, retention periods and who the information will be shared with. This is known as "privacy information" and it must be provided at the time the data is collected.

Right of rectification

Individuals can ask for any inaccurate personal data to be rectified, or completed if it is incomplete. There are some circumstances where the organisation does not have to comply with this request and this is covered in greater depth in Chapter 10. If you are in doubt, check with your Supervisory Authority.

Right to restrict processing

Individuals have the right to request the processing of their data is restricted or suppressed. There are some circumstances where the organisation does not have to comply with this request.

Right to data portability

Individuals have the right to obtain and reuse any of the personal data that they have provided to a Controller for their own purposes.

Right to object

In certain circumstances, individuals have the right to object to their personal data being processed. This is particularly evident in relation to direct marketing. There are some circumstances where the organisation does not have to comply with this request.

Automated decision making and profiling

There are particular rules in GDPR that relate to decisions made solely by automated means (i.e. without any human involvement) or automated processing when it is used to evaluate certain things about an individual. Article 22 imposes additional rules to protect individuals which include restrictions on the use of automated decision making unless it is:

- necessary to enter into or perform a contract (e.g. credit reference agencies);
- authorised by a law that applies to the Controller (e.g. safeguarding DBS checks);
- based on the individual's explicit consent (e.g. joining a golf club).

Appendix 2

GDPR terminology A–Z

Accountability	The ability to demonstrate compliance with the GDPR (through putting appropriate technical and organisational measures in place such as privacy policies, privacy impact assessments and privacy be design).
Archive	A collection of information (sometimes known as records) with a local focus or on a particular theme. Can include: letters, reports, minutes, registers, maps, photographs and films, digital files, sound recordings.
Binding Corporate Rules (BCRs)	A set of rules that allow multinational organisations to transfer personal data from within the EU to their affiliates outside the EU.
Biometric data	Personal data relating to physical, physiological or behavioural characteristics that allow or confirm the unique identification of that person (e.g. fingerprints, facial images or retina scans).
Consent (of the Data Subject)	Any freely given, specific, informed and unambiguous indication that the Data Subject agrees. This can be by a statement or by a clear affirmative action which signifies their agreement.
Cross Border Processing	Personal data that is processed by organisations with establishments in either one more than one Member State; or where personal data is processed by a single establishment in the Union but that substantially affects or is likely to substantially affect Data Subjects in more than one Member State.
Data Breach	Any accidental or unlawful destruction, loss, alteration, unauthorised disclosure or access of a subject's data.
Data concerning health	Personal data related to the physical or mental health of a natural person, including the provision of health care services, which reveal information about their health status.
Data Controller	The natural or legal person, public authority, agency or other body which, alone or jointly with others, determines the purposes and means of the processing.
Data Minimisation	The principle of collecting only that personal data which the organisation requires in order to achieve the intended purpose (this data should be adequate, relevant, limited to what is necessary and kept up to date).
Data Processor	Any natural or legal person, public authority, agency or other body which processes personal data on behalf of the Controller. This can include the Data Controller and their staff, a sub-contractor or outsourced platforms such as MS Office 365.

Data Protection Authority	The national authority who protects data privacy.
Data Protection by Design and Data Protection by Default	The basis on which all Data Controllers operate. Producers of products, services and applications are encouraged to take individuals rights into at the design and development stage. Internal policies and procedures should be adopted to meet this aspiration. These measures should include the ability of the controller to create and improve security features and provide transparent information to the Data Subject so that they can monitor the processing.
	The principles of data protection by design and by default should also be taken into consideration in the context of public tenders.
Data Protection Officer	An appointed individual who works to ensure an organisation implements and complies with the policies and procedures set by GDPR. A Data Protection Officer is obligatory if processing is carried out by a public authority; or the "core activities" of a Data Controller/Processor either require "regular and systematic monitoring of Data Subjects on a large scale", or consist of processing of special categories of data or data about criminal convictions "on a large scale".
Data Subject	An identified or identifiable individual person whose personal data is being collected, held or processed (whether it relates to their private, professional, or public life).
Data Protection Impact Assessment (DPIA)	A tool to help identify and minimise the data protection risks in new projects.
Encrypted Data	Personal data which has been translated into another form or code so that only people with specific access can read it.
Enterprise	A natural or legal person engaged in an economic activity, irrespective of its legal form, including partnerships or associations regularly engaged in an economic activity.
EU-US Privacy Shield	A set of GDPR standards that allow for the legal transfer of personal data between the EU and US for commercial reasons.
Fairness Principle	A controller must use personal data in a way that is fair and not detrimental, unexpected or misleading to the individuals concerned.
Filing System	Any structured set of personal data which are accessible according to specific criteria, whether centralised, decentralised or dispersed on a functional or geographical basis.

(Continued)

Genetic data	Personal data relating to inherited or acquired genetic characteristics which give unique information about the physiology or the health of that individual.
Group of Undertakings	A controlling undertaking and its controlled undertakings.
Health data	Personal data related to an individual's physical or mental health including the provision of health care services.
Information Society Service	Any service normally provided for remuneration, at a distance, by electronic means and at the request of a recipient (e.g. social media). This type of service is defined in Directive (EU) 2015/1535 Article 1(1)(b).
Integrity and Confidentiality Principle	Personal data must be processed using appropriate technical, organisational and security measures.
International Organisation	An organisation and its subordinate bodies governed by public international law, or any other body which is set up by, or on the basis of, an agreement between two or more countries.
Legal Person	A human being, firm, or government agency that is recognised as having privileges and obligations.
Legitimate Interests	Where there is justification for the processing because it will benefit either society as a whole or a particular company (e.g. an online shopping company processing client delivery addresses).
Main Establishment for the Controller	The place, in the Union, where a Processor organisation's central administration or decision-making function is housed.
Main Establishment for the Processor	Where an organisation's central administration or main processing activities take place.
Natural Person	A living and breathing individual human being.
Personal Data	Any information relating to an identified or identifiable natural person who can be identified, directly or indirectly by reference to an element of that data (e.g. name, identification number, location, an online identifier or to one or more factors specific to their physical, physiological, genetic, mental, economic, cultural or social identity).
Personal Data Breach	A breach of security which leads accidental or unlawful destruction, loss, alteration, unauthorised disclosure of, or access to, personal data. This can be during processing, transmission or storage.
Pii – Personally Identifiable Information	Information that can be used to identify, contact, or locate a single person, or to identify an individual either on its own or when combined with other information.

Privacy Impact Assessment	A tool used to identify the privacy risks.
Privacy Notice	A document setting out purposes for processing, retention periods for personal data, and who it will be shared with. This is privacy information must be provided at the time of data collection.
Purpose Limitation Principle	The principle that information may only be used for the specified, explicit and legitimate purposes for which the data was collected and not for any other purpose. Further use may only take place if it is compatible with your original purpose, you have consent to do so or there is a clear basis in law.
Processing	An operation or set of operations that is performed on personal data or on sets of personal data, whether or not it is by automated means (e.g. collection, recording, organisation, structuring, storage, adaptation or alteration, retrieval, consultation, use, disclosure by transmission, dissemination or otherwise making available, alignment or combination, restriction, erasure and destruction).
Profiling	Any form of automated processing of personal data that involves the use of that data to evaluate certain personal aspects. In particular where it is used to analyse or predict aspects of that person's performance at work, economic situation, health, personal preferences, interests, reliability, behaviour, location or movements.
Pseudonymisation	The processing of personal data in such a manner that the personal data can no longer be attributed to a specific Data Subject without the use of additional information, provided that such additional information is kept separately and is subject to technical and organisational measures to ensure that the personal data are not attributed to an identified or identifiable natural person.
Recipient	A natural or legal person, public authority, agency or another body, to whom the personal data are disclosed (may/may not be a third party).
Relevant and reasoned objection	An objection to a draft decision as to whether there is an infringement of this Regulation, or whether envisaged action in relation to the Controller or Processor complies with this Regulation, which clearly demonstrates the significance of the risks posed by the draft decision as regards the fundamental rights and freedoms of Data Subjects and, where applicable, the free flow of personal data within the Union.
Representative	A person within the Union who is chosen or appointed to act or speak for a Controller or Processor based outside the Union.

(Continued)

(Cont.)

Special categories of Data	Sensitive personal data such as racial or ethnic origin, political opinions, religious or philosophical views, trade union membership, sexual orientation. It also includes health, genetic and biometric data where they are being processed to uniquely identify an individual.
	Personal data relating to criminal convictions and offences is not included, but similar extra safeguards apply to this type of processing.
Subject Access	The right of the subject to obtain or request certain information relating to their personal data from the Data Controller.
Supervisory Authority	An independent public authority within each member state who monitors the application of GDPR.
Supervisory Authority concerned	The Supervisory Authority where the Controller or Processor is established or where the Data Subjects reside. Or the authority to whom a complaint has been lodged.
Third party	An organisation or person (other than the Data Subject, Controller, Processor) who is authorised to process personal data by the Data Controller/Processor.
Territorial Scope	The geographical scope of the GDPR includes the members of the European Union and their dependant territories, European Economic Area (EEA) states (Iceland, Lichtenstein and Norway) and countries seeking to join the EU.
Transfer	The movement of personal data to countries outside the EU/EEA or to international organisations (this includes viewing data hosted in another location).
With Due Regard to The State of The Art	An "allowance" that permits Data Controllers and Processors to take into account available technology, cost of implementation when putting in place technical and organisational measures to protect the rights of Data Subjects. These may be balanced against the nature, scope, context and purposes of processing and any potential risks to the Data Subject.

Chapter 3

The GDPR Articles and Recitals

This chapter studies the 99 Articles of GDPR and summarises the main points in each GDPR Article in plain language. Rather confusingly (for the purpose of this book), the Regulation is divided into 11 chapters, each of which comprises a number of articles. The more complex chapters are subdivided into sections. The legislation also includes Recitals that support the interpretation or implementation of the Articles.

The Recitals of GDPR

The 173 Recitals of GDPR are used to interpret the Articles and provide further insights into the function and purpose of each of the GDPR articles. The Recitals provide examples of when and how the Articles should be interpreted. These Recitals are written in relatively easy to understand format and so there is no requirement to reproduce them in this book. Table 3.1 provides a cross reference for those who wish to study the relevant Recitals for each of the Articles of GDPR

Table 3.1 Cross Reference of GDPR Articles and Recitals

Chapter	Articles	Relevant Recitals
Chapter 1 General Provisions	1	1,2,3,4,5,6,78,9,10,11,12
	2	13, 14,15,16,17,18,19,20,21,27
	3	22,23,24,25
	4	15,24,26,28,29,30,31,34,35,36,37
Chapter 2 Principles	5	39
	6	39,40,41,42,43,44,45,46,47,18,19,50,171
	7	32,33,42,43
	8	38
	9	46,51,52,53,54,55,56
	10	50
	11	57

(Continued)

Table 3.1 (Cont.)

Chapter	Articles	Relevant Recitals
Chapter 3 Rights of the Data Subject	12	58,59,60,73
	13	60,61,62
	14	60,61,62
	15	63,64
	16	65
	17	65,66
	18	67
	19	66
	20	68
	21	69,70
	22	71,72,91
	23	73
Chapter 4 Controller and Processor	24	74,75,76,77
	25	78
	26	79
	27	80
	28	81
	29	13,82
	30	82
	31	75,76,77,78,79,83
	32	85,87,88
	33	86,87,88
	34	75,84,89,90,91,92,93
	35	94,95,96
	36	97
	37	97
	38	97
	39	98,99
	40	100
	41	
	42	
	43	

Chapter 5 Transfers of Personal
    Data to Third Countries or
    International Organisations
	44	101,102

	45	103,104,105,106,107
	46	108,109
	47	110
	48	115
	49	111,112,113,114,115
	50	116
Chapter 6 Independent Supervisory Authorities	51	117,118,119,120
	52	117,118,120,121
	53	121
	54	117,121
	55	122

Chapter	Articles	Relevant Recitals
	56	124,127,128
	57	122,123,132,133,137
	58	122,129,131
	59	
Chapter 7 Cooperation and Consistency	60	124,125,130
	61	123,132,133
	62	126,134
	63	135
	64	136
	65	136
	66	137,138
	67	139
	68	139
	69	136,139
	70	140
	71	
	72	
	73	
	74	
	75	
	76	
Chapter 8 Remedies, Liability and Penalties	77	141
	78	141,143
	79	141,145
	80	142
	81	144
	82	146,147
	83	148,149,150,151,152
	84	149,150,151,152
Chapter 9 Provisions Relating to Specific Processing Situations	85	153
	86	154
	87	155
	88	156,157,158,159,160,161,162,163
	89	164
	90	165
	91	
Chapter 10 Delegated and Implementing Acts	92	166,167,168,169,170
	93	
Chapter 11 Final Provisions	94	171
	95	173
	96	
	97	
	98	
	99	

The GDPR Articles explained "in a nutshell"

Article	Subject Area		Explanation of Main Points in the Article
GDPR CHAPTER I – General Provisions			
Article 1	Subject-matter and objectives	• • •	Introduction to GDPR. Discussion of the rights of individuals to protection of their personal data. Reasons behind the introduction of the legislation (to protect personal data, harmonise EU regulations and allow free movement of data). More information on GDPR can be found in Chapter 1 of this book.
Article 2	Material scope	• •	Where GDPR applies (in the processing of personal data as part of a filing system or if wholly/partly processed by automated means). Where the regulation does not apply: ○ if it is purely for personal or household use. ○ for processes that fall outside EU law. ○ activities relating to freedom, security and justice. ○ crime prevention, investigation, detection or prosecution of criminal offences. ○ criminal penalties ○ public security. • Links to other legislation (EC) No 45/2001 and Electronic Commerce Directive 2000/31/EC.
Article 3	Territorial scope	•	The legislation applies: ○ where either the Controller or Processor are based in the EU. ○ if the Data Subject is in the EU and processing relates to goods or services or monitoring behaviour. The Regulation also applies to overseas dependencies.
Article 4	Definitions	•	Definitions of the key terms used in GDPR (an A-Z of these terms can be found in the Appendix to Chapter 2 of this book). Member States have different national legislation for freedom of expression.

Article	Subject Area	Explanation of Main Points in the Article
GDPR CHAPTER II – Principles		

Article 5	Principles relating to processing of personal data	• The principles of GDPR.
		• Data should be:
		   ○ processed lawfully, fairly and in a transparent manner.
		   ○ collected for a specified, explicit and legitimate reason.
		   ○ only further processed if this is compatible with the original purpose for which the information was collected.
		   ○ adequate, relevant and limited to what is necessary.
		   ○ accurate and kept up to date (if necessary).
		   ○ kept in a form that allows Data Subjects to be identified for no longer than is necessary for the purposes for which the personal data are processed.
		   ○ processed in a way that ensures the data is kept secure (protected from unauthorised or unlawful processing, accidental loss, destruction or damage).
		
		• The Controller is responsible for, and should be able to demonstrate compliance with the GDPR.
		
		  This demonstration of compliance is a new requirement under GDPR

Article 6	Lawfulness of processing	• For the data to be processed lawfully one of the following must apply:
		   ○ **consent** must have been given by the Data Subject.
		   ○ there is a **contract** between the Controller and Data Subject (or an intention to make a contract).
		   ○ the Controller needs to comply with a **legal obligation**.
		   ○ it is to protect the **vital interests** of a natural person.
		   ○ it is in the **public interest**.
		   ○ it is in the **legitimate interests** of the Controller or a third party (but the Data Subject's interests can override this).
		
		• EU or Member State law sets out the basis for lawful and fair processing with which the Controller must comply.

(Continued)

Article	Subject Area	Explanation of Main Points in the Article
		• This article does not apply to processing carried out by public authorities in the performance of their task. • The regulation allows for Member States to introduce more specific provisions for: ○ Freedom of expression and information. ○ Public access to official documents. ○ National identification numbers. ○ Employment. ○ Safeguards and derogations for archiving. ○ Obligations of secrecy. ○ Churches and religious associations. • Legal/legislative measures should be clear and precise so that those to whom it relates can understand the need to abide by it. • If Controllers wish to use the data for a second purpose then they must either have consent or the processing must be compatible with the original purpose (unless the law requires this second processing).
Article 7	Conditions for consent	• Controllers must be able to demonstrate that the Data Subject has consented to processing. • Requests for consent should be in clear and plain language and an intelligible and easily accessible form. • Data Subjects have the right to withdraw consent at any time. • It should be as easy to withdraw as to give consent. • Consent must be clearly distinguishable from the other matters. • When assessing whether consent is freely given account will be taken as to whether the performance of a contract is conditional on consent particularly if additional personal data is collected. If obtaining consent could be considered an infringement of GDPR then it is not binding. This area is quite complex and you should refer to the GDPR Recitals or obtain legal advice.
Article 8	Conditions applicable to child's consent in relation to	• If consent is used to offer information society services (e.g. online sellers of goods and services or and social media) directly to a child

Article	Subject Area	Explanation of Main Points in the Article
	information society services	then the processing of the personal data of that child is only lawful where the child is at least 16 years old (13 years old in UK).
		• If the child is under 16 years processing will only be lawful if consent has been given by a person with parental responsibility for the child. The Controller must verify that consent has been given.
		• The general contract law of Member States still applies to children's consent.
Article 9	Processing of special categories of personal data	• Member States may create:
		○ new laws/agreements to protect personal data in relation to national employment law.
		○ their own rules for Controllers/Processors who are subject to obligations of professional secrecy.
		• Processing the following categories of personal data is prohibited:
		○ health data.
		○ data about a person's sex life/sexual orientation.
		○ genetic or biometric data to uniquely identify a person.
		○ political opinions.
		○ racial or ethnic origins.
		○ religious or philosophical beliefs.
		○ trade union membership.
		Except when:
		○ the Data Subject has given explicit consent.
		○ processing is for employment, social security or social protection.
		○ to protect the vital interests of the Data Subject (e.g. if they are incapable of giving consent).
		○ processing is carried out by a body/organisation of its member's data and that data is only shared with members of the organisation (e.g. foundations, associations and political, philosophical, religious or trade union not-for-profit bodies).
		○ the Data Subject has already made the data public.
		○ processing is necessary for a legal claim or judicial act.
		○ processing is in the public interest (but still respecting the rights and interests of the Data Subject).

(Continued)

Article	Subject Area		Explanation of Main Points in the Article
		○	processing is necessary for preventive or occupational medicine.
		○	the data is processed by a professional who is subject to an obligation of professional secrecy.
		○	processing is necessary for public health reasons.
		○	processing is for archiving purposes in the public interest.
		•	Member States may introduce further conditions, including limitations, regarding the processing of genetic data, biometric data or data concerning health where they choose to do so.
			In all the cases, processing should be proportionate and appropriate safeguards must be in place to protect the individual's rights.
Article 10	Processing of personal data relating to criminal convictions and offences	•	Only an official authority can process data about criminal convictions and offences or related security measures.
		•	Official authorities are responsible for keeping a register of criminal convictions.
Article 11	Processing which does not require identification	•	If the reason for processing does not require the Data Subject to be identified then the Controller is not be obliged to obtain additional information in order to identify them.
		•	The Controller should inform Data Subjects when it can demonstrate that it is not able to identify them.
		•	Where processing does not require identification then the individual's rights (Articles 15–20) do not apply unless the Data Subject provides additional information so they can be identified.

GDPR CHAPTER III – Rights of the Data Subject

Section 1 – Transparency and Modalities

Article	Subject Area		Explanation of Main Points in the Article
Article 12	Transparent information, communication and modalities for the exercise of the rights of the Data Subject	•	Data Controllers should provide information about their data processing activities and help Data Subjects to exercise their rights of access/rectification/erasure.
			The Data Controller may ask the Data Subject for proof of identity before providing a response to a request. Where additional information is requested the deadline for response will start on receipt of this information.

- Any response should be provided free of charge.
- Responses should be concise, transparent, intelligible, in an easily accessible form and use clear and plain language.
- Responses must include details relating to the individual's right to lodge a complaint or seek a judicial remedy.
- Controllers should respond to a subject access request without undue delay (one month) they may take no more than three months.
- If the request is made in electronic form then the information may be provided in the same way unless a different format has been requested (it should be machine-readable where appropriate).
- Unfounded/excessive requests may be refused or a charge imposed as long as the Controller can prove that the request is manifestly unfounded/excessive.
- The Data Controller may only refuse to act on a request if they can demonstrate that they cannot identify the Data Subject.
- If the Data Controller is not going to take action, they must inform the Data Subject within 30 days of receipt of a request.
- In the future a standardised procedure or format for responses may developed by the Commission.

 Data Controllers must reply to a Subject Access Request within 30 days of receipt. In complex cases this may be extended as long the Data Subject is informed of the delay within one month.

Section 2 – Information and Access to Personal Data

Article 13	Information to be provided where personal data is collected from the Data Subject	• When collecting personal data, the Controller shall provide:

  - their (or their representative's) identity and contact details.
  - the DPO's contact details.
  - the purpose for which the personal data will be processed.

(Continued)

Article	Subject Area	Explanation of Main Points in the Article

- the legal basis for processing.
- the Controller or third party's legitimate interests.
- details of the recipients or categories of recipients with whom the data is shared.
- details of any adequacy decision/safeguards in place if the Controller intends to transfer personal data to a third country/international organisation.
- details of the period for which the data will be stored, or the criteria used to determine that period.
- confirmation of the individual's rights of: access, rectification, restriction of processing as well as the right to object to processing and the right to data portability.
- where the processing is based on consent (or explicit consent) it must be made clear to the Data Subject that they have the right to withdraw consent at any time.
- confirmation of the Data Subject's right to lodge a complaint with a Supervisory authority.
- clarification as to whether data provided as a statutory or contractual requirement, or if it is a requirement necessary to enter into a contract.
- whether the Data Subject is obliged to provide the personal data and of the possible consequences of failure to provide such data.
- whether the data will be subject to automated decision-making, including profiling (meaningful information about the logic involved, as well as the significance and envisaged consequences should be provided).

- Where the Controller intends to process the personal data other than for the original purpose the Data Subject must be informed of this change before processing can commence.

    - any new purpose will be subject to the requirements above unless the subject already has this information.

Article	Subject Area	Explanation of Main Points in the Article
Article 14	Information to be provided where personal data has not been obtained from the Data Subject	• Where the personal data is not obtained from the Data Subject, Controllers are still obliged to provide the Data Subject with the following information: ○ the Controller (or their representative's) identity and contact details. ○ the DPO's contact details. ○ the purpose for which the data is processed. ○ the legal basis for processing. ○ the categories of data concerned. ○ details of the recipients or categories of recipients of the data. ○ details of any adequacy decision/safeguards in place if the Controller intends to transfer data to a third country/international organisation. ○ the period for which the data will be stored (or the criteria used to determine that period). ○ what the legitimate interests of the Controller (or third party) are. ○ the Data Subject's rights (access, rectification, erasure, restriction of processing as well as the right to object to processing and the right to data portability). ○ the Data Subject's right to withdraw consent at any time if processing is based on consent or explicit consent. ○ the Data Subject's right to lodge a complaint with a Supervisory Authority. ○ the source of the personal data and whether it came from publicly accessible sources (if applicable). ○ whether the data will be subject to automated decision-making, including profiling. 　▪ In this case meaningful information about the logic involved, as well as the significance and the envisaged consequences of such processing for the Data Subject should be provided. • The information above should be provided within a reasonable period after obtaining the personal data (within one month at the latest); or at the time of first communication to the Data Subject or when the data is first disclosed to another recipient.

(Continued)

Article	Subject Area	Explanation of Main Points in the Article
		• Where the Controller intends to process the personal data other than for the purpose for which it was originally gathered then the Data Subject must be informed of this change before processing can commence.
		• If the obligation to inform the data, subject is likely to make achieving the objective of processing impossible or it will seriously impair the objectives then the Controller should take appropriate measures to protect the rights, freedoms and legitimate interests of the Data Subjects.
		• If obtaining or disclosure is expressly laid down by the EU or a Member State and appropriate measures are in place to protect the Data Subject's rights then there is no need to inform the Data Subject.
		• Where the personal data must remain confidential subject to an obligation of professional secrecy then the Data Subject does not need to be informed.
		• The conditions above do not apply where the Data Subject already has the information or if providing the information is impossible or would involve a disproportionate effort.

 You can only use this exemption for information that was provided by a party other than the Data Subject **as long as** appropriate safeguards are in place.

Article	Subject Area	Explanation of Main Points in the Article
Article 15	Right of access by the Data Subject	• The Data Subject has the right to receive confirmation that their data is being processed by a Controller **and should** be given access to any personal data being processed. • Data Controllers should provide Data Subjects with the following information: ○ the purpose of processing. ○ the categories of personal data concerned. ○ the recipients or categories of recipient to whom the personal data have been or will be disclosed (particularly if recipients are in third countries or international organisations). ○ the period for which the data will be stored (or the criteria used to determine that period).

Article	Subject Area	Explanation of Main Points in the Article

		○ the Data Subject's rights to rectification, erasure or to restrict or object to the processing.
		    ○ the Data Subject's right to complain to the Supervisory Authority.
		    ○ information about the source of the personal data where it was not collected from the Data Subject.
		    ○ information about whether the data will be subject to automated decision-making, including profiling (including meaningful information about the logic involved, the significance and the envisaged consequences of such processing for the Data Subject).
		
		• Where personal data is transferred to a third country or to an international organisation, the Data Subject has the right to be informed of the safeguards taken in relation to the transfer.
		• The Controller shall provide the Data Subject with a free copy of their personal data.
		
		    ○ if any further copies are required the Controller may charge a reasonable fee to cover administrative costs.
		    ○ if the request is made by electronic means the information should be provided in a commonly used electronic form (unless requested otherwise by the Data Subject).
		
		• The right of individuals to obtain a copy of their personal data should not adversely affect the rights and freedoms of others.

Section 3 – Rectification and Erasure

Article	Subject Area	Explanation of Main Points in the Article
Article 16	Right to rectification	• The Data Subject has the right to ask the Controller to rectify inaccurate personal data about to themselves without undue delay. • As long as the purpose of processing permits it, the Data Subject has the right to ask the Data Controller to make incomplete personal data completed (e.g. by providing a supplementary information).
Article 17	Right to erasure ("right to be forgotten")	• The Data Subject has the right ask the Controller to erase data about them without undue delay.

(Continued)

Article	Subject Area	Explanation of Main Points in the Article

- The Controller is obliged to erase personal data without undue delay where one of the following applies:

  - the personal data is no longer necessary for the purpose for which it was collected or processed.
  - the Data Subject has withdrawn the consent on which the processing is based and there is no other legal ground for the processing.
  - the Data Subject objects to the processing (and processing is carried out on grounds of consent or by automated means) and there are no overriding legitimate grounds for the processing.
  - the personal data has been unlawfully processed.
  - a legal obligation in EU or Member State law has instructed that the personal data be erased.
  - the personal data was collected in order to offer information society services to a child.

- Where the Controller has made the personal data public and is subsequently obliged to erase the personal data, they shall take reasonable steps to inform other Controllers that the Data Subject has requested the erasure (e.g. asking them to remove links to and copies or replicas of that personal data).

  - the Data Controller may take into account available technology and cost when complying with this requirement.

- The right to be forgotten does not apply where processing is necessary:

  - to exercise the right of freedom of expression and information.
  - to comply with a legal obligation which requires processing by EU or Member State law.
  - to perform a task in the public interest.
  - to exercise the official authority vested in the Controller.
  - for reasons of public interest in the area of public health.

Article	Subject Area	Explanation of Main Points in the Article
		○ for archiving purposes in the public interest or for scientific, historical, or statistical purposes in so far as the right to be forgotten is likely to make the achievement of the objectives of processing impossible. ○ to establish, exercise or defend a legal claim. • Member States determine the limits of free expression under their national laws. Beware, it is possible that data may be processed under freedom of expression in some Member States but not in others. If in doubt check with the Supervisory Authority.
Article 18	Right to restrict processing	• If one of the following applies then the Data Subject has the right to instruct the Controller to restrict processing: ○ the Data Subject contests the accuracy of the personal data. ■ processing may be restricted for a period so that the Controller can verify the accuracy of the personal data. ○ the processing is unlawful but the Data Subject doesn't want the data erased they may request that its use is restricted instead. ○ the Controller no longer needs the personal data, but the Data Subject needs it for a legal claim. ○ the Data Subject has objected to processing and pending the verification whether the Controller's legitimate grounds override the Data Subject's rights. • Where processing has been restricted the data may only be processed(excluding storage) under the following conditions: ○ with the Data Subject's consent. ○ for a legal claim. ○ to protect the rights of another natural or legal person. ○ for reasons of public interest of the EU or of a Member State. • Where a Data Subject has restricted processing, they must be informed by the Controller before any restriction is lifted.

(Continued)

Article	Subject Area	Explanation of Main Points in the Article
Article 19	Notification obligation regarding rectification, erasure, or restriction of processing of data	• The Controller shall inform each recipient of data of the details of any "rectification", "erasure" or "restriction of processing" requests it receives. Unless this proves impossible or involves disproportionate effort. • The Controller shall inform the Data Subject who the recipients of the data are if the Data Subject requests it.
Article 20	Right to data portability	• The Data Subject has the right to receive a copy of any data that they provided to a Data Controller about themselves. It should be provided in a structured, commonly used and machine-readable format. • The Data Subject has the right to transmit this data to another Controller without hindrance where: ○ processing is based on consent (or explicit consent). ○ processing is based on a contract and the processing is carried out by automated means. • In exercising their right to data portability, the Data Subject has the right to ask for the personal data to be transmitted directly from one Controller to another (where this is technically feasible). • The right of data portability shall not prejudice an individual's the right to be forgotten. ○ the right does not apply to processing for a task in the public interest or where a Controller exercises their official authority. • The right to data portability should not adversely affect the rights and freedoms of others.

Section 4 – Right to Object and Automated Individual Decision-Making

Article 21	Right to object	• The Data Subject has the right to object **at any time** to their personal data being processed when it is based on legitimate or public interest or the exercising of the Controller's official authority (this includes objecting to any profiling based on those provisions).

Article	Subject Area	Explanation of Main Points in the Article
		• Where an objection is made the Controller may no longer process the personal data unless they can demonstrate compelling legitimate grounds that override the interests, rights and freedoms of the Data Subject. • The Data Subject has the right to object at any time to the processing of personal data for direct marketing purposes (including profiling related to direct marketing). ○ where the Data Subject has objected to processing for direct marketing purposes, their data may no longer be processed for marketing. • The Data Subject's rights to object to processing shall be explicitly brought to their attention when the organisation first communicates with them. ○ The information shall be presented clearly and separately from any other information. • The Data Subject may exercise his or her right to object to processing by automated means where appropriate. • Where personal data is processed for scientific, historical research or statistical purposes the Data Subject has the right to object to their data being processed. • Where processing is necessary for a task in the public interest then the subject does not have the right to object to processing.
Article 22	Automated individual decision-making, including profiling	• The Data Subject has the right not to be the subject of a decision based solely on automated processing (including profiling) unless: ○ the decision is necessary to enter into or to perform a contract between them and a Data Controller. ○ the decision is authorised by EU or Member State law. ○ the decision is based on the Data Subject's explicit consent. • Where automated decision-making or profiling is permitted the Data Controller must safeguard the Data Subject's rights, freedoms and legitimate interests.

(Continued)

Article	Subject Area	Explanation of Main Points in the Article
		• Where automated decision-making or profiling is permitted the Data Controller must provide both the right for human intervention and provide opportunities to the subject to express their point of view/contest any decision. • Automated decision-making shall not be based on special categories of personal data unless consent or public interest applies and there are suitable safeguards in place.

Section 5 – Restrictions

Article 23	Restrictions	• EU or Member State law may restrict the rights of the Data Subject when they consider it is necessary and proportionate to safeguard:

- ○ national security.
- ○ defence.
- ○ public security.
- ○ prevention, investigation, detection or prosecution of criminal offences or the execution of criminal penalties (including to guard against or prevent threats to public security).
- ○ other important objectives of general public interest, in particular an important economic or financial interest including monetary, budgetary and taxation matters, public health and social security.
- ○ protection of judicial independence and judicial proceedings.
- ○ prevention, investigation, detection and prosecution of breaches of ethics for regulated professions.
- ○ monitoring, inspection or regulatory functions connected to the exercise of official authority.
- ○ protection of Data Subject or the rights and freedoms of others.
- ○ enforcement of civil law claims.

• Legislative measure shall contain specific provisions relating to:

- ○ the purpose of the processing or categories of processing.
- ○ the categories of personal data.
- ○ the scope of the restrictions introduced.

Article	Subject Area	Explanation of Main Points in the Article
		○ the safeguards to prevent abuse or unlawful access or transfer.
		○ the specification of the Controller or categories of Controllers.
		○ the storage periods and applicable safeguards taking into account the nature, scope and purposes of the processing or categories of processing.
		○ the risks to the rights and freedoms of Data Subjects.
		○ the right of Data Subjects to be informed about the restriction, unless it may be prejudicial to the purpose of the restriction.

GDPR CHAPTER IV – Controller and Processor

Section I – General Obligations

Article	Subject Area	Explanation of Main Points in the Article
Article 24	Responsibility of the Controller	• Data Controllers must be able to **demonstrate** that processing is in accordance with the GDPR by putting suitable technical and organisational measures in place. • Controllers may take into account the nature, scope and context of the processing and the likelihood of the risks to individuals actually happening. • Measures should include implementing appropriate (proportionate) data protection policies. • Compliance may be demonstrated by either adhering to an approved code of conduct (see Article 40) or obtaining an approved certification (see Article 42).

Article 25	Data protection by design and by default	• Principles such as data minimisation and pseudonymisation should be implemented in an effective manner.
		• Appropriate safeguards should be integrated into processing both when determining the means of processing and when the processing takes place.
		• Controllers can take into account the risks and likelihood of any potential breach as well as the state of the art, the cost of implementation and the nature, scope, context and purposes of processing when designing a system.
		• The default should be to only to process personal data that is necessary for a specific purpose. There should be limits on:
		  ○ the amount of personal data collected.
		  ○ the extent of the processing.
		  ○ the period it is stored or accessible.

(Continued)

Article	Subject Area	Explanation of Main Points in the Article
		• Personal data may not be made accessible to an indefinite number of people without the intervention of a human being (this should be a default setting).
		• Compliance with this requirement may be demonstrated by obtaining an approved certification (see Article 42).
Article 26	Joint Controllers	• Where two or more Controllers jointly determine the purpose and means of processing, they are **joint Controllers** (they can decide between themselves their respective responsibilities).
		• The roles and relationships of each joint Controller should be clear.
		• The Data Subject should be made aware of the roles and relationships of the joint Controllers.
		• The Data Subject may exercise their rights against any of the Controllers.
		• Joint Controllers should designate a contact point for Data Subjects.
Article 27	Representatives of Controllers or Processors not established in the Union	• Where the Controller/Processor is based outside the EU they should appoint a representative who is based inside the Union as their first point of contact for GDPR enquiries.
		• The representative and Data Subjects should be in the same Member State.
		• The Controller/Processor shall make it clear that the representative is to be addressed in addition to or instead of the Controller/Processor on all issues related to processing.
		• Legal actions may still be initiated against the Controller/Processor.
		• A representative within the EU is not required if:
		○ processing is occasional and unlikely to result in a risk to individuals rights and freedoms **and** does not include large scale processing of special categories of data or of data about criminal convictions/offences.
		○ the Processor/Controller are a public authority or body.
Article 28	Processor	• A Data Controller may only appoint a Processor who can demonstrate that they are compliant with the GDPR legislation.

- If a Processor determines the purposes and means of processing then they shall be considered to be a Controller in respect of that element of data.
- There should be a legally binding contract between data Processors and their Controllers.
- Contracts with Processors shall be in writing, including in electronic form.
- The contract may be based, in whole or in part, on standard contractual clauses and must stipulate the following:

  - processing will only take place on the documented instructions from the Controller.
  - those who process the personal data are committed to or have a statutory obligation of confidentiality.
  - measures to maintain the security of data.
  - measures required to enable the Controller to respond to requests from the Data Subject.
  - security measures.
  - how to respond to Data Breaches.
  - requirements to delete or return all the personal data at the end of the contract period unless further storage is required by law.
  - information required to demonstrate compliance with the regulation.
  - the Processor's responsibility to inform the Controller if an instruction infringes the regulations.

- A Processor may not engage another Processor without the written authorisation of the Controller.
- Where a Processor engages sub-contractor then that contract should contain the same data protection obligations as set out in the original contract with the Controller.

  - should a "sub Processor" fail to fulfil its data protection obligations, the initial Processor shall be liable.

- Compliance may be demonstrated by either adhering to an approved code of conduct (see Article 40) or obtaining an approved certification (see Article 42).

Article	Subject Area		Explanation of Main Points in the Article
Article 29	Processing under the authority of the Controller or Processor	•	The Processor may not process the data unless instructed to do so by the Controller unless they are required to do so by law.
Article 30	Records of processing activities	•	Each Controller (and their representative if appropriate) should keep a record of processing activities which contains the following information:
		○	the name and contact details of the Controller (their DPO, representative or any joint Controllers).
		○	the purpose of processing.
		○	the categories of data being processed.
		○	who the data will be disclosed to.
		○	any safeguards in place if the data is transferred to a third country or international organisation.
		○	the time limits within which each category of data should be erased.
		○	a general description of the security measures in place.
		•	Each Processor (and their representative if appropriate) shall keep a record of all categories of processing activities carried out on their behalf, which includes:
		○	the name and contact details of the Processor or Processors.
		○	the name and contact details of each Controller (and, where applicable, the Controller's representative, and their DPO).
		○	the categories of processing carried out on behalf of each Controller.
		○	the details of any third country or an international organisation with whom data is shared and any safeguards in place.
		○	a general description of the security measures in place.
		•	These records of processing activities shall be in writing, including in electronic form.
		•	The record should be made available to the Supervisory Authority on request.

Article	Subject Area	Explanation of Main Points in the Article
		The obligations listed do not apply to an organisation that employs fewer than 250 persons **unless** the processing is not occasional, it is likely to result in a risk to the rights and freedoms of the Data Subjects or includes special categories of data or data relating to criminal convictions/offences.
Article 31	Cooperation with the Supervisory Authority	• All Controllers and Processors must cooperate with the Supervisory Authorities.

Section 2 – Security of personal data

Article	Subject Area	Explanation of Main Points in the Article
Article 32	Security of processing	• Processing may only take place on the instructions of the Data Controller. • Data Controllers and Processor should take steps to ensure processing is secure. • Controllers and Processors must implement security measures that are appropriate to the risk to the data. • Any risk (e.g. accidental/unlawful destruction, loss, alteration, unauthorised disclosure/access) may be balanced against the state of the art and the costs of implementing the measures. • Security measures may include: ○ pseudonymisation. ○ encryption. ○ confidentiality, integrity, availability and resilience of processing systems and services. ○ an ability to restore the availability and access to personal data in a timely manner in the event of an incident. ○ regular testing. • Compliance may be demonstrated by either adhering to an approved code of conduct (see Article 40) or obtaining an approved certification (see Article 42).
Article 33	Notification of a personal Data Breach to the Supervisory Authority	• The Data Controller must report any Data Breach to the relevant Supervisory Authority as soon as possible and within 72 hours at the most.

(Continued)

Article	Subject Area		Explanation of Main Points in the Article
		•	A breach report should provide information about the company, the nature of the breach, the number and categories of data concerned, the likely consequences and the details of the DPO.
			Many Supervisory Authorities have an online breach report format. It is recommended that organisations check what should be reported and ensure that internal breach forms contain this information.
		•	All Data Breaches must be documented.
		•	If the Data Breach is unlikely to result in a risk to the rights and freedoms of Data Subjects then it need not be reported but must be logged.
		•	Data Processors need to inform their Data Controllers of a breach as soon as possible after it occurs in order that the Data Controller can report the breach.
Article 34	Communication of a personal Data Breach to the Data Subject	•	Any organisation that suffers a high-risk Data Breach, which is likely to have a significant impact on their Data Subject's rights and free-doms, must inform the Data Subject without delay.
		○	the information should be provided in clear and plain language describing the nature of the breach and its likely consequences.
		•	The Data Subject may not need to be informed if:
		○	the Controller has appropriate protection measures in place (e.g. encryption).
		○	the Controller has taken measures to ensure that any risk is no longer likely to materialise.
		○	it would involve disproportionate effort to inform every Data Subject.
		▪	in which case a public notice may be required.
		•	If the Controller has not already informed the Data Subject of a breach the Supervisory Authority may require them to do so.

Article	Subject Area	Explanation of Main Points in the Article

Section 3 – Data Protection Impact Assessment and prior consultation

Article	Subject Area	Explanation of Main Points in the Article
Article 35	Data Protection Impact Assessment	• Organisations who plan to introduce new technologies in high-risk data processing should carry out a Data Protection Impact Assessment (DPIA) before processing. For example, if processing involves: ○ evaluation of personal aspects based on automated processing and decision-making (e.g. profiling). ○ large scale processing of special categories of data or data relating to criminal convictions and offences. ○ systematic monitoring of a publicly accessible area on a large scale. • A DPIA should provide the following information: ○ a systematic description of the envisaged processing operations and the purposes of the processing. ○ an assessment of the necessity and proportionality of the processing operations in relation to the purposes. ○ an assessment of risks to Data Subjects' rights and freedoms. ○ measures envisaged to demonstrate the organisation has addressed the risks and ensured that personal data is protected (e.g. safeguards, security measures and mechanisms). • The Controller should consult with their DPO (where there is one) when carrying out a DPIA. • Where appropriate the Controller may seek the views of Data Subjects. • The DPIA should be reviewed regularly. • The Supervisory Authority will publish a list of the types of processing operations which require a DPIA to be completed and those which do not. • Where a law covers the processing operation in question, and a DPIA has already been carried (e.g. as part of a general impact assessment) then a further assessment is not required.

(Continued)

Article	Subject Area	Explanation of Main Points in the Article
Article 36	Prior consultation	• Member States will consult their Supervisory Authority when planning new laws or regulatory measures which relate to processing personal data.
		• Member State law may require Controllers to consult with, and obtain prior authorisation from, the Supervisory Authority to process data in the public interest (e.g. social protection/ public health).
		• Where a DPIA indicates that the planned processing will be particularly high-risk then the organisation should consult their Supervisory Authority before proceeding.
		• The following information should be provided to Supervisory Authorities as part of prior consultation:
		○ the responsibilities of the Controller, joint Controllers and Processors involved.
		○ the purpose and means of the intended processing.
		○ measures and safeguards in place.
		○ the contact details of the DPO (where applicable).
		○ the Data Protection Impact Assessment (DPIA).
		○ any other information requested by the Supervisory Authority.
		• If the planned processing planning could infringe the GDPR, then the Supervisory Authority must offer advice within eight weeks (14 weeks if the processing is particularly complicated).

Section 4 – Data Protection Officer

Article	Subject Area	Explanation of Main Points in the Article
Article 37	Designation of the Data Protection Officer	• A Data Protection Officer (DPO) is required where:
		○ processing is carried out by a public authority or body.
		○ the core activities of the Controller/Processor involve regular and systematic monitoring of Data Subjects on a large scale.
		○ the core activities of the Controller/Processor involve processing special categories of data and criminal convictions data on a large scale.

Article	Subject Area	Explanation of Main Points in the Article
		• The DPO should be appointed on the basis of professional qualities as well as expert knowledge of data protection law and practices and their ability to carry out the tasks listed in Article 39 below.
		• One DPO may serve a number of organisations or several public authority or bodies.
		• Associations and bodies representing categories of Controllers or Processors may require a DPO to be appointed.
		• The DPO may be a staff member in the Controller/Processor organisation or may fulfil the tasks through a service contract.
		• The Controller or the Processor is required to publish their DPO's contact details.
		• The Controller/Processor is required to share their DPO's contact details with the Supervisory Authority.
Article 38	Position of the Data Protection Officer	• The DPO must be involved in all aspects of data protection in the organisation.
		• The DPO should be given the resources necessary to carry out their tasks (e.g. access to personal data and processing operations, and ongoing training).
		• The DPO should not be given instructions in how to carry out their DPO role.
		• The DPO should not be dismissed or penalised for performing their role.
		• The DPO should directly report to the highest management level.
		• Data Subjects should be able to contact the DPO about all issues relating to processing of and to the exercise of their rights.
		• The DPO shall be bound by secrecy or confidentiality in performing their task.
		• The DPO may fulfil other roles within the organisation as long as they do not result in a conflict of interests.
Article 39	Tasks of the Data Protection Officer	• The DPO should have the following tasks:
		○ to inform and advise the Controller, Processor and their employees of their obligations.
		○ to monitor compliance with GDPR and other data protection legislation.

(Continued)

Article	Subject Area	Explanation of Main Points in the Article
		○ to monitor compliance with the Controller/Processor's data protection policies (including assigning responsibilities, awareness-raising, training of staff and completing Data Audits).
		○ to provide advice on DPIAs where requested and monitor its performance.
		○ to cooperate with the Supervisory Authority.
		○ to act as the contact point for the Supervisory Authority on processing, prior consultation, and to consult with regard to any other matter.
		• The DPO shall pay due regard to the risk associated with processing operations, taking into account the nature, scope, context and purposes of processing.

Section 5 – Codes of Conduct and Certification

Article	Subject Area	Explanation of Main Points in the Article
Article 40	Codes of conduct	• Suitable codes of conduct may be drawn up by Member States, Supervisory Authorities, the European Data Protection Board and the Commission.
		• Associations and other bodies who represent categories of Controllers or Processors may prepare, amend or extend codes of conduct relating to:
		○ fair and transparent processing.
		○ legitimate interests of Controllers in specific contexts.
		○ collection of personal data.
		○ pseudonymisation of personal data.
		○ information provided to the public and to Data Subjects.
		○ Data Subjects exercising their rights.
		○ information provided to, and the protection of, children.
		○ the manner in which the consent is obtained from those with parental responsibility for children.
		○ measures and procedures in respect of privacy by design and default.
		○ measures to ensure security of processing.
		○ mechanisms to notify the Supervisory Authority of Data Breaches and the communication of these details to Data Subjects.

Article	Subject Area	Explanation of Main Points in the Article
		○ transferring personal data to third countries/international organisations.
		○ out-of-court proceedings and dispute resolution procedures for disputes between Controllers and Data Subjects.
		• Controllers or Processors who are not subject to GDPR may also adhere to such codes of conduct by making binding and enforceable commitments to apply appropriate safeguards.
		• Any code of conduct shall contain mechanisms to permit the monitoring of compliance with the code.
		• If a draft code of conduct relates to processing activities in one Member State then the Supervisory Authority in that state may register and publish the code. If the draft code of conduct relates to processing activities in several Member States then the Supervisory Authority will submit it to the European Data Protection Board who will provide an opinion and seek approval from Commission for the approved code of conduct to be adopted.
		• The Commission will publish approved codes.
		• The European Data Protection Board will keep a register of all approved codes of conduct, amendments and extensions which should be publicly available.
Article 41	Monitoring of approved codes of conduct	• Monitoring compliance with a code of conduct may be carried out by a body with an appropriate level of expertise relating to the subject-matter.
		• Monitoring bodies will be accredited by the competent Supervisory Authority providing they have:
		○ demonstrated their independence and expertise in the subject-matter.
		○ established procedures to assess the eligibility of Controllers and Processors, to monitor their compliance and to periodically review its operation.
		○ established procedures and structures to handle complaints about infringements of the code, the manner in which the code has been implemented and made those

(Continued)

Article	Subject Area	Explanation of Main Points in the Article
		procedures and structures transparent to Data Subjects and the public.
		○ demonstrated to the satisfaction of the competent Supervisory Authority that its tasks and duties do not result in a conflict of interests.
		• The competent Supervisory Authority shall submit the draft criteria for accreditation to the European Data Protection Board.
		• A monitoring body shall suspend, exclude or take other appropriate action if a Controller or Processor infringes the code.
		○ The monitoring body shall inform the competent Supervisory Authority of what has taken place and why.
		• The competent Supervisory Authority may revoke the accreditation of a monitoring body if the conditions for accreditation are not, or are no longer, met or where actions taken by the body infringe this Regulation.
		• Processing carried out by public authorities and bodies does not require adherence to an approved code of conduct.
Article 42	Certification	• Suitable data protection certification mechanisms, data protection seals and marks may be established up by Member States, Supervisory Authorities, the European Data Protection Board and the Commission.
		• Data protection certification mechanisms, seals or marks may be used to demonstrate that appropriate safeguards have been put in place by Controllers or Processors who are not subject to this Regulation (i.e. third countries/ international organisations).
		• Certification shall be voluntary and the process shall be transparent.
		• Certification does not reduce the Controller or Processor's responsibility to comply with GDPR.
		• Certification shall either be issued by a certification body (see Article 43) or by the competent Supervisory Authority.
		• If the criteria are approved by the European Data Protection Board, this may result in

Article	Subject Area	Explanation of Main Points in the Article
		a common certification, the European Data Protection Seal.
		• A Controller/Processor who submits to the certification mechanism shall provide the certification body with all information and access to its processing activities necessary for the certification procedure.
		• Certification shall be issued for a maximum of three years.
		• Certification may be renewed provided that the relevant requirements continue to be met or may be withdrawn where they are no longer met.
		• The European Data Protection Board shall maintain a public register of all certification mechanisms and data protection seals and marks.
Article 43	Certification bodies	• Certification bodies who have an appropriate level of expertise in relation to data protection may issue and renew certification.
		• These certification bodies shall be accredited by the Supervisory Authority or the national accreditation body (or both).
		• Certification bodies shall be accredited only where they have:
		○ demonstrated their independence and expertise to the satisfaction of the competent Supervisory Authority.
		○ undertaken to respect the criteria referred to in Article 42(5).
		○ established procedures to issue, review and withdraw certification, seals and marks.
		○ established procedures and structures to handle complaints about infringements and to make those procedures and structures transparent to Data Subjects and the public.
		○ demonstrated that their tasks and duties do not result in a conflict of interests.
		• The competent Supervisory Authority will set the criteria for the accreditation of certification bodies (these details shall be made public).
		• Certification bodies are responsible for assessment leading to certification or the withdrawal of certifications.
		• Accreditation may be issued for a maximum of five years and may be renewed on the same conditions.

(Continued)

Article	Subject Area	Explanation of Main Points in the Article
		• Certification bodies will provide the Supervisory Authorities with the reasons for granting or withdrawing certifications. • The competent Supervisory Authority or the national accreditation body may revoke an accreditation where the conditions are not, or are no longer, met or where actions taken by a certification body infringe this Regulation. • The Commission may lay down technical standards for certification mechanisms and data protection seals and marks, and mechanisms to promote and recognise those certification mechanisms, seals and marks.

GDPR CHAPTER V – Transfers of Personal Data to Third Countries or International Organisations

Article	Subject Area	Explanation of Main Points in the Article
Article 44	General principle for transfers	• Personal data may only be transferred to a third country or to an international organisation if they abide by the conditions laid down in Articles 45–50. • All the provisions in this Chapter shall be applied to ensure that the protection of natural persons is not undermined.
Article 45	Transfers on the basis of an adequacy decision	• The European Commission may affirm that a territory, one or more specified sectors within a third country, an international organisation or a third country's data processing practices are "adequate". ○ Where the adequacy rule is in place any data transfer does not require specific authorisation. • When assessing if there is an adequate level of protection, the Commission shall take account: ○ the rule of law, respect for human rights and fundamental freedoms, relevant legislation and the access of public authorities to personal data. ○ the implementation of such legislation, data protection rules, professional rules and security measures, including rules for the onward transfer of personal data to another third country or international organisation.

Article	Subject Area	Explanation of Main Points in the Article
		◦ case-law, as well as effective and enforceable Data Subject rights and effective administrative and judicial redress for the Data Subjects. ◦ the existence and functioning of an independent Supervisory Authority in the country concerned. ◦ any international commitments the country or international organisation concerned has entered into in particular in relation to data protection. • The implementing act will specify any territorial or sectoral applications and provide a mechanism for a periodic review (at least every four years), which takes into account developments in that period. • The Commission will monitor developments in third countries and international organisations that could affect their adequacy decisions. • The Commission may repeal, amend or suspend adequacy decision. • The Commission may enter into consultations with the third country or international organisation with a view to remedying an adequacy rule. • The Commission shall publish a list of the third countries, territories and specified sectors within a third country and international organisations with an adequate level of protection in the Official Journal of the European Union and on its website. • Decisions adopted by the Commission shall remain in force until amended, replaced or repealed.
Article 46	Transfers subject to appropriate safeguards	• In the absence of an adequacy decision a Controller/Processor may only transfer personal data to a third country or an international organisation if the Controller/Processor has provided appropriate safeguards, and there are enforceable Data Subject rights and effective legal remedies available. • Appropriate safeguards include: ◦ legally binding, enforceable instruments between public authorities/bodies. ◦ binding corporate rules. ◦ standard data protection clauses adopted by the Commission.

(Continued)

Article	Subject Area	Explanation of Main Points in the Article
		<ul><li>○ standard data protection clauses adopted by a Supervisory Authority and approved by the Commission.</li><li>○ an approved code of conduct or approved certification together with binding and enforceable commitments from the Controller/Processor in the third country to apply these safeguards particularly in regard to Data Subjects' rights.</li></ul><ul><li>Subject to authorisation from the Supervisory Authority, the appropriate safeguards referred to above may also be provided by:</li></ul><ul><li>○ contractual clauses between the Controller/Processor and the Controller/Processor or recipient of the personal data in the third country/international organisation.</li><li>○ provisions to be inserted into administrative arrangements between public authorities or bodies which include enforceable and effective Data Subject rights.</li></ul><ul><li>Supervisory Authorities may apply the consistency mechanism.</li><li>Authorisations shall remain valid until amended, replaced or repealed, if necessary, by the Supervisory Authority.</li></ul>
Article 47	Binding corporate rules	<ul><li>A Supervisory Authority may approve binding corporate rules provided that they are:</li></ul><ul><li>○ legally binding, apply to and are enforced by every member concerned of the group of undertakings engaged in a joint economic activity, including their employees.</li><li>○ expressly confer enforceable rights on Data Subjects with regard to the processing of their personal data.</li><li>○ specify at least:</li><ul><li>▪ the structure and contact details of the group and its members.</li><li>▪ the type of data transfers, categories of data, type of processing and its purposes, the type of Data Subjects affected and the identity of the third country/countries in question.</li></ul></ul>

- their legally binding nature, both internally and externally.
- the application of GDPR and the requirements in respect of onward transfers to bodies not bound by the binding corporate rules.
- the rights of Data Subjects with regard to processing and the means to exercise those rights.
- the acceptance by the Controller/ Processor of liability for any breaches of the binding corporate rules by any member not established in the Union.
- how the information on the binding corporate rules is provided to the Data Subjects.
- the tasks of any DPO or any other person in charge of monitoring compliance within the group of undertakings as well as monitoring training and complaint-handling.
- the complaint procedure.
- the mechanisms within the group to ensure verification of compliance.
- mechanisms for reporting and recording changes to the rules and reporting those changes to the Supervisory Authority.
- cooperation mechanisms with the Supervisory Authority to ensure compliance.
- mechanisms for reporting any legal requirements to the competent Supervisory Authority if they are likely to have a substantial adverse effect on the guarantees provided by the binding corporate rules.
- data protection training of personnel with permanent or regular access to personal data.

- The Commission may specify the format and procedures for the exchange of information between Controllers, Processors and Supervisory Authorities for binding corporate rules.

(Continued)

Article	Subject Area	Explanation of Main Points in the Article
Article 48	Transfers or disclosures not authorised by Union law	• In addition to any of the allowable circumstances for third country data transfers, as set out above (Articles 44–50) a court in a third country may rule that personal data should be transferred out of the EU. • Such a court ruling will only be enforceable if there is an international agreement between the third country and the EU or EU Member State.
Article 49	Derogations for specific situations	• Under certain circumstances it is possible to transfer personal data to a non-approved third country, even if appropriate safeguards or binding corporate rules are not in place. • Transfer personal data to a non-approved third country may happen in the following circumstances: ○ the person whose data is being transferred has specifically consented to it, after being informed of the risks. ○ the transfer is necessary for a legal claim. ○ the transfer is necessary for a contract between the Data Subject and Controller or the Controller and another natural or legal person. ○ the transfer is necessary to save the person's life, and they're unable to consent to it. ○ the transfer is necessary for important reasons of public interest (recognised in law). ○ the transfer is necessary for the establishment, exercise or defence of legal claims. ○ the transfer is made from a register which according to Union or Member State law is intended to provide information to the public as long as it does not involve the entirety of the personal data or entire categories of the personal data contained in the register. • In the absence of an adequacy decision, Union or Member State law may, for reasons of public interest, set limits to the transfer of specific categories of personal data to a third country or an international organisation.

Article	Subject Area		Explanation of Main Points in the Article
Article 50	International cooperation for the protection of personal data	•	The Commission and Supervisory Authorities shall take appropriate steps to develop international cooperation mechanisms with third countries and international organisations through:
		○	international mutual assistance.
		○	stakeholder engagement in discussion and activities aimed at furthering international cooperation.
		○	promoting the exchange and documentation of personal data protection legislation and practice, including on jurisdictional conflicts with third countries.

GDPR CHAPTER VI – Independent Supervisory Authorities

Section 1 – Independent Status

Article 51	Supervisory Authority	•	Each Member State has one or more independent public authority "Supervisory Authority". (SA) to monitor the application of GDPR in their Member State.
		•	Each SA contributes to the consistent application of GDPR throughout the Union by cooperating with other SAs and the Commission.
		•	If a Member State has more than one SA (e.g. Germany), one will be designated as the lead.
Article 52	Independence	•	Each SA is completely independent.
		•	Members of SAs exercise their powers in accordance with GDPR and are free from external influence.
		•	Member States shall ensure that SAs are appropriately resourced so that they can perform their task, and select their own staff.
		•	SAs shall have a separate, public annual budget.
Article 53	General conditions for the members of the Supervisory Authority	•	SA members should be appointed through a transparent procedure.
		•	Each member shall have the qualifications, experience and skills to perform their duties and exercise their powers.
		•	The duties of a member end at the expiry of their term of office, resignation or compulsory retirement, in accordance Member State law.
		•	A member shall be dismissed only in cases of serious misconduct or if they no longer fulfil the conditions required to perform their duties.

(Continued)

Article	Subject Area		Explanation of Main Points in the Article
Article 54	Rules on the establishment of the Supervisory Authority	•	Member States will legislate to set up their SA including the necessary qualifications, rules and procedures terms of office, and other conditions as appropriate.
		•	Staff in the SA shall be subject to a duty of professional secrecy (during and after their term of office) in relation to information they become aware of during their term of office.
		•	Member States may create their own rules in relation to obligations of professional secrecy for Controllers/Processors that are subject as long as the Commission is informed of these rules.

Section 2 – Competence, tasks and powers

Article	Subject Area		Explanation of Main Points in the Article
Article 55	Competence	•	Each SA must be able and allowed to carry out all the tasks assigned to them by the Regulation.
		•	SAs may not supervise processing activities of courts acting in their judicial capacity.
Article 56	Competence of the lead Supervisory Authority	•	Where data processing takes place across borders, the SA of the EU Member State in which the organisation is based (or does most of its processing) will be the lead SA.
		•	Complaints or allegations of infringement will be handled by the SA of the Member State in which the incident occurred. If this is not the lead SA then the SA concerned must inform the lead SA and ask if they wish to deal with the incident itself, or let the reporting SA handle it. The lead SA has three weeks to make this decision.
		•	When engaged in cross-border data processing the organisation should only communicate with the lead SA.
Article 57	Tasks	•	Each SA has the following tasks:
		○	monitor and enforce the application of GDPR.
		○	promote public awareness and understanding of the risks, rules, safeguards and rights in relation to processing (especially activities addressed specifically to children).
		○	advise on legislative and administrative measures which relate to the protection of rights and freedoms in respect of processing.

Article	Subject Area	Explanation of Main Points in the Article
		○ promote awareness of the SA's obligations to Controllers/Processors.
		○ upon request, provide information to any Data Subject about how to exercise their rights under the Regulation
		○ cooperate with SAs in other Member States.
		○ handle complaints, investigate the matter and inform the complainant of the progress and outcome of the investigation.
		○ cooperate with other SAs to ensure the regulation is applied and enforced in a consistent manner.
		○ conduct investigations on how GDPR is being applied.
		○ monitor developments in information and communication technologies and commercial practices.
		○ adopt standard contractual clauses.
		○ establish and maintain a list in relation to the requirement for Data Protection Impact Assessment.
		○ give advice on the processing operations.
		○ encourage the drawing up of codes of conduct.
		○ draft and publish the criteria for the accreditation of a body to monitor codes of conduct and create a certification body.
		○ provide opinion and approval of codes of conduct which provide sufficient safeguards.
		○ encourage the establishment of data protection certification mechanisms and of data protection seals and marks and approve the criteria of certification.
		○ conduct periodic reviews of certifications issued.
		○ accredit a body to monitor codes of conduct and a certification body.
		○ authorise contractual clauses and provisions.
		○ approve binding corporate rules (see Article 47).
		○ contribute to the activities of the European Data Protection Board.

(Continued)

Article	Subject Area	Explanation of Main Points in the Article
		○ keep internal records of infringements and of measures taken.
		○ fulfil any tasks related to the protection of personal data.
		• Each SA shall make the complaints process as simple as possible. Providing an electronic complaint submission form as well as other complaints mechanisms.
		• SAs shall provide their services free of charge for both the Data Subject and, where applicable, the DPO.
		• Where requests are manifestly unfounded or excessive, in particular because of their repetitive character, the SA may charge a reasonable fee based on administrative costs, or refuse to act on the request. The SA is responsible for demonstrating that the request is manifestly unfounded or excessive.
Article 58	Powers	• SAs have the following powers:
		○ Investigative powers (gaining access to a Data Controller/Processor's premises and equipment).
		○ Corrective powers (issuing warnings and fines for infringement).
		○ Advisory powers (opinions to parliament about data protection issues).
		Examples of the use of these powers by a number of Supervisory Authorities can be found in Chapter 1, Table 1.1.
Article 59	Activity reports	• Each SA is required to prepare an annual report on its activities which is transmitted to the national parliament, the government and other authorities as well as being made public.

GDPR CHAPTER VII – Cooperation and Consistency

Section 1 – Cooperation

Article 60	Cooperation between the lead Supervisory Authority	• The lead SA must cooperate with the other SAs and exchange all relevant information.
		• The lead SA may request mutual assistance when carrying out an investigation or monitoring the implementation of a measure concerning a Controller/Processor in another State.

Article	Subject Area	Explanation of Main Points in the Article

		• The lead SA shall communicate all relevant information to the other SAs concerned.
		
		  ◦ If another SA raises a concern of an objection to a draft decision then the matter will be submitted to the consistency mechanism.
		  ◦ If it intends to follow the objection a revised draft decision will be presented by the lead SA to the other SA.
		  ◦ Where none of the SAs concerned object to the draft decision then the lead SA and the SAs concerned shall be deemed to be "in agreement" with that draft decision and shall be bound by it.
		
		• The lead SA shall adopt the decision.
		• The lead SA shall notify the Controller or Processor at their main establishment of the decision.
		• The lead SA shall inform the other SAs concerned and the European Data Protection Board of their decision.
		• The SA with whom a complaint has been lodged shall inform the complainant on the decision.
		
		  ◦ Where a complaint is dismissed or rejected, the SA with whom the complaint was lodged shall adopt the decision and notify both the complainant and the Controller.
		  ◦ Where the lead SA and the SAs concerned agree to dismiss or reject parts of a complaint and to act on other parts of that complaint, a separate decision shall be adopted for each part.
		  ◦ The lead SA shall notify the main establishment or single establishment of the Controller/Processor on the territory of its Member State and shall inform the complainant.
		  ◦ The SA of the complainant shall adopt the decision for the part concerning dismissal or rejection of that complaint, and shall notify it to that complainant and shall inform the Controller/Processor thereof.

(Continued)

Article	Subject Area	Explanation of Main Points in the Article
		• After being notified of the decision of the lead SA the Controller/Processor shall take the necessary measures to ensure compliance with the decision.
		○ The Controller/Processor shall notify the lead SA of the measures taken to comply with the decision. The lead SA shall inform the other SAs concerned.
		• Where a SA has reasons to consider that there is an urgent need to act in order to protect the interests of Data Subjects, the urgency procedure referred to in Article 66 will apply.
		• The SA shall provide the information to each other by electronic means, using a standardised format.
Article 61	Mutual assistance	• SAs are required to help each other implement the Regulation. This includes providing each other with all necessary information.
		○ the information requested shall be provided in a standardised format.
		○ a fee may not be charged.
		• If one SA asks another for help a response must be received within one month.
		○ If a response is not received the requesting SA may adopt a provisional measure in that Member State.
		• Requests can only be refused under very specific circumstances, including:
		○ if it is outside of the SA's capability, powers or abilities.
		○ complying with the request would infringe the regulation.
		• Reasons for any refusal must be given.
Article 62	Joint operations of Supervisory Authorities	• SAs may conduct joint operations including joint investigations and joint enforcement measures (e.g. where a Controller/Processor is established in several Member States).
		• A SA from one Member State may grant some of their powers a SA in another state.
		• The host Member State is liable for the action of any staff from another supervising authority working on their behalf.

Article	Subject Area		Explanation of Main Points in the Article
Section 2 – Consistency			
Article 63	Consistency mechanism	•	SAs shall cooperate with each other and the Commission to ensure the Regulation is applied consistently.
Article 64	Opinion of the European Data Protection Board	•	The European Data Protection Board will issue an opinion where a SA takes certain actions. These include where a SA wishes to:
		○	approve a code of conduct covering data processing activities across several Member States;
		○	authorise certain contractual clauses to allow organisations to transfer data to non-approved third countries;
		○	approve binding corporate rules to allow companies to transfer data to non-approved third countries.
		•	Member States are responsible for determining the limits of free expression under national law.
		✐	This can mean that information may be processed under freedom of expression in some Member States but not in others.
Article 65	Dispute resolution by the Board	•	If there is a disagreement among SAs about how to implement the GDPR then the European Data Protection Board may make a binding decision on the matter. For example, if:
		○	a SA has raised an objection to a draft decision of the lead authority or the lead authority has rejected an objection.
		○	where there are conflicting views on which of the SAs concerned is competent for the main establishment.
		○	where a competent SA does not request the opinion of the Board or does not follow the opinion of the Board.
		•	Any European Data Protection Board binding decision shall be adopted within one month (two for complex matters) and the SAs will be notified. The decision will be published on the Board's website.
		•	The lead SA must adopt the final decision of the board without undue delay and at the latest by one month after being notified of the decision.

(Continued)

Article	Subject Area	Explanation of Main Points in the Article
Article 66	Urgency procedure	• In exceptional circumstances (e.g. a SA considers that there is an urgent need) temporary laws may be put in place to mitigate risks. • Such laws may be in place for a maximum of three months. • The SA must inform other SAs and the board of these circumstances. • A SA who has acted in this manner may request an urgent opinion or an urgent binding decision from the European Data Protection Board, giving reasons for requesting such opinion or decision. • Any SA may request urgent action from the European Data Protection Board if another SA has failed to take appropriate action.
Article 67	Exchange of information	• The Commission can pass implementing acts in order to specify how information is exchanged between SAs, and between SAs and the European Data Protection Board.

Section 3 – European Data Protection Board

Article	Subject Area	Explanation of Main Points in the Article
Article 68	European Data Protection Board	• The European Data Protection Board (the Board) is made up of the head of one Supervisory Authority from each EU Member State. • The Board is represented by its Chair. • The European Commission may attend European Data Protection Board meetings but may not vote.
Article 69	Independence	• The European Data Protection Board acts independently when performing its tasks or exercising its powers, neither seeking nor taking instructions.
Article 70	Tasks of the Board	• The European Data Protection Board ensures that the Regulation is consistently applied through monitoring, advice, opinion. • The Board also examines questions, issues guidelines, recommendations and best practice as appropriate. • The Board is also responsible for: ○ the establishment of data protection certification mechanisms, seals and marks. ○ accreditation of certification bodies. ○ maintaining a public register of accredited bodies and accredited Controllers or Processors. ○ providing the Commission with an opinion on certification requirements.

Article	Subject Area	Explanation of Main Points in the Article
		• The Board promotes cooperation and the effective bilateral and multilateral exchange of information, training and best practice.
		• The Board, issues and maintains a publicly accessible electronic register of decisions made by Supervisory Authorities/courts.
		• Recommendations made by the Board are forwarded to the Commission and made public.
		• Where appropriate the Board consults with interested parties and give them the opportunity to comment. The results of any consultation are made publicly available.
Article 71	Reports	• The European Data Protection Board produces an annual report which is made public. This report includes a review of the practical application of the guidelines, recommendations, best practice and details of any disputes that it has made a judgement on.
Article 72	Procedure	• The Board makes its decisions by a simple majority vote.
		• The Board may change its rules or adopt new operational arrangements by a two-thirds majority vote.
Article 73	Chair	• A Chair and two deputy chairs are elected from members of the Board by a majority vote.
		• Chairs and Deputies may serve two, 5-year terms maximum.
Article 74	Tasks of the Chair	• The tasks of the Chair of the European Data Protection Board are to:
		○ convene meetings of the Board.
		○ prepare Board agendas.
		○ notify the Supervisory Authorities of the Board's decisions.
		○ ensure the Board acts in a timely manner.
Article 75	Secretariat	• The European Data Protection Supervisor provides a secretariat for the European Data Protection Board (under the instruction of the Chair of the Board).
		• The secretariat provides analytical, administrative and logistical support to the Board including, the day-to-day business of the Board, communications, translation, meeting preparation, drafting and publication of documentation.
		• The secretariat has separate reporting lines to the European Data Protection Supervisor's staff.
		• Secretariat support to the board is subject to a Memorandum of Understanding.

(Continued)

Article	Subject Area	Explanation of Main Points in the Article
Article 76	Confidentiality	• The discussions of the European Data Protection Board are confidential if appropriate. • Some of the documents submitted to members of the Board may be made available to the public in accordance with Regulation (EC) No 1049/2001.

GDPR CHAPTER VIII – Remedies, Liability and Penalties

Article	Subject Area	Explanation of Main Points in the Article
Article 77	Right to lodge a complaint with a Supervisory Authority	• Every Data Subject shall have the right to lodge a complaint with a Supervisory Authority which may be based in the Member State of: ○ the Data Subject's habitual residence. ○ the Data Subject's place of work. ○ the place of the alleged infringement. • The Supervisory Authority must keep complainants informed about the progress and the outcome of their complaint.
Article 78	Right to an effective judicial remedy against a Supervisory Authority	• Individuals have the right to take a Supervisory Authority to court to seek remedies against them (e.g. if it has not handled a complaint properly). • The court will be in the EU Member State in which the Supervisory Authority is based.
Article 79	Right to an effective judicial remedy against a Controller or Processor	• Individuals have the right to lodge a complaint with a Supervisory Authority **and** the right to take the Data Controller/Processor to court if they think that their rights have been infringed as a result of processing which was not in compliance with GDPR. • Proceedings against a Controller/Processor can be in a court either in the EU Member State where the Data Controller/Processor is based or the State in which the individual is based.
Article 80	Representation of Data Subjects	• When an individual brings a court case against a Supervisory Authority, Data Controller or Processor, they have the right to be supported by a not-for-profit organisation (as long as the organisation is involved in data protection and has objectives that serve the public interest). • EU Member States must also allow this organisation to lodge complaints with Supervisory Authorities on behalf of individuals.

Article	Subject Area	Explanation of Main Points in the Article
Article 81	Suspension of proceedings	• If a Member State court is dealing with a case against a Data Controller/Processor and it becomes aware that there is a related case pending against the same Data Controller/Processor in a different EU Member State then the first court should contact the second court to confirm this. ○ The second court may then suspend proceedings.
Article 82	Right to compensation and liability	• Anyone who has been damaged by an infringement of GDPR has a right to compensation from Data Controller/Processor making the infringement. • Data Controllers involved in data processing are liable for the damage caused by that processing if they infringe the Regulation. • Data Processors are only responsible for the damage they cause by: ○ infringing parts of GDPR specifically addressed to data Processors. ○ acting against the instructions of their Data Controller. • Controllers/Processors are only exempt from liability if they can prove that they are not in any way responsible for the event giving rise to the damage. • Where more than one (or both) Controller or Processor are involved in the same processing and they are responsible for any damage then each of them is liable for the entire damage. • Controllers/Processors are entitled to claim back part of the compensation which corresponds to the actions of another Controller/Processor.
Article 83	General conditions for imposing administrative fines	• Supervisory Authorities may fine a Data Controller/Processor for infringing the GDPR. • Fines are designed in part to serve as a deterrent and therefore should be effective, proportionate and dissuasive. • The Supervisory Authority takes several factors into account when deciding whether to impose a fine, and how much a fine should be. These factors include: ○ the seriousness of the infringement. ○ whether it was intentional or negligent.

(Continued)

Article	Subject Area	Explanation of Main Points in the Article

- whether any steps were taken to limit the damage done.
- the number of Data Subjects.
- the degree to which the Controller/Processor is responsible.
- any relevant previous infringements.
- the degree of cooperation taken to remedy matters and mitigate against adverse effects.
- the categories of personal data affected.
- how the Supervisory Authority became aware of the infringement.
- if the Controller/Processor notified the infringement.
- if there the Controller/Processor had previous orders against them that relate to the same subject-matter and they complied with those measures.
- any other aggravating or mitigating factors.

- Fines may be imposed in addition to, or instead of, advisory and corrective measures.
- Fines of **€10,000,000**, or up to **2% of the total worldwide annual turnover** of the preceding financial year, **whichever is higher** may be imposed for infringements such as:

  - a breach of the rules on gaining a child's consent for online services.
  - failure to integrate appropriate data protection mechanisms into a data processing system.
  - failure to submit all necessary information as part of a certification process.

- Other infringements attract a maximum fine of up to **€20,000,000**, or up to **4% of the total worldwide** annual turnover, **whichever is higher.** Examples include:

  - failure to properly gain consent where it is required.
  - failure follow the rules when processing special category data
  - not complying with the Supervisory Authority.

- Member States may lay down the for fines on public authorities.

Article	Subject Area		Explanation of Main Points in the Article
Article 84	Penalties	•	Member States shall implement a separate system of penalties to deter infringement of the GDPR in addition to the fines set out in the Regulation.

GDPR CHAPTER IX – Provisions Relating to Specific Processing Situations

Article	Subject Area		Explanation of Main Points in the Article
Article 85	Processing and freedom of expression and information	•	Member States are responsible for determining the limits of free expression under their own national laws (including journalistic, academic, artistic or literary expression). This may include changes to:
		○	rights of the Data Subject.
		○	role of the Controller and Processor.
		○	the transfer of personal data to third countries or international organisations.
		○	the power of independent Supervisory bodies.
		•	Data may be processed for the purposes of free expression in some Member States but not in others.
		•	Member States shall notify to the Commission of any provisions it has adopted without delay.
Article 86	Processing and public access to official documents	•	Personal data held in official documents may be processed.
		•	In these circumstances the member State is responsible for striking a balance between the right of the public to access this information and the individual's right to privacy.
Article 87	Processing of the national identification number	•	Member States may apply their own conditions to the processing of national identification numbers.
		○	Identity numbers may only be used where there are suitable safeguards in place.
Article 88	Processing in the context of employment	•	Member State employment laws fall outside GDPR.
		•	Member States should strike a balance between national employment laws and an individual's right to privacy.
		•	Member States may develop for more specific rules to ensure the protection of individual's rights and freedoms in respect employment in particular for:
		○	recruitment.
		○	contracts of employment.
		○	management.

(Continued)

Article	Subject Area	Explanation of Main Points in the Article
		○ planning and organisation of work. ○ workplace equality and diversity. ○ health and safety at work. ○ protection of employer's or customer's property. ○ the exercise and enjoyment of rights and benefits related to employment. ○ termination of employment.
Article 89	Safeguards and derogations relating to processing for archiving purposes in the public interest, scientific or historical research purposes or statistical purposes	• There are certain purposes for which personal data may be processed in the public interest, outside of the GDPR's standard requirements. • Suitable safeguards should be put in place where rights are removed for data being processed in the public interest (e.g. where an individual's rights would make the activity impossible or seriously impair the achievement of the specific purpose). • Where processing is for scientific/historical research or statistical purposes the following rights may not apply: 　○ Right of access. 　○ Right to rectification. 　○ Right to restrict processing. 　○ Right to object. • Where processing is for archiving purposes in the public interest. The following rights may not apply: 　○ Right of access. 　○ Right to rectification. 　○ Right to restrict processing. 　○ Right to object. 　○ Right to erasure. 　○ Right to data portability. • The rights of the Data Subject must be safeguarded in the above cases and safeguards shall ensure that technical and organisational measures are in place in to ensure respect for the principle of data minimisation. This may include pseudonymisation. • Where further processing is required but the Data Subjects do not need to be identified a method of removing the identity should be used. • Where processing serves at the same time another purpose, any derogations apply only to processing for the purposes referred above.

Article	Subject Area	Explanation of Main Points in the Article
Article 90	Obligations of secrecy	• Member States may create their own rules in relation to Controllers or Processors that are subject to obligations of professional secrecy (e.g. Banks and Law Firms) as long as they inform the Commission. • Those rules shall apply only with regard to personal data which the Controller/Processor has received as a result of or has obtained in an activity covered by that obligation of secrecy.
Article 91	Existing data protection rules of churches and religious associations	• Churches and religious associations or communities may apply their own data protection rules provided that they are in line with this Regulation. • Churches or religious associations may be supervised by an independent Supervisory Authority (provided that it fulfils the conditions of this regulation).

GDPR CHAPTER X – Delegated Acts and Implementing Acts

Article	Subject Area	Explanation of Main Points in the Article
Article 92	Exercise of the delegation	• GDPR gives the European Commission power to pass particular acts which may be used to make changes to existing laws. • This delegation of power is conferred on the Commission for an indeterminate period of time. • The European Council and Parliament can revoke this power at any time. • The European Parliament and to the Council should be notified simultaneously as soon as the Commission adopts a delegated act. • A delegated act shall enter into force only if no objection has been expressed by either the European Parliament or the Council within a period of three (max six) months.
Article 93	Committee procedure	• A committee (defined in Regulation (EU) No 182/2011) will be set up to assist with the application of the regulation. Articles 5 and 8 of Regulation (EU) No 182/2011 apply to this committee.

GDPR CHAPTER XI – Final Provisions

Article	Subject Area	Explanation of Main Points in the Article
Article 94	Repeal of Directive 95/46/EC	• GDPR repeals Directive 95/46/EC. • Any references to Directive 95/46/EC should be taken as a reference to GDPR. • References to the Working Party on the Protection of Individuals (WP29) should be taken as references to the European Data Protection Board.

(Continued)

Article	Subject Area	Explanation of Main Points in the Article
Article 95	Relationship with Directive 2002/58/EC	• GDPR does not place additional burdens on telecoms providers who process data under the ePrivacy Directive (2002/58/EC).
		🖝 At the time of writing there was uncertainty in the relationship between GDPR and the ePrivacy Directive. This will be subject to future clarification.
Article 96	Relationship with previously concluded Agreements	• Agreements relating to the transfer of personal data to third countries or international organisations may remain in force until they are updated or revoked as long as they were in place on 24 May 2016 and complied with EU law prior to that date.
Article 97	Commission reports	• The commission will review GDPR every four years. • The review will be reported to the European Parliament. • Commission reports will be made public and should examine: ◦ transfer of personal data to third countries/international organisations under adequacy conditions. ◦ examination of third countries national regulations. ◦ how cooperative and consistent independent Supervisory Authorities have been. • The reports may take into account any European Parliament positions or findings. • National supervisory bodies and member states may be required to provide information for these reports. • The commission may make recommendations for changes to the regulations in light of technological advancements.
Article 98	Review of other Union legal acts on data protection	• Other legislation may be updated to protect personal data in a way that is consistent with GDPR. Particularly where processing is done by EU bodies or it relates to the free movement of data.
Article 99	Entry into force and application	• GDPR is effective from 25 May 2018.

Chapter 4

Applying **GDPR** to your organisation

This chapter discusses the building blocks that are needed in order to apply GDPR to a business.

The key is to ensure that you have responsible data practices in place that comply with GDPR. There are three steps to take: Build awareness; Understand the data you hold; and Communicate the information.

How does **GDPR** apply to my business?

You need to ask yourself the question "Do we collect, use, store or do anything else with the personal information of employees, customers or both?". If the answer is yes then GDPR applies to you and you must therefore understand what your role is in the processing of that data. In some countries you will need to be registered with your Supervisory Authority.

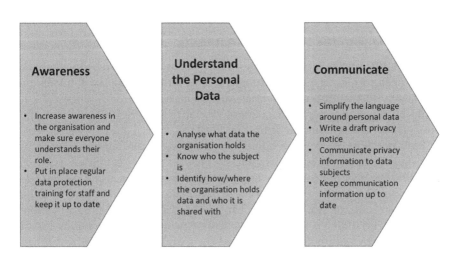

Figure 4.1 GDPR Building Blocks

Review any previous registration

An established business will already be aware that it processes personal data and should have been working in compliance with the previous national data protection legislation. Many Supervisory Authorities accept registration under previous legislation as meeting the GDPR criteria.

Even if there is more work to do by being compliant with the previous law, organisations are already on the way to working in compliance with GDPR. This is because many of the new rules and themes build on the previous laws. Examples of additional tasks that may be required include:

- Check the registration with the Supervisory Authority.
- Develop Privacy Notices and data protection policies if none exist.
- Undertake a Data Audit to understand who has access to the data, where it is shared and how it is disposed of.

If the organisation did not work in compliance with the previous data protection legislation then it will need to do quite a lot of work to make sure it complies with all the statutory obligations. Compliance with GDPR will be part of this.

If the organisation works with sensitive personal information including things like health, race/ethnicity, political opinions, religious or philosophical beliefs then additional work will be required in order to comply with the new law because the rules relating to special categories of information such as this are more stringent.

To help organisations, many of the Supervisory Authorities produce packages of tools and resources on their websites. A link to the UK ICO resources is in the Resources Section (see Resource Link 4.1).

Registering with the Supervisory Authority

If the GDPR applies to your business or organisation then you should check if you need to register with your Supervisory Authority. This will usually be the Supervisory Authority in which the business is based. Alternatively, it could be the authority in the country the Data Subjects are based in if the business is registered outside of Europe.

It is not possible to give advice on the system throughout Europe as each nation approaches registration differently. Some countries, such as UK, place a legal obligation on Data Controllers to register and pay a Data Protection Fee, while other countries like France maintain a list of Data Controllers but do not make a charge. Germany has adopted a sector-specific registration system and Ireland has maintained its previous list of registrations but insists the Data Protection Commission is informed when a DPO is appointed.

UK registration

CASE STUDY 4.1   REGISTRATION WITH THE SUPERVISORY AUTHORITY

In a recent survey of small business owners attending a business net-working event in the UK 46% had not yet registered with the ICO.

The requirement to register in UK is different to the requirement under the 1998 DPA. Many SMEs and businesses are still unaware that they need to register. In many cases they think they are too small for the legislation to apply or they are fearful of doing something wrong so have chosen to do nothing.

There are very few businesses in the UK to whom the legislation does not apply (see the following list of exempt organisations). Controllers who had a registration in UK under the 1998 DPA will not have to pay the new fee until their previous registration expires.

Every other organisation in UK needs to register with the ICO irrespective of whether they are a business, social group or charity. This is because by holding personal information in a filing system of any sort (whether it is something as simple as an order book for the butcher or a complicated computer database for an insurance company) you fall under the GDPR legislation.

Registration is simple and should take about 10–15 minutes. It is simply a matter of going to the Supervisory Authority's website and filling in an online form. Failure to register is likely to result in a fine. A link to the UK ICO registration tool is in the Resources Section (Resource Link 4.2).

Within the UK there are 4 registration tiers. Annual fees for these tiers are between £40 and £2,900. The exact amount an organisation is required to pay will generally depend on how many people the business employs and what the annual turnover is. The tiers in UK are:

- **Exempt organisations and individuals** – Not for profit organisations, small pension funds, members of the House of Lords and selected (or prospective) representatives such as MPs and councillors are exempt from registration with the UK ICO.
- **Tier 1 organisations** – Tier 1 organisations include all charities, pubic authorities or businesses who employ less than 10 staff and have an annual turnover of less than £632,000. The annual fee for tier 1 organisations is £40.

- **Tier 2 organisations** – Tier 2 organisations include businesses who employ less than 250 staff and have an annual turnover of less than £36 million. The annual fee for tier 2 organisations is £60.
- **Tier 3 organisations** – Tier 3 organisations include businesses who employ more than 250 staff and have an annual turnover of more than £36 million. The annual fee for tier 3 organisations is £2,900.

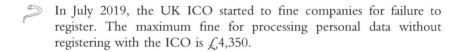 In July 2019, the UK ICO started to fine companies for failure to register. The maximum fine for processing personal data without registering with the ICO is £4,350.

Decide if you are a Controller or Processor

Once you have identified that the Regulations applies to your business, then the next step is to work out whether you are a "Controller" or "Processor" of the personal data (in some cases organisations may be both a Controller and a Processor). Chapter 5 contains detailed information on Controllers and Processors including discussion of their roles and responsibilities.

The term "Processing" means obtaining, recording or holding data or carrying out any operation on information or data in GDPR. This can include:

- Organising, adapting or altering information or data.
- Use, retrieval or consultation of information or data.
- Disclosure of information.
- Alignment, combination, blocking, erasure or destruction of information or data.

Data Controller

A "Data Controller" is the person or organisation who (alone or jointly) determines the purpose for which data is processed and the manner in which it is processed. An organisation making the following decisions is a Data Controller:

- To collect data in the first place.
- Which items of data to collect.
- The purpose or purposes the data are to be used for.
- Which individuals to collect data about.
- The legal basis for collecting data.
- Whether to disclose the data, and if so, who to.
- Whether subject access and other individuals' rights apply.
- Whether to make non-routine amendments to the data.
- How long to keep the data.

The Controller has overall responsible for the data. It is the Controller who should have a GDPR compliant contract with their Processor(s). The controlled will define their Processor's legal obligations (e.g. the requirement to maintain records of personal data and processing activities) and set out who has legal liability if there is a Data Breach.

Data Processor

The "Data Processor" can be any person (other than an employee of the Data Controller) who processes the data on behalf of the Data Controller. Data Processors make the following decisions:

- How to store the data.
- Which IT systems or other methods to use to collect the data.
- The details of the security that will surround the personal data.
- What means to use to transfer the data between organisations.
- What means will be used to retrieve data.
- The method for ensuring a retention schedule is adhered to.
- The means used to delete or dispose of the data.

Build awareness

Once you understand what data you hold and your role you can start to build awareness. Everyone who deals with someone else's personal data needs to be aware of what the data is and understand their role is in keeping it safe. This means that the owners/board members/governors/trustees who lead the organisation have as much of a role to play as the staff who actually work with the information on a daily basis.

Personal data is defined in Article 4(1) of the GDPR (*Article 4, EU GDPR, "GDPR Definitions"*). Quote 4.1 provides the exact text.

QUOTE 4.1   ARTICLE 4(1) OF GDPR – PERSONAL DATA

"Personal data" means any information relating to an identified or identifiable natural person ("data subject"); an identifiable natural person is one who can be identified, directly or indirectly, in particular by reference to an identifier such as a name, an identification number, location data, an online identifier or to one or more factors specific to the physical, physiological, genetic, mental, economic, cultural or social identity of that natural person;   *Article 4 (1)*

There is more information in Chapter 6 to help the reader understand Personal Data. I recommend that readers who have no idea whether the data that their organisation processes comes under the category of "personal data" read Chapter 6 first.

Regular briefing, updates and training are the best way to achieve this awareness throughout the business. It is preferable to make these updates relevant to the organisation and an individual's role within it. However, if you cannot develop business specific training there are many generalist data protections and GDPR training packages available on the internet. Chapter 14 provides suggestions for staff training and links are provided to the companion website (www.pppmanagement.co.uk/resources), which has more training assets for the reader.

Understand the data

Businesses will hold personal data on a range of individuals. Including customers, staff, owners, suppliers and third parties. In order to understand the data your organisation holds you will need to identify all the various types of personal data that the business gathers about the individuals it interacts with. This will range from simple forms of personal data such as names and email addresses or telephone numbers to more complicated special categories of information such as medical or bank information and photographs.

CASE STUDY 4.2   EXEMPLAR HOLISTICS

Exemplar Holistics is a small holistic therapy company with one or occasionally two members of staff. The company offers, massage, complementary therapies and podiatry services to NHS and private patients. The company is registered with a number of medical insurance companies as a recognised provider. The business operates from 3 locations, as part of a self-employed therapy team in a clinic in the town centre (they rent a room), a converted room in the lead therapist's home and as a mobile service in patients own homes.

Case study example – personal information sources

In this chapter we use Exemplar Holistics as our case study on which to expand the issue of understanding personal data within a business context. The details of all the case studies in the book are in the Case Studies section on the companion website.

The case study company holds personal information on the following individuals:

- The business owner.
- Patients.
- Clinic employees.
- Patients' emergency contacts.
- Staff emergency contacts.
- The clinic.
- Suppliers.
- Named individuals (Local Authority/NHS/other organisations).

Although it is only a small organisation, because the business processes sensitive information it recognises that it needs to make a record of its processing activities (in accordance with Article 30(2) of GDPR). It will therefore make a list of what this personal data comprises (from simple contact details and names for some individuals such as suppliers to more complex and sensitive data which includes medical or financial information for patients).

To capture all the types of data involved we completed a simple table (Table 4.1) which shows what information is held on each category of Data Subject. This information is documented so that appropriate measures can be put in place to manage and protect the data.

Table 4.1 Examples of Personal Data Held by Exemplar Holistics

Type of Personal Data	Patients	Suppliers	Staff	Clinic	NHS Insurers, LA, etc
Name	X	X	X	X	X
Phone Number	X	X	X	X	X
Marital Status	X		X		
Family Details	X		X		
Email Address	X	X	X	X	X
Emergency Contact	X		X		
Residence Access	X		X		
Bank Information	(online payments)	X	X	X	X
Medical Conditions	X				
Medical History	X		X		
Reason for Treatment	X				
Mental Health Status	X				

The movement of data within the business was then discussed by asking a series of questions.

1. How is the information gathered?
2. Where do you store the gathered information?
3. Is it processed (or updated) any further or just filed?
4. Do other organisations provide personal information?
5. Is the information shared with other organisations?
6. Are there any standalone systems that also contain personal information?
7. Are references provided or received?

This enables Table 4.2 to be completed.

Draw up a simple data flow diagram

A simple data flow diagram (see Figure 4.2) will help to look at the systems used to process information, from which you are able to decide where possible vulnerabilities in the business are. The diagram also captures who the

Table 4.2 Personal Data Movement Questions – Exemplar Holistics

Data Flow Questions	Answers	Choose from
How is the information gathered?	Paper Application Forms for customers	Paper Application forms, Electronic Application Forms, Staff application forms (Paper or Digital)
Where is the gathered information stored?	Paper Files, Computer Files	Email Files, Paper Customer Files, Paper Staff Files, Electronic Files, Management information, Administration, Bank Payments System, Website
Is it processed (or updated) any further or just filed?	Updated after Each Treatment	Processed Further, Updated, Filed
Do other organisations provide personal information?	NHS	Names of other Organisations who provide information (Photographers, Press, Credit Reference Agencies, Other bodies, Pensions, HMRC, Payroll, Crime Prevention/ Safeguarding)
Is the information shared with other organisations?	Crime Prevention	Names of other Organisations who Receive Information (see above)
Are there any standalone systems that also contain personal information?	Facebook	CCTV, Accounting System, Facebook, Twitter, Instagram, other Processors, sub-Processors etc.
Are References Provided or Received	Provided and Received	Provided, Received

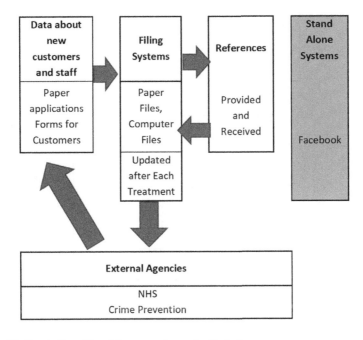

Figure 4.2 Simple Date Flow Diagram – Exemplar Holistics

organisation shares information with as well as who is responsible for it (e.g. is it processed in house or does someone else do the work on your behalf).

The areas to consider are information storage, sharing and disposal.

From this data flow diagram and the personal data gathering questions the business was able to create a data map. Figure 4.3 shows a high-level data map for data relating to patients of Exemplar Holistics:

Data Audit

In a larger organisation, once they know which elements of personal information are processed and whether it is a Controller or Processor, the next step is to complete a Data Audit. It is helpful to have the flow diagrams and questionnaire above to populate the initial audit findings.

There is no right or wrong way to complete a Data Audit, although many consultants or advisors will direct you to their preferred solution. Organisations should select an approach that best suits their business.

Sometimes it may be possible to gather all staff together and brainstorm or interview individual specialists on a 1:1 basis. The work can be completed by

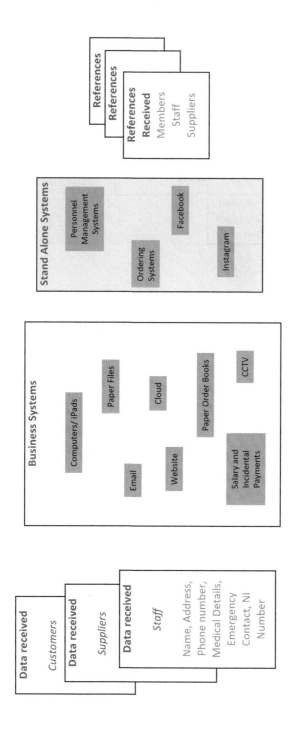

Figure 4.3 High Level Data Map Diagram – Exemplar Holistics

a team or given to one person to complete. Noticeboards, sticky notes or a database programme such as Excel can be used.

At the end of this work a database will have been produced that identifies every piece of personal data that the organisation holds. Showing:

- Who the Data Subject is.
- What the source of personal data is (is it collected or received?).
- The approximate volume of data held.
- How often the data is processed (per day/week/month).
- A description of each item of personal data to be processed.
- Whether the organisation is a Processor or Controller.
- What the purpose of processing is.
- What the lawful basis of processing is.
- What the retention period is.
- The category of the data.
- What format the data is held in (electronic/paper).
- How the data is transferred to others (if it is).
- The geographic location of the processing.
- If the data processed by automated means.
- Who has access to the data.

The answers to the questions below will help the organisation to put a suitable data management system in place.

- Are third parties or Data Processors involved?
- Is there any cross-border processing (within the EU or internationally)?
- Are there any privacy risks?
- What is the risk to rights and freedoms of Data Subjects?
- Does the organisation have an appropriate Privacy Notice?
- Have the organisation applied data limitation policies?
- How does the organisation ensure accuracy?
- Have the organisation ensured data minimisation?
- Have the organisation implemented storage limitation?
- What security have the organisation in place?
- Where the organisation get consent how the organisation asks for and record consent?
- How the organisation record and manage ongoing consent?

Other questions to ask are who is going to be your Data Protection Officer and how you will review, monitor and update your data protection plans and policies.

The important thing to remember is that it will take time to get the audit right. Depending on the size of the organisation the completed document may be several pages in length (our latest audit ran to 27 A3 pages).

Once complete the audit will need to be checked by departments for accuracy and to highlight any changes that have occurred since it was first completed. Figure 4.4 (opposite) is an example of a Data Audit capturing patient personal data.

Understand the risks

Once you have recorded, identified and mapped the data collection task you will be able to complete an analysis of the systems that you use to hold this data. There are 3 types of possible security risk:

- **Physical risks** such as losing memory sticks or paper files.
- **Procedural risks** such as the wrong person getting access to personal data.
- **Software risks** such as the risks from hacking or failure of the system.

All of these risks should be identified for each element of data that is held.

CASE STUDY 4.3   CCTV RISK ANALYSIS

At Exemplar Holistics the patient is photographed on CCTV entering the property for safeguarding reasons. In this case the CCTV risks include:

- Failure of the user to access the system.
- Remote access by an unauthorised user.
- Loss of data.
- Updating of data.
- Inadequate data deletion.
- Failure to register with the ICO.
- Failure to display ICO Registration.

Keep the data safe

All staff within the organisation should be made aware of what personal data the organisation holds and the systems it is held on. Who has access to this information will depend on their role.

Keeping data safe is discussed at length in Chapter 11. Some steps that organisations could take to ensure staff keep data safe would be to incorporate the following guidance into your data safety policy:

	Type	Source	Legal basis	Originally	Updated	Retention Period	Determined by	How Held	Shared With	Sensitive Data
Patients	Name	Individual	Contract	First Consultation	None	Last Treatment + 8 Years	Industry Practice	Hard Copy + Mobile Phone	NHS/ Insurer	No
	Address	Individual	Contract	First Consultation	As required	Last Treatment	Industry Practice	Hard Copy	Updated after each treatment	No
	Family Details	Individual	Consent	First Consultation	As required	Last Treatment	Industry Practice	Hard Copy	Updated after each treatment	No
	Marital Status	Individual	Consent	First Consultation	As required	Last Treatment	Industry Practice	Hard Copy	Updated after each treatment	No
	Contact Details	Individual	Contract	First Consultation	As required	Last Treatment + 8 Years	Industry Practice	Hard Copy + Mobile Phone	Updated after each treatment	No
	Health Details	Individual	Contract	First Consultation	Updated after each treatment	Last Treatment + 8 Years	Industry Practice	Hard Copy	Updated after each treatment	Yes
	Medical Conditions	Individual	Contract	First Consultation	Updated after each treatment	Duration of Service	Industry Practice	Hard Copy	Updated after each treatment	Yes
	Treatment Information	Therapist	Contract	Each Consultation	Updated after each treatment				NHS/ Insurer	Yes
	Photograph	CCTV System	Vital Interests (Safeguarding)	First Consultation	As required	6 months from date	Industry Practice	IT System	Police/ Safeguarding	No
	Bank Account	Individual	Consent	First Consultation	As required	Last Treatment	Industry Practice	Quickbooks	Updated after each treatment	No
	Insurance/NHS	Individual	Consent	First Consultation	As required	Last Treatment + 8 Years	Industry Practice	Hard Copy	Updated after each treatment	No
Emergency Contact	Name	Individual	Vital Interests	First Consultation	As required	Last Treatment	Industry Practice	Hard Copy		No
	Contact Details	Individual	Vital Interests	First Consultation	As required	Last Treatment	Industry Practice	Hard Copy		No

Figure 4.4 Extract from Exemplar Holistics Data Audit Table

- Anonymise or redact personal data where possible or where appropriate.
- Be conscious of what is on the screen when others can see.
- Be mindful of individuals with duplicated or similar names.
- Be mindful of possible vulnerability when using off site Wi-Fi to log in to emails etc.
- Complete a simple risk analysis of the systems the organisation uses; concentrating on physical, procedural and software security.
- Delete/shred or securely dispose of personal data that is no longer required.
- Do not share personal data with others unless authorised.
- Only keep personal data for the minimum amount of time necessary.
- Password protect portable memory devices containing personal data and keep them safe.
- Report any Data Breach as soon as it occurs.
- Seek guidance on information security when required.

How to respond to Data Breach

Breaches can be either accidental or deliberate. A simple Data Breach is an occasion when:

- personal data is lost, destroyed, corrupted or disclosed.
- someone accesses personal data or passes it on without proper authorisation.
- personal data is made unavailable, for example, when it has been encrypted by ransomware, or accidentally lost or destroyed.

Each organisation needs to have a plan in place to respond to breaches that come to light. All breaches should be properly recorded, investigated and remedial action should be taken where appropriate. Not every Data Breach needs to be reported to the ICO,

Organisations have a duty to report personal Data Breaches to the Supervisory Authority within 72 hours of becoming aware of the breach. They are also obliged to inform the individuals concerned without undue delay if it is likely that there will be a high risk of the breach adversely affecting their rights and freedoms. More information on Data Breaches is in Chapter 8.

 All staff should know how to respond to a Data Breach.

Sharing information electronically

Organisations are not permitted to share personal data without a lawful reason. This includes passing on another person's email address or phone number to a third party without permission.

CASE STUDY 4.4   SHARING INFORMATION INCORRECTLY

The Gloucestershire Police Force was fined £80,000 by the UK ICO in June 2018 after it sent out a bulk email that identified victims of non-recent child abuse. The force was investigating allegations of abuse relating to multiple victims when in December 2016, an officer sent an update on the case to 56 recipients by email. The email addresses were entered in the "To" field and all concerned were able to see the names of the other potential victims.

To comply with GDPR, organisations should make sure that when they create a process or system, they "design in" privacy considerations to ensure that personal data is only stored and shared when it is needed. Particularly with emails, the SAs recommend that BCC is used for large groups of individuals. Chapter 9 contains more guidance on sharing information electronically.

Data protection training

Everyone who deals with personal data needs to be aware of GDPR and other Data Protection Legislation and their responsibilities under it. Regular training of personnel involved in data processing is essential. Different organisations will approach the issue of staff training in their own way. This will depend on the complexity of the business and the number of individuals involved. More details on training can be found in Chapter 14.

Retaining and deleting data

One of the key tenants of GDPR is the "data minimisation" rule. This means that organisations can no longer keep records for prolonged periods unless they have good reasons to do so. When creating a data retention policy:

- Do not keep personal data for longer than it is needed.
- Develop a policy setting standard retention periods wherever possible.
- Carefully consider how you would respond to a challenge to your retention of data.
- Decide how individuals can exercise their "right to erasure" if the data is no longer required.

- Periodically review the data held and either erase, anonymise or delete it when identification of the subject is no longer required.
- Document any data that will be kept for longer because it is for public interest archiving, scientific or historical research, or statistical purposes.

Think about – and be able to justify – how long you keep personal data. This will depend on your original purpose for holding the data.

Know how individual can to exercise their rights

Because individuals have a right to access the data that an organisation holds on them there should be a clear system in place to facilitate this.

There are 3 possible routes for individuals to take to access information. The most appropriate access choice will depend on what information the individual wants.

The three types of request are:

- A Subject Access Request (SAR), which must be answered by the organisation within one month of receipt. This could be used if an individual wants to know what personal data an organisation holds about them to check it for accuracy.
- A Freedom of Information Request which must be responded to with 20 working days. This request is used when an individual or organisation is conducting research and wish to get specific information from a public body about their business.
- A Request to access a specific type of record e.g. medical/educational record. The timeline for this is in line with industry guidelines. Requests to access specific records may be used when the individual wants to see their medical/school record.

An SAR can only be submitted by the subject (or someone with parental responsibility for the subject or an authorised representative). More guidance on individuals' rights of access can be found in Chapter 13.

Communication

The final step in GDPR preparation is communication. Everyone you deal with should know in clear unambiguous terms what data you hold and why you hold it. Businesses should communicate with their Data Subjects in a transparent and easy to understand manner.

This communication is achieved through Privacy Notices, policies, procedures, notices and staff training.

Privacy Notices

One of the ways to achieved this is through the use of a Privacy Notice or statement (which is discussed in depth in Chapter 7). The term "Privacy Notice" is used to describe the way an organisation looks after an individual's privacy and it can be provided in a range of ways. It is not necessary to restrict privacy information to a single notice or page on the organisation's website.

Some of the ways the organisation can provide privacy information are:

- Using signage – for example an information poster in a public area.
- Electronically – in text messages; on websites; in emails; in apps.
- In writing – through printed media; printed adverts; contact or medical forms such as financial applications or job applications.
- Orally either face to face or on the telephone (make this is documented).

It is considered good practice to use the same medium that was used to collect personal data to deliver privacy information. So, where data is collected on a paper form the organisation should make a privacy statement on that form. Where an online form is completed a pop up may appear as the individual completes the form. The organisation can then complement this basic privacy information with more detailed information which is contained on the organisation's website. This is referred to as a blended approach.

Whatever approach is taken the organisation should remember to focus on the individual when making decisions how to deliver privacy information.

Checking how well you are doing with your preparations

Supervisory Authorities and many consultancy practices offer on-line help and guidance on how to achieve or check on progress towards compliance. These online checklists which generate a short report which will provide suggestions of actions that could be taken as well as links to additional guidance. The link to the UK ICO self-assessment checklist is at in the Resources Section (Resource 4.3).

In order to complete this self assessment you will need to be able to answer the following questions about the business:

1. Do you record what personal data you hold?
2. Do the people you hold personal data on know that you have it and understand how you use it?
3. Do you only collect the personal data is needed?

4. How long do you keep personal data for?
5. How do you keep personal data accurate and up-to-date?
6. How do you keep personal data secure?
7. Have you considered how people can to exercise their rights regarding the personal data you hold about them?
8. Do you and your staff (if you have any) know your data protection responsibilities?

Chapter 5

Data Controllers, Data Processors and the Data Protection Officer

The most important thing for any enterprise involved in the processing of personal data is for them to know if they are a Data Controller or Data Processor. This is because the roles and responsibilities that they have in relation to that data are different depending on whether they are the Controller or Processor. Some organisations may even find that they are both a Controller and a Processor.

This chapter discusses the role of a Controller, Processor and Data Protection Officer (DPO). These are individuals who are responsible for processing personal data (any information that relates to an **identifiable** person who could be directly or indirectly identified through this data). Personal data can include names, contact details, CCTV, photographs, car registrations, as well as date of birth, credit card details etc. Even if the amount of data that the organisation holds is very small, the organisation **must** still ensure that it complies with GDPR.

Irrespective of how it is held (paper files, on a phone or in a computer database), all the data that is on file is covered by the legislation.

To determine whether you are a Controller or Processor, you will need to consider your role and responsibilities in relation to your data processing activities.

CASE STUDY 5.1   CONTROLLERS AND PROCESSORS

A large health club has many therapists, personal trainers and support staff. It decides to use a payroll company to pay salaries. The health club tells the payroll company when to pay the wages and provides all the information for the salary slip and payment. They also indicate when a staff member leaves or has a pay rise and what hours they have worked. The payroll company provides the IT system and stores the employees' data. In this case, the health club is the Data Controller and the payroll company is the Data Processor.

The principles of data protection are essentially the same whether you are a small business or a multinational corporation. Because it is the risk that particular businesses and types of data processing pose rather than the size of the organisation that is relevant. Many of the actions organisations should take are practical and straightforward. Those who handle particularly sensitive data, or process personal data in potentially intrusive ways, pose the greatest risk and should take the most care.

Definition of processing

We have seen in previous chapters that when used in GDPR, "Processing" can include obtaining, recording or holding the data. But it can also include any operations that are performed on the data such as those in Figure 5.1 below. Definitions these terms can be found in Appendix 2, at the end of Chapter 2.

Many of the essentials of data processing applied before GDPR came into force and have been known about for a long time. GDPR seeks to build on those principles by keeping fairness, transparency, accuracy, security, data minimisation and respect for the rights of the individual whose data you are processing at the forefront of every organisation's consciousness.

Much of the criticism about GDPR focused on the perceived burdens it will place on SMEs and smaller organisations. SMEs have limited time and resources to dedicate to compliance and the SAs have recognised and kept this in mind when adopting their regulatory approach.

In actuality, the principles in GDPR provide an opportunity to scale the task of compliance to the risk posed by processing activities. Many of the principles actually reinforce actions businesses are already engaged in such as record keeping.

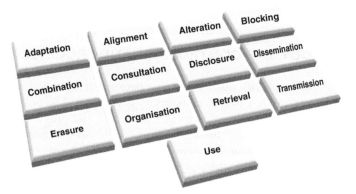

Figure 5.1 Data Processing Terms

Data Controllers

The organisation who has overall control and who can choose what the purpose of the processing is and how it is done (the means) is known as the Controller. In essence the Controller is the decision maker and it is up to them what information is collected and why it needs to be done.

The term Data Controller is defined in Article 4(7) of the GDPR (*Article 4, EU GDPR, "GDPR Definitions"*). The exact text is extracted in Quote 5.1.

QUOTE 5.1   ARTICLE 4(7) OF GDPR – DATA CONTROLLER

"Controller" means the natural or legal person, public authority,   Article 4(7)
agency or other body which, alone or jointly with others,
determines the purposes and means of the processing of
personal data; where the purposes and means of such processing
are determined by Union or Member State law, the controller or
the specific criteria for its nomination may be provided for by
Union or Member State law;

The organisation that makes the decisions on "Why, What and How" is a Data Controller (see Figure 5.2).

But a Controller isn't only concerned with choosing what information to gather (and subsequently "process"); they are also responsible for the

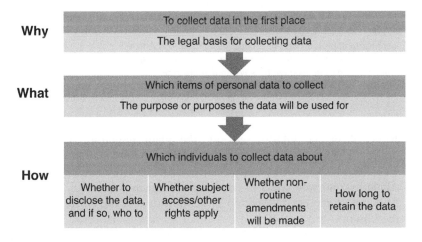

Figure 5.2 Data Controller Decisions

processing of the information. This is their role whether or not they actually do the processing or if it is done by another organisation on their behalf.

The Data Controller's responsibilities

Under GDPR, Data Controllers have the highest level of data protection responsibility. It is the Data Controller who has the responsibility for the security of the data throughout the system. They must be able to demonstrate their compliance with the data protection principles and make sure that their processing is carried out in line with GDPR using appropriate organisational and technical control measures. In order to demonstrate compliance, they may follow an approved code of conduct or certification scheme.

The responsibilities of the Data Controller are defined in Article 24 of the GDPR (*Article 24, EU GDPR, "Responsibility of the controller"*). The exact text is extracted in Quote 5.2.

QUOTE 5.2   ARTICLE 24 OF GDPR – DATA CONTROLLER RESPONSIBILITIES

Taking into account the nature, scope, context and purposes of processing as well as the risks of varying likelihood and severity for the rights and freedoms of natural persons, the controller shall implement appropriate technical and organisational measures to ensure and to be able to demonstrate that processing is performed in accordance with this regulation. Those measures shall be reviewed and updated where necessary	*Article 24.1*
Where proportionate in relation to processing activities, the measures referred to in paragraph 1 shall include the implementation of appropriate data protection policies by the controller.	*Article 24.2*
Adherence to approved codes of conduct as referred to in Article 40 or approved certification mechanisms as referred to in Article 42 may be used as an element by which to demonstrate compliance with the obligations of the controller.	*Article 24.3*

Chapter 4 of the GDPR sets out the main responsibilities for Data Controllers. These responsibilities are summarised here:

* Abide by approved codes of conduct (laid out in Article 40).
* Appoint a representative within the Union (if they are not established in the Union).
* Conduct a Data Protection Impact Assessment (DPIA) if new processing in is likely to result in a high risk to the rights and freedoms of natural

persons. Consulting the Supervisory Authority if the Controller is not able to mitigate these risks.

- Cooperate with the relevant Supervisory Authority/ies.
- Ensure that data protection by design and by default is at the core of the business.
- Keep adequate records of processing activities.
- Maintain the security of processing activities.
- Notify the Data Subject (where necessary) if a personal Data Breach occurs.
- Notify the Supervisory Authority if a personal Data Breach occurs.
- Nominate a Data Protection Officer (where necessary).
- Obtain certification from the national Supervisory Authority (renewed every three years).
- Provide safeguards when transferring personal data to third countries or international organisations.
- Register with a certification body (this may be used as an element to demonstrate compliance with the requirements).

 Controllers in the UK must register and pay the data protection fee to the ICO unless they are exempt.

Data Controller's considerations and codes of conduct

Data Controllers are encouraged to adopt the "data minimisation" rule. Whereby only the personal data that is required is processed. Data may only be used for the specific purpose for which it is gathered and should not be made accessible to others unless permission has been given for this to happen.

When considering their role, a Data Controller should take into account the amount of data collected, its accessibility, the extent of processing and how long it will be stored for.

The Controller may strike a balance between available technology and cost against the risks to the data or the likelihood of any risk to the rights and freedoms of the Data Subject, which are posed by the processing.

These costs and technological advancements may change over time and the therefore the Controller is obliged to implement appropriate data protection measures both at the outset and at the time of the processing. Measures may either be technical or organisational e.g. data minimisation and pseudonymisation.

To help Data Controllers in their role provision is made in the legislation for trade bodies or associations to be formed. These organisations may adopt codes of conduct in respect of GDPR which will demonstrate their compliance. This is further described in Article 40 of the GDPR (*Article 40, EU GDPR, "Codes of Conduct"*). The exact text is extracted in Quote 5.3:

QUOTE 5.3   ARTICLE 40 OF GDPR – CODES OF CONDUCT

Associations and other bodies representing categories of controllers or processors may prepare codes of conduct, or amend or extend such codes, for the purpose of specifying the application of this Regulation, such as with regard to:	Article 40.2
• fair and transparent processing;	Article 40.2(a)
• the legitimate interests pursued by controllers in specific contexts;	Article 40.2(b)
• the collection of personal data;	Article 40.2(c)
• the pseudonymisation of personal data	Article 40.2(d)
• the information provided to the public and to data subjects;	Article 40.2(e)
• the **exercise** of the rights of data subjects;	Article 40.2(f)
• the information provided to, and the protection of, children, **and** the manner in which the consent of the holders of parental responsibility over children is to be obtained;	Article 40.2(g)
• the measures and procedures referred to in Articles 24 and 25 and the measures to ensure security of processing referred to in Article 32;	Article 40.2(h)
• the notification of personal data breaches to supervisory authorities and the communication of such personal data breaches to data subjects;	Article 40.2(i)
• the transfer of personal data to third countries or international organisations;	Article 40.2(j)
• out-of-court proceedings and other dispute resolution procedures for resolving disputes between controllers and data subjects with regard to processing, without prejudice to the rights of data subjects pursuant to Articles 77 and 79	Article 40.2(k)

Who has ultimate responsibility?

Where a Controller uses a Data Processor, then it is the Controller who retains overall responsibility for the data. The Controller is required to make sure that their Processor is compliant. Any contract between them should identify the Processor's legal obligations (e.g. to maintain records of personal data and processing activities). The contract should also make it clear who is legally liable in the event of a Data Breach.

Recording processing activities

Each Controller and their representative are required to maintain a record of all their processing activities (ROPA). The obligation to record your processing activities is contained in Article 30 of the GDPR.

This record must be in written form but the exact format may be chosen by the organisation (it can be in physical or electronic form). The ROPA should reflect the day to day reality of how you process personal data and should contain the following information:

- "Actors" involved (Controller, Processors, representative, joint Controller, etc.)
- A description of the categories of Data Subjects.
- A description of the categories of personal data.
- Details of any data transfer guarantees.
- Details of the categories of recipients to whom the personal data have been or will be disclosed (including recipients in third countries or international organisations).
- General description of the technical and organisational security measures.
- Name and contact details of the Data Controller and the Data Protection Officer (or the joint Controllers/the Controller's representative where appropriate).
- Retention periods and envisaged time limits for different categories of data.
- Security measures.
- The purpose or aim of the processing.

Both Controllers and Processors should have a copy that relates to all the activities they carry out on personal data.

> Many Supervisory Authorities have created tools to help organisations record their activities. If your national authority has not produced a guide, the Resources Section of this book contains links to the UK and French SA tools (Resource 5.1).

The obligations above apply to organisation that employ more than 250 people. However smaller organisations are required to comply if the processing; is likely to result in a risk to the rights and freedoms of Data Subjects, is not occasional or includes special categories of data or criminal convictions and offences.

Penalties for non-compliance

If a Controller does not comply with GDPR, then individuals or Supervisory Authority can hold them to account. The Supervisory Authority can insist that the company caries out remedial action or impose a fine for non-compliance.

The amount that you can be fined is significant!

The Controller's role in reporting Data Breaches

The Data Controller must deal effectively with any Data Breach, but you do not need to report every breach to the Supervisory Authority. In the event of a Data Breach, the Data Controller should consider the likelihood and severity is of a risk to people's rights and freedoms as a result of the breach. If there is a risk then you need to report the matter to both the ICO and the individual. You will find more about Data Breaches in Chapter 12 of this book.

Can I be a joint Data Controller?

Just because one organisation provides a service to another it does not automatically become a Data Processor. It could still be a Data Controller in its own right. If a number of controllers jointly determine the purposes and means of the processing of the same personal data, then they will be joint Controllers. However, they are not joint controllers if they are processing the same data for different purposes. GDPR includes explicit requirements which are directed at Joint Controllers.

CASE STUDY 5.2   JOINT CONTROLLERS

An office CCTV camera system is operated by a tenant jointly with the building owner. Both are involved in deciding how the CCTV system is run and what the images it captures are used for. The tenant and the building owner are joint Data Controllers in relation to personal data processed in operating the system.

The decision on whether an organisation is a Controller will depend on the degree of control it exercises over the processing operation (e.g. an accountancy firm working on a client's behalf is a Data Controller of any personal information in their client's books).

When deciding who will take primary responsibility for complying with GDPR from a number of joint Controllers they must arrange the matter between themselves and then make the information available to individuals.

 All the joint Controllers will still be responsible for compliance and action may be taken against any controller if there is a breach of those obligations.

Registering as a Data Controller

The Supervisory Authorities have adopted different approaches to Data Controller registration and therefore it is recommended that the reader seeks guidance from their national body.

In the UK, under the 2018 Data Protection (Charges and Information) Regulations, every organisation that processes personal information is required to pay a fee to the Information Commissioner's Office (ICO). There are a few exemptions such as charities but it is recommended ed that you check on the ICO website to see if you are exempt rather than assume you are.

Controllers who were already registered under the 1998 Act will not need to pay the new fee until their previous registration expires. All other business should register with the ICO as a priority. The task is not expensive or time consuming. The majority of small businesses will find that registration will cost approx. £40 and it will take no more than 10–15 minutes to complete the online form.

This new regulation applies to every organisation or sole trader. You are breaking the law if, as a Controller, you process or are responsible for someone processing personal data and you have either not paid a fee or paid an incorrect amount. **The maximum penalty is a £4,350 fine**.

The list of registered organisations

Most Supervisory Authorities maintain a list of registered organisations. The UK ICO website has a tool that you can search to find out if an organisation is registered with them. This link is can be found in the Resources section (Resource 5.2) (https://ico.org.uk/about-the-ico/what-we-do/register-of-fee-payers/).

When registering with the Supervisory Authority you should be aware that it is a public service, so if you use a domestic address for your business and do not wish this to go on the public register you need to provide an alternative address.

If you process personal data only for one (or more) of the following reasons you are likely to be classed as an exempt organisation:

- Accounts and records.
- Advertising, marketing and public relations.
- Judicial functions.
- Not-for-profit organisations.
- Personal, family or household affairs.

- Processing without an automated system such as a computer.
- Public registers.
- Staff administration.

Data Processors

Whether you are a Controller or Processor will depend on the degree of control you exercise over the processing operation. If you do have no reason of your own to process data and you only act on a client's instructions, you are most likely to be a Processor. The term Data Processor is defined in Article 4(8) of the GDPR (*Article 4(8), EU GDPR, "GDPR Definitions"*). The exact text is extracted in Quote 5.4.

QUOTE 5.4   ARTICLE 4(8) OF GDPR – DATA PROCESSOR

"Processor" means a natural or legal person, public authority,   Article 4(8)
agency or other body which processes personal data on behalf of
the controller;

The Data Processor can be any person (other than an employee of the Data Controller) who processes the data on behalf of the Data Controller. The Data Processor can have some control over the technical aspects of how a service is delivered and make decisions on the "details means and methods" (see Figure 5.3).

Where a Processor is judged to be the organisation that determines the purpose and means of processing of a particular data set, then they are considered to be a Controller in respect of that data processing activity.

   Watch out! Just because one organisation provides a service for another does not always mean that it is a Data Processor. It could be a Data Controller in its own right, depending on the degree of control it exercises over the processing operation.

The Data Processor's responsibilities

Processors may only act under the authority of a Controller. The Processor and anyone with access to the personal data may not process the data unless they have been instructed to do so by the Controller (except when they are required to do so by law). This relationship must be governed by a binding legal contract which places a number of requirements on the Processor:

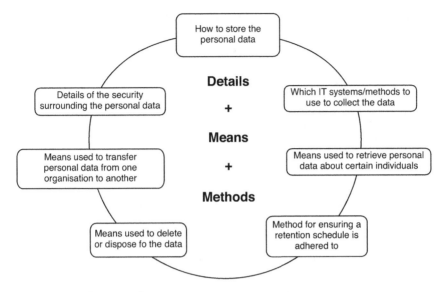

Figure 5.3 Data Processor Decisions

- Processors are not permitted to engage another processor (sub-Processor) or make changes to a sub processor without the express permission of the Data Controller (in writing before the event).
- Should another Processor be required to carry out processing activities on behalf of the Controller then they will be bound by the same contract as the main Processor.
- Should that "sub-Processor" fail to fulfil its obligations, the initial processor remains fully liable to the Controller for that other Processor's obligations.
- Processors are obliged to notify the Controller if they become aware of a personal Data Breach of the problem as soon as possible. The Controller is responsible for reporting the matter to the ICO and individual concerned where necessary and for investigating the matter.

The contract between a Controller and Processor should stipulate a number of matters as defined in Article 28(3) of the GDPR (*Article 28.3, EU GDPR, "General Responsibilities of Processors"*). The exact text is extracted in Quote 5.5.

QUOTE 5.5   ARTICLE 28(3) OF GDPR – GENERAL RESPONSIBILITIES OF PROCESSORS

Processing by a processor shall be governed by a contract or other legal act under Union or Member State law, that is binding on the processor with regard to the controller and that sets out the subject-matter and duration of the processing, the nature and purpose of the processing, the type of personal data and categories of data subjects and the obligations and rights of the controller. That contract or other legal act shall stipulate, in particular, that the processor:	*Article 28.3*
processes the personal data only on documented instructions from the controller, including with regard to transfers of personal data to a third country or an international organisation, unless required to do so by Union or Member State law to which the processor is subject; in such a case, the processor shall inform the controller of that legal requirement before processing, unless that law prohibits such information on important grounds of public interest;	*Article 28.3 (a)*
• *ensures that persons **authorised** to process the personal data have committed themselves to confidentiality or are under an appropriate statutory obligation of confidentiality;*	*Article 28.3 (b)*
• *takes all measures required pursuant to Article 32;*	*Article 28.3 (c)*
• *respects the conditions referred to in paragraphs 2 and 4 for engaging another processor;*	*Article 28.3 (d)*
• *taking into account the nature of the processing, assists the controller by appropriate technical and organisational measures, insofar as this is possible, for the fulfilment of the controller's obligation to respond to requests for exercising the data subject's rights laid down in Chapter III;*	*Article 28.3 (e)*
• *assists the controller in ensuring compliance with the obligations pursuant to Articles 32 to 36 taking into account the nature of processing and the information available to the processor;*	*Article 28.3 (f)*
• *at the choice of the controller, deletes or returns all the personal data to the controller after the end of the provision of services relating to processing, and deletes existing copies unless Union or Member State law requires storage of the personal data;*	*Article 28.3 (g)*
• *makes available to the controller all information necessary to demonstrate compliance with the obligations laid down in this Article and allow for and contribute to audits, including inspections, conducted by the controller or another auditor mandated by the controller.*	*Article 28.3 (h)*

Approved codes of conduct

Processors should provide guarantees to the Controller that they have suitable technical and organisational measures in place to meet the requirements of GDPR. A way of providing these guarantees would be if a Processor adheres to an approved "code of conduct" or a "certification" system approved by the European Data Protection Board or Supervisory Authority.

Recording processing activities

Each Processor (and their representative if necessary) are required to maintain a written record of all the categories of processing activities that they carry out for a Controller. This record should be made available to the Supervising Authority if required and should contain the following information:

- The name and contact details of the Processor(s) and of each Controller on behalf of which the Processor is acting, as well as details of their Data Protection Officer.
- The categories of processing which are being carried out on behalf of each Controller.
- Where transfers of personal data are made to a third country/international organisation, the details of that country/international organisation and documentation relating to safeguards that are in place.
- A general description of the technical and organisational security measures.

A record is not required for an organisation that employs fewer than 250 people so long as the processing is occasional, unlikely to result in a risk to the rights and freedoms of Data Subjects, or does not relate to special categories of data, criminal convictions or offences.

Security of processing

Individuals and Supervisory Authorities (such as the ICO) can hold both Controllers and Processors to account if they fail to comply with their responsibilities under the GDPR.

The Controller and Processor are both responsible for putting in place appropriate levels of security.

When assessing the appropriate level of security, the risks of the processing activity will be taken into account. The following should be in place as appropriate:

- Confidential processing systems and services.
- Encryption of personal data.
- Processing systems and services that are available and resilient.
- Maintaining the integrity of processing systems and services.
- Pseudonymisation.
- Regular testing, assessment and evaluation of the effectiveness of security measures.
- Control of access to ensure that processing is only carried out on the instructions of the Controller.
- The ability to restore the availability and access to personal data in a timely manner in the event of a physical or technical incident.

Data Protection Officer (DPO)

A Data Protection Officer (DPO) provides expert professional knowledge of data protection law and IT security and should be appointed on the basis of professional qualities. The precise scope and detail of the DPO role will depend on the size of the organisation and the complexity of the processing it is engaged in.

Contrary to much of the advice in the media and on line. GDPR does **not** require every business to have a DPO. The decision on whether to appoint a DPO is not based on the size of the company but what the core processing activities of the organisation are.

The DPO's roles and responsibilities are outlined in Section 4 of the GDPR. A DPO is only required in certain circumstances as stated in Article 37 (*Article 37, EU GDPR, "Designation of a DPO"*). The exact text is extracted in Quote 5.6.

QUOTE 5.6   ARTICLE 37(1) OF GDPR – DESIGNATION OF A DPO

The controller and the processor shall designate a data   Article 37.1
protection officer in any case where:

- *the processing is carried out by a public authority or body, except for courts acting in their judicial capacity;*
- *the core activities of the controller or the processor consist of processing operations which, by virtue of their nature, their scope and/or their purposes, require regular and systematic monitoring of data subjects on a large scale; or*
- *the core activities of the controller or the processor consist of processing on a large scale of special categories of data pursuant to Article 9 and personal data relating to criminal convictions and offences referred to in Article 10.*

Who needs a DPO?

Public bodies are always obliged to appoint a DPO. Other organisations only need a DPO if their activities involve processing sensitive personal data on a large scale or a form of data processing that will have a far-reaching effect on the Data Subjects' rights.

Appointing a DPO

Groups and companies have two choices of how they appoint their DPO. They can either nominate an internal (employee) or external DPO. There are many companies offering "DPO As A Service".

It is possible for a group of businesses to choose to appoint a single DPO. As long as the person nominated is easily accessible for the Supervisory Authorities, employees and external Data Subjects.

Companies may also choose to appoint a DPO on a voluntary basis to help with data protection even if they aren't obliged to by the GDPR.

Whoever is nominated as the DPO, both the Controller and Processor are required to publish the contact details of their DPO and communicate these details to the Supervisory Authority.

The impartiality of the DPO

The main condition for selecting a DPO, is to make sure the role is impartial. Where you appoint an internal DPO there must not be a conflict of interest because of their work in the business.

Controllers and Processors need to make sure that:

*   They ensure the DPO is involved in all personal data matters.
*   They support the DPO in their tasks by providing the resources and access to personal data and processing operations that they require.
*   They ensure that the DPO operates independently without instruction as to how to carry out the task (DPOs should not be dismissed or penalised by the Controller or the Processor for performing their tasks).

In order that oversight is maintained the DPO shall:

*   Report directly to the highest management level.
*   Be bound by secrecy or confidentiality while performing their task.
*   Be free to fulfil other tasks and duties as long as they do not result in a conflict of interests.

Data Subjects should be free to contact the DPO on all issues related to the processing of their personal data and to the exercise of their rights under the Regulation.

Tasks of the DPO

The DPO should take into account the nature, scope, context and purposes of processing when performing their tasks and be mindful of the risk associated with the processing operations.

The DPO shall have at least the following tasks:

- Inform and advise the Controller or the Processor and the employees who carry out processing of their obligations with regard to data protection.
- Monitor compliance with data protection regulations and internal policies, including the assignment of responsibilities, awareness-raising, training staff involved in processing operations, and carrying out audits.
- Provide advice and monitoring where requested for Data Protection Impact Assessments.
- Act as the contact point for the Supervisory Authority.
- Cooperate with the Supervisory Authority.

Chapter 6

Analysing what personal data you hold

This chapter discusses what data can be termed as "personal data" and then outlines the various types of personal data that an organisation may process. The chapter goes on to describe how data can be used to identify a person and how it is managed within an organisation.

This will help the reader to:

* Identify what categories of personal data their organisation holds.
* Understand how they process that personal data.
* Recognise whether the data they hold directly or indirectly identifies the Data Subject.

What is personal data?

For information to be considered as personal data it must relate to a living human being who can be identified by that data.

Personal data is defined in Article 4(1) of the GDPR (*Article 4, EU GDPR, "GDPR Definitions"*). The exact text is extracted in Quote 6.1.

QUOTE 6.1   ARTICLE 4(1) OF GDPR – PERSONAL DATA

"Personal data" means any information relating to an identified or   *Article 4(1)*
identifiable natural person ("data subject"); an identifiable natural
person is one who can be identified, directly or indirectly, in particular
by reference to an identifier such as a name, an identification
number, location data, an online identifier or to one or more factors
specific to the physical, physiological, genetic, mental, economic,
cultural or social identity of that natural person.

Information about a limited company or organisation that has a "legal personality" separate to its owners/directors does not constitute personal data.

There are many types of personal data and Figure 6.1 shows some of the most common types covered by the GDPR legislation. (In this book, this is referred to as the personal data honeycomb).

With some types of personal information, such as a photograph, it is clear that a person can be directly identified from the information. For other information types it will be more difficult to decide if the person can be identified from it and what the effect of processing the information will be. This is because even without a name you can use data to learn or record something about that individual. Such data "relates to" an individual and is therefore classed as personal information.

In order to assess whether the data fits this definition you should consider the following points about the information.

The impact on the individual

If the data is occasionally processed to learn something about an individual, even though it was not the primarily purpose for processing that data it classes as personal data because it has an impact on the individual in question. See Case Study 6.1a.

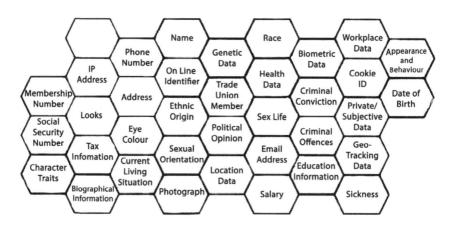

Figure 6.1 Types of Personal Data

CASE STUDY 6.1A   CONSIDERING INFORMATION IN RELATION TO AN INDIVIDUAL – USE OF THE DATA HAS AN IMPACT ON THE INDIVIDUAL

A school process anonymised exam results for records and then used cohort results to decide teachers' bonuses. This data would be personal data.

Relating the data to the individual

Data can contain references to an identifiable individual, or be linked to them, but not "relate to" them because it is not about that individual, but about another topic entirely. Depending on the circumstances, this data may or may not be personal data. See Case Study 6.1b.

CASE STUDY 6.1B   CONSIDERING INFORMATION IN RELATION TO AN INDIVIDUAL – DATA DOES NOT RELATE TO THE INDIVIDUAL

Information collected by email relating to a HR meeting to discuss a member of staff is about the meeting and not the staff member, and therefore is not personal information.

Does the purpose for which the data is being processed make the information personal data?

If the data is used to make decisions about a person or to learn, evaluate or treat them in in a certain way, then even if it does not contain their details it should be treated as personal data. See Case Study 6.1c.

CASE STUDY 6.1C   CONSIDERING INFORMATION IN RELATION TO AN INDIVIDUAL – THE PURPOSE FOR WHICH THE DATA IS BEING PROCESSED MAKES THE INFORMATION PERSONAL DATA

Details about the times that staff "log on" to their work computer when used to corroborate their timesheet will become personal data.

Is the content about or linked to an individual?

If the information is about a particular individual or their activities, it is personal data. See Case Study 6.1d.

CASE STUDY 6.1D   CONSIDERING INFORMATION IN RELATION TO AN INDIVIDUAL – THE CONTENT IS ABOUT OR LINKED TO AN INDIVIDUAL

Medical and educational records are about individuals and therefore are personal data.

Is the information accurate?

Even if the information about an individual is inaccurate it still relates to the person and is therefore personal data.

Is the data an opinion about an individual?

Irrespective of the accuracy of the opinion it would be considered as personal data.

Has the purpose of processing changed in the hands of a second organisation?

If the purpose changes then information that may not have been personal data may become personal information. See Case Study 6.1e.

CASE STUDY 6.1E   CONSIDERING INFORMATION IN RELATION TO AN INDIVIDUAL – THE PURPOSE OF PROCESSING THE INFORMATION CHANGES IN THE HANDS OF A SECOND ORGANISATION

A photograph is taken of children playing in the park on a sunny day and published on the local paper's Twitter page as part of a story about keeping active in high temperatures. Included in the photograph is a child who should be in school. The photographer did not process the photograph to learn anything about any of the individuals and therefore, in their hands the data is not personal data. The child's photograph was recognised by staff in his school and a truancy report was generated and a copy of the article placed on his file. While being processed by the school the photograph is being used to record, learn or decide something about the individual. For this reason, it would be personal data.

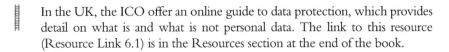 In the UK, the ICO offer an online guide to data protection, which provides detail on what is and what is not personal data. The link to this resource (Resource Link 6.1) is in the Resources section at the end of the book.

Common identifiers

Common identifiers are pieces of information which may allow the individual to whom the information in question relates to be identified from their online activities. As well as the individual's name these may include location data, an identification number or an online identifier as described on p. 127.

Special categories of information

Some categories of personal data are more sensitive than others. These categories require a greater level of protection and are referred to as "special categories of personal data". This is broadly similar to the category "sensitive personal data" in previous legislation but it now includes biometric data. Processing this type of information is prohibited unless an exemption applies.

In order to lawfully process special category data, you need both a lawful basis under Article 6 (see Quote 6.2) and a separate condition for processing special category data under Article 9 (see Quote 6.3).

QUOTE 6.2   ARTICLE 6 OF GDPR – LAWFUL BASIS FOR PROCESSING

Processing shall be lawful only if and to the extent that at least one of the following applies: *Article 6(1)*

- *the data subject has given consent to the processing of his or her personal data for one or more specific purposes;*
- *processing is necessary for the performance of a contract to which the data subject is party or in order to take steps at the request of the data subject prior to entering into a contract;*
- *processing is necessary for compliance with a legal obligation to which the controller is subject;*
- *processing is necessary in order to protect the vital interests of the data subject or of another natural person;*
- *processing is necessary for the performance of a task carried out in the public interest or in the exercise of official authority vested in the controller;*
- *processing is necessary for the purposes of the legitimate interests pursued by the controller or by a third party, except where such interests are overridden by the*

interests or fundamental rights and freedoms of the data subject which require protection of personal data, in particular where the data subject is a child.{shall not apply to processing carried out by public authorities in the performance of their tasks}

Member States may maintain or introduce more specific provisions to adapt the application of the rules of this Regulation.   *Article 6(2)*

The basis for the processing referred to in point (c) and (e) of paragraph 1 shall be laid down by: *Article 6(3)*

- *Union law; or*
- *Member State law to which the controller is subject.*

The purpose of the processing shall be determined in that legal basis or, as regards the processing referred to in point (e) of paragraph 1, shall be necessary for the performance of a task carried out in the public interest or in the exercise of official authority vested in the controller. That legal basis may contain specific provisions to adapt the application of rules of this Regulation, inter alia: the general conditions governing the lawfulness of processing by the controller; the types of data which are subject to the processing; the data subjects concerned; the entities to, and the purposes for which, the personal data may be disclosed; the purpose limitation; storage periods; and processing operations and processing procedures, including measures to ensure lawful and fair processing such as those for other specific processing situations as provided for in Chapter IX. The Union or the Member State law shall meet an objective of public interest and be proportionate to the legitimate aim pursued.

Where the processing for a purpose other than that for which the personal data have been collected is not based on the data subject's consent or on a Union or Member State law which constitutes a necessary and proportionate measure in a democratic society to safeguard the objectives referred to in Article 23(1), the controller shall, in order to ascertain whether processing for another purpose is compatible with the purpose for which the personal data are initially collected, take into account, inter alia: *Article 6(4)*

- *any link between the purposes for which the personal data have been collected and the purposes of the intended further processing;*
- *the context in which the personal data have been collected, in particular regarding the relationship between data subjects and the controller;*

(continued)

- the nature of the personal data, in particular whether special categories of personal data are processed, pursuant to Article 9, or whether personal data related to criminal convictions and offences are processed, pursuant to Article 10;
- the possible consequences of the intended further processing for data subjects;
- the existence of appropriate safeguards, which may include encryption or pseudonymisation.

QUOTE 6.3   ARTICLE 9 OF GDPR – PROCESSING OF SPECIAL CATEGORIES OF PERSONAL DATA

Processing of personal data revealing racial or ethnic origin, political opinions, religious or philosophical beliefs, or trade union membership, and the processing of genetic data, biometric data for the purpose of uniquely identifying a natural person, data concerning health or data concerning a natural person's sex life or sexual orientation shall be prohibited.   Article 9(1)

Paragraph 1 shall not apply if one of the following applies: Article 9(2)

- the data subject has given explicit consent to the processing of those personal data for one or more specified purposes, except where Union or Member State law provide that the prohibition referred to in paragraph 1 may not be lifted by the data subject;
- processing is necessary for the purposes of carrying out the obligations and exercising specific rights of the controller or of the data subject in the field of employment and social security and social protection law in so far as it is authorised by Union or Member State law or a collective agreement pursuant to Member State law providing for appropriate safeguards for the fundamental rights and the interests of the data subject;
- processing is necessary to protect the vital interests of the data subject or of another natural person where the data subject is physically or legally incapable of giving consent;
- processing is carried out in the course of its legitimate activities with appropriate safeguards by a foundation, association or any other not-for-profit body with a political, philosophical, religious or trade union aim and on condition that the processing relates solely to the members or to former members of the body or to persons who have regular contact with it in connection with its purposes and that the personal data are not disclosed outside that body without the consent of the data subjects;

- processing relates to personal data which are manifestly made public by the data subject;
- processing is necessary for the establishment, exercise or defence of legal claims or whenever courts are acting in their judicial capacity;
- processing is necessary for reasons of substantial public interest, on the basis of Union or Member State law which shall be proportionate to the aim pursued, respect the essence of the right to data protection and provide for suitable and specific measures to safeguard the fundamental rights and the interests of the data subject;
- processing is necessary for the purposes of preventive or occupational medicine, for the assessment of the working capacity of the employee, medical diagnosis, the provision of health or social care or treatment or the management of health or social care systems and services on the basis of Union or Member State law or pursuant to contract with a health professional and subject to the conditions and safeguards referred to in paragraph 3;
- processing is necessary for reasons of public interest in the area of public health, such as protecting against serious cross-border threats to health or ensuring high standards of quality and safety of health care and of medicinal products or medical devices, on the basis of Union or Member State law which provides for suitable and specific measures to safeguard the rights and freedoms of the data subject, in particular professional secrecy;
- processing is necessary for archiving purposes in the public interest, scientific or historical research purposes or statistical purposes in accordance with Article 89(1) based on Union or Member State law which shall be proportionate to the aim pursued, respect the essence of the right to data protection and provide for suitable and specific measures to safeguard the fundamental rights and the interests of the data subject.

Personal data referred to in paragraph 1 may be processed for the purposes referred to in point (h) of paragraph 2 when those data are processed by or under the responsibility of a professional subject to the obligation of professional secrecy under Union or Member State law or rules established by national competent bodies or by another person also subject to an obligation of secrecy under Union or Member State law or rules established by national competent bodies.	Article 9(3)
Member States may maintain or introduce further conditions, including limitations, with regard to the processing of genetic data, biometric data or data concerning health.	Article 9(4)

These bases do not have to be linked but you **must** determine them before you begin processing. It is good practice to document your decision for future reference.

By documenting your decision, you will be able to demonstrate that you comply with the 7th principle of GDPR.

What are special categories of information?

Special categories of information include the following types of data:

- Biometric data (where it is used for identification).
- Information about ethnicity.
- Genetic data.
- Health data.
- Political opinions.
- Information about race.
- Religious or philosophical beliefs.
- Sex life or sexual orientation.
- Trade union membership.

 If you process genetic or health data there are certain additional regulations that you should follow. It is recommended that you look at recitals 34, 35 and 51–54 of GDPR.

Exceptions to the prohibition on processing

There are a number of occasions where the prohibition of processing does not apply. These include where:

- Processing is in the legitimate interests of a political, philosophical, religious or trade union body.
- Processing is for employment/social reasons in the vital interests of the Data Subject (or another person) and the Data Subject is not capable of giving consent
- Security/protection law (see Article 9(2) (b), (h), (i) and (j)).
- The data relates to information that the Data Subject has already made public about themselves (for example on social media).
- The subject has given explicit consent.
- Processing is necessary for a legal claim/defence.
- Processing it is necessary for reasons of public interest in the area of public health.
- Processing is necessary for reasons of substantial public interest (See Article 9(2)(g)).

- Processing is necessary for:

  - preventive or occupational medicine.
  - the assessment of the working capacity of the employee.
  - medical diagnosis.
  - provision of health or social care or treatment.
  - the management of health or social care systems and service.

- Processing is for archiving purposes in the public interest, scientific or historical research purposes or statistical purposes

 Data about criminal convictions and offences require a higher level of protection and are subject to separate safeguards as set out in Article 10 of GDPR.

What is processing?

Personal data needs to be processed in some way in order to fall under GDPR. Processing can be either when information is held in some type of manual filing system and processed by a human being or when data is held in an electronic form and processed in part or wholly by automatic systems.

Unstructured paper records that are not (or are not intended to be) part of structured filing system are not covered by the legislation unless they are being held by a public authority.

Processing is defined in Article 4(2) of the GDPR (*Article 4, EU GDPR, "GDPR Definitions"*). The exact text is extracted in Quote 6.4.

QUOTE 6.4   ARTICLE 4(2) OF GDPR – PROCESSING

*"Processing" means any operation or set of operations which is   Article 4(2)
performed on personal data or on sets of personal data, whether or not
by automated means, such as collection, recording, organisation,
structuring, storage, adaptation or alteration, retrieval, consultation, use,
disclosure by transmission, dissemination or otherwise making available,
alignment or combination, restriction, erasure or destruction.*

What does GDPR mean by identified?

GDPR applies to any data by which a living person may be identified. Therefore, if you can distinguish one individual from another then that person is "identified" or is "identifiable". It doesn't matter if this identification occurs directly or indirectly. Very often combination of a person's name together with another type of information such as postcode will be enough to identify them.

CASE STUDY 6.2   IDENTIFYING AN INDIVIDUAL BY NAME

It would not necessarily be possible to identify a person from the statement Chris Smith works for company x in High Wycombe. By adding more information such as "Chris Smith with brown hair" then the individual can be identified.

 In order to identify servicemen with the same name, the Armed Forces use a unique identifier such as a Service Number in conjunction with the name such as Smith 123, Smith 562 etc.

There may be occasions where you still need to retain the information but no longer need to identify the individuals. In this case the legislation recommends that you anonymise the data wherever possible to limit the risk to Data Subjects. Anonymisation should be done in such a way that the Data Subject can no longer be identified from the data you have. It should not be possible re-identify the individuals to which the data refers.

If you use pseudonymisation, the information remains personal data and therefore is still within the scope of the GDPR.

Information about a deceased person is not considered to be personal data and is therefore not covered by the regulation.

Online identifiers

Online "identifiers" are also classed as personal data. An online identifier is information that relates to a device that an individual is using. The use of which can leave traces. These traces may then be combined with unique identifiers and other information on a server and used to create profiles of individuals from which it is possible to identify them. Examples of online identifiers are:

- Account handles.
- Advertising IDs.
- Applications.
- Cookies.
- Device fingerprints.
- Internet protocol (IP) addresses.
- MAC addresses.
- Pixel tags.
- Protocols.
- Radio frequency identification (RFID) tags.
- Other tools.

CASE STUDY 6.3   IDENTIFYING AN INDIVIDUAL BY AN ONLINE IDENTIFIER

An individual's Twitter, or other social media username uniquely identifies that individual and is sufficient to identify them (whether or not the name is anonymous or nonsensical). Therefore, the username is classed as personal data because it distinguishes one individual from another.

Online identifiers may be used to distinguish one user from another, possibly by creating profiles of the individuals to identify them. You should consider if online identifiers (on their own or in combination with other information) can be used to identify an individual and whether these are available to those who are processing the data.

Other ways to identify an individual

There are other ways to identify an individual. These include the use of physical factors such as in Case Study 6.4 where the colour of a person's hair and place of work were used to identify them in addition to their name.

CASE STUDY 6.4   INDIRECT IDENTIFICATION USING PHYSICAL CHARACTERISTICS

If an individual is not known to the operators of a CCTV system, but they are able to distinguish that individual on the basis of physical characteristics (height, gait etc), that individual has been "identified" in an indirect manner.

In this manner a combination of factors that are specific to that person such as cultural, economic, genetic, mental, physical, physiological or social characteristics can tell you about the person and therefore help to identify them.

Occasionally you may hold information and it is not clear if it contains personal data or not. In this case it is considered good practice to treat the information collected as though it is personal data.

Direct vs indirect identification

Sometimes you may be able to identify an individual solely from the personal data that you are processing and it is clear that the person can be identified. In other situations, the information you hold may indirectly identify an individual or your information could be combined with information from another source (even the individual themselves) and then used to identify them. Table 6.1 shows examples of direct and indirect identification.

When releasing or disclosing information you should consider all of the means that anyone is likely to use to identify that individual. This is important because the information you release or disclose could be linked with other information to identify someone.

Two parts of an organisation may process information, which allows an individual to be identified even though the information is anonymized for one party. In Case Study 6.5 the recruiting manager cannot identify the individual from the application that they receive. However, the individual can still be identified if the application form is combined with the information that is held by the school office manager.

If it is not immediately obvious if an individual can be identified from the information held you should consider all the factors in play and treat the information accordingly.

> The key point of indirect identification is that when information is combined with other information it allows an individual to be identified.

Table 6.1 Direct and Indirect Identification

Direct Identification	Indirect Identification
Name	Car registration number and/or VIN
Address and postcode	National insurance number
Telephone number	Passport number
Corporate and personal email address	Age
Elements of dates (except year) related to an individual	A combination of significant criteria such as age, occupation, place of residence
Medical Record or Card numbers	Geographic/regional location
Account numbers	CCTV Images when the individual is not known to the Processor
Certificate/licence numbers	Highly visible characteristics of the individual (e.g., ethnicity)
Full-face photographic images	Race
Internet protocol (IP) address numbers	Number of children
Biometric identifiers, including fingerprints and voiceprints	Uncommon characteristics of the individual
Web universal resource locators (URLs)	Rare health condition

Personal data in the case study organisation

In order to analyse what personally identifiable data an organisation holds you need to look at both the documents you use to gather information from the Data Subjects and the programmes your staff use.

CASE STUDY 6.5   IDENTIFICATION USING INFORMATION HELD ELSEWHERE IN THE ORGANISATION

A teacher applies for a job in a school. The Office Manager removes the first page of the application and saves it in their "Job Applications" folder to which there is restricted access. They then save the remainder of the application which is identified only by a random application number in the "Post X Recruitment folder" and send this to the manager in charge of recruiting for that post. A note of the random application numbers attributed to each application is saved in the Job Applications folder. The information is still available within the organisation and therefore the individual can be identified.

Deciding what information can be used to identify a person

When you have considered what information you process and whether this can be used to identify someone, you should document any assessment you have made (as part of your demonstration of compliance). It will also mean that a later stage you can revisit what you have looked at and reassess whether or not the information you hold can be used to identify someone.

As part of the assessment you will consider what means are likely to be used to identify the individual taking into account all factors, such as:

• Available technology at the time of the processing and at the current time.
• Changes to the public availability of certain records.
• Technological or security developments.
• The perceived value of the record.
• The cost of identification.
• The time required for identification.

Figure 6.2 shows the personal data captured by Exemplar Holistics, the case study company introduced in Chapter 5.

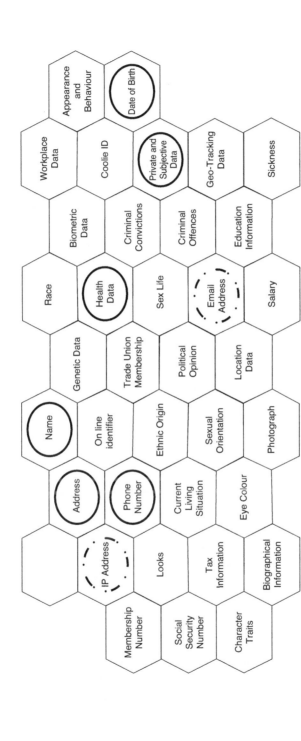

Figure 6.2 Exemplar Holistics Personal Data Analysis

By looking at the means available to identify an individual and how readily available they are you should be able to understand if your processing poses a risk to individuals.

 You should look deeper into this than merely considering what an ordinary person may do. A determined person (such as a hacker or someone with malicious intent) may have a particular reason to want to identify individuals and will take more time and have more capable tools at their disposal. This is especially important if the information is about a highly personal matter or your client list includes high profile public figures.

Fill in the personal data grid for your organisation

By following the advice in this chapter, you will be able to fill in the grid used in Figure 6.3 for your own organisation. A blank version of this form is on the companion website (www.pppmanagement.co.uk/resources).

Once you have analysed what personal data you hold the next step is to analyse your data. You can do this is by completing a simple Data Audit you will be able to start to capture information such as its sources, where it is stored and who it is passed to or shared with.

To prepare for Data Audit, you will need to be able to answer the following questions:

• What information is gathered?
• What is the source of the information?
• What is lawful basis for processing the information?

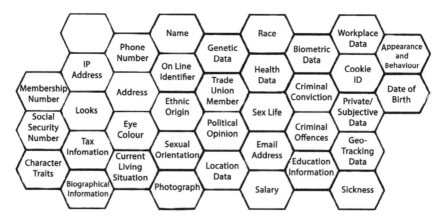

Figure 6.3 Personal Data in Your Organisation

- When is the information collected?
- When is the information updated?
- How long is the information held for?
- What determines the retention period?
- How is the information held/stored?
- Who is it shared with?
- How is it disposed of?
- Does the information include special categories of data?

A customisable template for this questionnaire is on the companion website (www.pppmanagement.co.uk/resources). Data Audits, data maps and data analysis are discussed in greater detail in Chapter 8, p. 147.

Chapter 7

Privacy Policies and Notices

Why do I need a Privacy Policy?

GDPR requires companies and organisations to provide transparent and accessible information about the personal data that they process whenever they collect such data from individuals. The easiest way to provide this information is to have a comprehensive Privacy Policy.

The most appropriate way to deliver this information will depend on the size of your business and the complexity of the information you collect. It may require just a simple Privacy Notice displayed in a prominent position or conversely, a more detailed suite of Privacy Policies that are several pages long.

You can also choose whether to give your privacy information orally, in writing, through signage or electronically. What you choose will depend largely on your audience, what you collect and how it is collected. Quite often the most appropriate way to share the information is using a "layered approach", which include a combination of:

- Icons and symbols on site (e.g. showing you have CCTV).
- Notices on display.
- A statement at the point of collection (e.g. a notice at the bottom of your joining form.
- Formal policy documents.
- A privacy dashboard.
- Video messages.

Most importantly you should ensure that however you deliver privacy information, you give a consistent message that is kept up to date.

What information should a privacy document contain?

What you put in your privacy documents will depend on how your business uses personal data. To make as easy as possible for your users you should share information in a logical order. Your privacy documents should include information about:

- How users can contact you.
- What purpose you process data for.
- The legal basis you have to processing their data.
- If you intend to share the data who the third-party recipients will be.
- Whether you intend to transfer data outside the EU.
- How long you intend to store the data.
- How users can exercise their rights under the GDPR.

Some of this information is always required, other information should be provided ONLY if it applies to your business. Tables 7.1 and 7.2 explain what information should be provided and when it is required.

Table 7.1 Information That Should Always Be Provided to Data Subjects

Information to be Provided	Details
The organisation's name and contact details	A clear statement of who the organisation is and how it can be contacted.
Your purpose for processing the information	List each different purpose you have for processing personal data (e.g. administration, security, marketing, order processing, etc.).
The lawful basis you have for the processing	Details of each lawful basis that you rely on (these are laid out in Article 6(1) of the GDPR).
How long you will keep the personal data	List your retention periods and where you don't have one tell people how you will decide on how long you keep their data.
What rights the individuals have in respect of the processing you do	The rights of access, rectification, erasure, restriction, objection, and data portability differ depend on your lawful basis for processing. You should make sure that what you tell people accurately reflects this. Where individuals have the right to object this must be explicitly brought to their attention clearly and separately from any other information.
The individual's right to complain to a Supervisory Authority (e.g. the ICO in UK) ▤ A list of EU Member State Supervisory Authorities is on p. 13.	Individuals have the right to complain to a Supervisory Authority, either in the country in which they live, where they work or the country where the infringement occurred. It is good practice to provide the contact details of your Supervisory Authority in your privacy documentation.

Table 7.2 Information That Is Only Required When It Is Applicable

Information to be provided	Details
The name and contact details of your representative	If you are based outside the EU you should provide the contact details of an organisation within the EU who are your representatives.
Contact details of your Data Protection Officer	Not all organisations are required to appoint a DPO. But where you have a DPO you should say how to contact this person in your privacy documentation.
Any legitimate interests you have for the processing	If you rely on legitimate interests as your legal basis for processing you should clearly explain in a separate section your interests are (Article 6(1)(f)).
Recipients, or categories of recipients of the personal data	Provide details of who you share people's personal data with. Including anyone who processes personal data on your behalf. You can either tell people the names of the organisations or the categories that they fall within.
Details when personal data will be transferred to any third countries or international organisations	If you transfer personal data to any countries or organisations outside the EU you should say whether the transfer is made on the basis of an adequacy decision by the European Commission. If the transfer is not made on the basis of an adequacy decision you should provide information about any safeguards you have in place. You must also inform people how to get a copy of these safeguards.
Statement on the individual's right to withdraw consent	Where you use consent as your basis for processing you should make a statement informing Data Subjects that they can withdraw their consent at any time. Consent must be as easy to withdraw as it is to give.
If individuals are under a statutory or contractual obligation to provide the personal data you should provide details of this	If Data Subjects are required by law, or as a condition of their contract, to provide you with personal data then you should make this clear (and provide details of what will happen if they do not provide that data). You should be clear about the types of personal data you require under this obligation.
Provide details of any automated decision-making, including profiling that will take place	Use simple, understandable terms to explain the rationale behind your decisions and how they might affect individuals (especially what

> information you use, why it is relevant and what the likely impact will be). You should be clear if any decisions are based solely on automated processing, describing the logic involved, it's significance and any envisaged consequences.

In the UK, if you think that processing personal data is in your legitimate interests, you are required to undertake a Legitimate Interests Assessment. The ICO provides some guidance on this on its website.

How should privacy information be presented?

Having a privacy document is one of the ways that you can comply with the key GDPR principle of transparency. If you already have a Privacy Policy in place that was written under previous legislation you will need to update it to comply with the GDPR.

The format of your privacy documentation, policy or notice is up to you. You can design a document using your own house style which aligns to your values and principles (making sure you follow any specific sectoral rules).

Your privacy information should be presented in a comprehensive, easily accessible style which is written in clear and simple language. Therefore, it should be written and presented effectively using use clear, straightforward language. Confusing terminology or legalistic language should be avoided (not everyone will have the same level of understanding as you do). It should be delivered in a style that your audience will understand and should be truthful and not offer counter-intuitive or misleading choices.

It is particularly important that you actively give privacy information if:

- You collect sensitive information.
- Your intended use is likely to be unexpected or objectionable.
- Providing personal information, or failing to do so, will have a significant effect on the individual.
- The information will be shared with another organisation in a way that individuals would not expect.

If you process large amounts of special category data or have a large number of legal reasons to process information (e.g. in a school) you may need separate detailed privacy documents for staff, students and parents.

Conversely, if your policy relates to a limited amount of data which is stored in a simple way you could consider a simple sign, which you can display on a noticeboard or in a prominent place (an example of this is in Figure 7.1).

Deciding what your privacy document includes

As outlined above, exactly what you put in your privacy documents will depend on how your business uses personal data. At the very minimum your privacy document needs to include:

- The name and contact details of the organisation.
- The purposes for processing.
- The lawful basis for processing.
- How long the personal data will be kept.
- What rights the individuals have in respect of the processing including their right to complain to the Supervisory Authority.

As outlined in Table 7.2, privacy documents may need to include the following (determined on a case by case basis):

- The name and contact details of a representative in EU.
- Contact details for the DPO.
- Details of any legitimate interests.
- Recipients, or categories of recipients of the personal data.
- Details when personal data will be transferred to any third countries or international organisations.
- A statement on the individual's right to withdraw consent.
- Details if individuals are under a statutory or contractual obligation to provide the personal data.
- Details of any automated decision-making, including profiling that will take place.

You could also consider including:

- Links between different types of data collected and the purpose that each is used for.
- The consequences for the individual if they do not provide information.
- Details of the security measures you have in place.
- What rights of access individuals have (if any).
- What will or will not be done with the data.

The act of writing a privacy document gives you an opportunity to assess exactly how you manage personal data in your organisation. It allows you to work out what personal information you hold, what you do with it (or what you plan to do

Village Butcher's Privacy Statement

We are ****** Village Butcher,{*address*}. We serve local
businesses and private households. This Privacy Statement tells
you how we collect, process and protect your personal information.

What information we hold	What we Use it for	Our Lawful Basis	When we delete it	Who we share it with
Your name, contact number and details of your orders	So that we can contact you about an order	It is Necessary for a contract we have with you	Historical data is deleted after 2 uears	Nobody
Information you have made public on social media	To communicate with you on social media	Your consent	You may exit the platform at any time	Other users of social media
Credit Card and bank details for account clients only	To take payments To manage our accounts	It is Necessary for a contract we have with you	Transactional infoamtion is kept for 6 years	Our accountant

What happens if you do not wish to share your data with us?
We will be unable to take orders on account from you.

Data Security
We are committed to keeping your data secure. We complete
regular scans of our computer systems and our computer software
is updated regularly.
Our hard copy order books are kept in a safe location.

Your Rights
You have the following rights in relation to the data we hold about
you:
The right to request a copy of the data we hold.
The right to know what data we hold.
The right to ask us to correct any data that is inaccurate or out of
date.
Please note we may ask you to confirm your identity before we
provide this data.

We do not transfer your personal information outside the UK.

This statement was issued on 1 September 2019.

© This statement was produced for us by Professional Procurement and
Project Management copyrighted solely for the use of "Village Butchers"

Figure 7.1 Simple Privacy Sign

with it). It provides a method to check that you collect only the information you need or if you are collecting more than you require. You will also be able to assess whether you will create new personal information as a result of processing.

By understanding this you will also be able to work out if you are the Controller or Processor (or both) in respect of this data. You may identify others who use the data and could identify multiple Data Controllers or Processors.

The ICO have a useful one-page Privacy Notice checklist, the details of which are available at Resource Link 7.1.

Benefits of a Privacy Policy

As well as the benefit of being able to demonstrate that you are operating under GDPR. A privacy notice is a mandatory requirement. There are other benefits to having an up-to-date, GDPR-compliant Privacy Policy.

Firstly, it provides an opportunity to review your data protection practices. This could benefit you as you could as a result be less likely to suffer a Data Breach or be subject to a complaint.

Secondly, in the event of a breach or complaint you can demonstrate to the Supervisory Authorities that you have done the right thing.

The final benefit is that your customers will feel that their personal data is safe and their rights are respected. This may help them to choose you ahead of the competition.

The layered approach

Privacy Policies and Notices should provide an understandable and effective communication of (sometimes) complex and important information to the people you are dealing with. It is no longer acceptable to hide behind a complex, multi-page document full of legal wording. Even where a detailed privacy notice or policy is required the terminology must be clear and concise.

It may be appropriate to simply make a statement to a Data Subject rather than provide a more complex document. The statement would describe how the organization collects, uses, retains and discloses personal information.

Alternatively, you could use "just in time notices", which give focused, headline information at the point that data is collected (e.g. application form).

Creating a Privacy Notice/statement

This section outlines the various sections that a privacy document or state-ment will require. There are many online offerings which you could adapt. Should you choose to do it yourself the task is relatively simple. The following sections include the information you should provide. There is a customisable privacy statement on the companion website for you to download free of charge.

Opening

In the opening section of your Privacy Notice/Policy you should include:

- The organisation name.
- Who the notice relates to (staff/patients/emergency contacts).
- Details of the date on which it is to be reviewed next.
- Introductory paragraphs showing why this policy is necessary/relevant.

Reason why the information is processed

You should provide information on why the organisation processes each item of personal information in a clear statement for example "we collect bank details for our staff in order to pay them" and "we collect your next of kin's name and telephone number so that we can contact them in an emergency if you are incapacitated".

Lawful basis on which information is processed

Each item of information may only be processed if the organisation has a "lawful basis" to do so. These are defined on pp. 121–122. You should include details of each of your lawful bases and may use any of the following lawful bases:

- Consent.
- Legitimate interests.
- Necessary for a contract.
- Legal obligation.
- Vital interests.
- Public interest.

If you are processing any "Special Categories of Personal Information", you must both one of the lawful bases listed above **as well as** one of the following reasons:

- Archiving purposes in the public interest, scientific or historical research purposes or statistical purposes.
- Employment, social security or social protection.
- Explicit consent.
- Legal claims.
- Medical purposes.
- Preventative or occupational medicine.

- Processing is part of the legitimate activities of a foundation, association or any other not-for-profit body with a political, philosophical, religious or trade union aim and relates solely to the members of the organisation.
- Public health.
- Substantial public interest.
- The Data Subject has already made the information public.
- Vital interest.

Consent

You must provide separate details for any information that is obtained on a consent basis. More detail on consent can be found on p. 143.

Storage information

You should provide details of how the organisation stores this information (e.g. paper copies, electronic files/emails, apps). This should include how long you plan to store the information and what you will do with it when you no longer need it.

Data collection information

You should give details of how the organisation collects information.

Data sharing information

Where you share information, you should give details of who you share information with and why you do this.

Individuals' rights of access

You need to provide clear information for individuals to request access to their personal data.

There should be a clear statement on what the individuals' rights are in respect of the data that they provide. Particularly, you should provide relevant (case specific) details of the following rights:

- The right to object to processing of personal data that is likely to cause, or is causing, damage or distress.
- The right to prevent processing if the purpose is direct marketing.
- The right to object to decisions being taken by automated means.
- The right to have inaccurate personal data rectified, blocked, erased or destroyed.
- The right to seek redress, either through the Supervisory Authority or through the courts.

Who to contact?

The organisation should provide details of the person in the organisation to contact to discuss anything in the organisation's Privacy Notice {name, number, email). This could be the CEO or DPO.

In order that the organisation can document that the Data Subject has read and understood their Privacy Notice, they may prepare a "declaration" for individuals to sign at the end of the document.

GDPR consent

GDPR contains a new definition of consent in Article 4(11) of the GDPR (*Article 4, EU GDPR, "GDPR Definitions"*). The exact text is extracted in Quote 7.1.

QUOTE 7.1   ARTICLE 4(11) OF GDPR – CONSENT

"Consent" of the data subject means any freely given, specific, informed and unambiguous indication of the data subject's wishes by which he or she, by a statement or by a clear affirmative action, signifies agreement to the processing of personal data relating to him or her.   Article 4(11)

Consent should not be used if you have another lawful basis to process information. To check if consent is appropriate you should consider whether you would still process the information if consent were to be withdrawn. If you would continue to process the information then consent is not the right basis for you.

Consent is not required for all aspects of personal data processing. Users should be able to make an informed choice about whether or not to give permission for their personal data to be processed. For some activities, it is always best to seek consent these include:

- Sending direct marketing emails to new customers.
- Using targeted advertising cookies.
- Storing sensitive personal data.

In July 2019, the Hellenic Data Protection Authority fined PwC €150,000 for unlawfully processing its employees' personal data using an "inappropriate legal basis" (PwC had selected "consent" instead of "contract" as it's lawful basis for processing employee data).

Consent is a freely given, affirmative choice

Data Subjects must have a genuine, free choice whether they consent or not. When you ask for consent you MUST offer them both options and it should be as easy to refuse consent as it is to grant it.

Users should be asked to make a positive choice. It is no longer acceptable to assume consent from a person's silence nor is it acceptable to offer users a pre-ticked box, or use statements like "by continuing to use our website, you consent to ..."

   Consent obtained under GDPR must be an opt in, not opt out.

Consent is limited to one type of processing

If you obtain consent for one type of processing this consent does not automatically transfer to another type of processing. You must get separate consent for each type of processing. This is referred to as "granular" consent (the ability to opt into some types of processing but not others).

Consent should be capable of being easily withdrawn

As well as being able to refuse to give consent, users must also be allowed to withdraw consent after they have given. For more information see Article 7(3) of the GDPR.

   It should be as easy to withdraw as to give consent.

Cookie consent

Cookies, small text files that download onto your smartphone, smart TV or computer when you click onto a website (or app), allow the website to recognise your device for the next time you access it and to store some information about your preferences or actions.

Empty Consent Box   Pre Filled Consent Box

Figure 7.2 Consent Boxes Must Not Be Pre-Filled

Individuals have the right to refuse to allow cookies to be placed on their device if these will reduce their online privacy. This means that cookie consent IS required for all websites and apps that are based in the EU because just about every website and app tracks users by using cookies to capture their data.

In order to comply with the legislation, the first time a user contacts your website you must provide:

- A clear statement that cookies are being used.
- An explanation of what the cookies are for and you use them.
- A clear mechanism to get their consent to store a cookie on their device.

To be valid, consent must be freely given, specific and informed. It must involve some form of unambiguous positive action such as ticking a box or clicking a link.

 The use of covert surveillance software or spyware that downloads to a device to track activities without the user's knowledge is also banned. (See the La Liga Case in Table 1.2, p. 10).

When is cookie consent not required?

Cookie consent is not required if it is purely needed to carry out a communication transmission over an electronic communications network, or to provide a service over the internet.

Cookies that are merely helpful but not essential (or are only essential for the provider and not the user/subscriber) still require consent.

It is good practice to provide users with information about cookies, even if consent is not required, e.g. where they are:

- On an internet shopping website to remember the goods a user wishes to buy.
- Session cookies, which provide security in an online service such as banking services.
- To ensure that the content of your page loads quickly and effectively by distributing the workload across several computers.

Information to obtain cookie consent

The information you give to users when obtaining consent should be clear and comprehensive. It should explain how the cookies work and what you use them for. The legislation does not specify exactly what you must provide nor how to provide it.

It is possible to use a third party checking service to see if your website is GDPR compliant. If you choose to go down this route, as with all things, do your research and check out all the alternatives.

You might be sharing personal data in more ways than you realise (e.g. a third-party database, (Microsoft's SQL Server), shopping cart software (Shopify), an automated email service (MailChimp).

Chapter 8

Recording your processing activities

It is important for a business to keep a record of all the activities that are being carried out. This will inevitably need to include a series of documents that describe the process you have in place to protect personal data. This is necessary both so that you have something for your own records and because it is required by the GDPR legislation. This series of documents is referred to as a Record of Processing Activities (ROPA).

Companies who keep a record of what data they hold, why it is held and who it is shared with are better able to manage their data. Such organisations can more easily demonstrate that they are working in compliance with the legislation.

The requirement to document your processing is new to GDPR.

Smaller organisations with fewer than 250 staff do not have to document their processing activities as long as their processing is:

- Occasional.
- Unlikely to result in a risk to the right and freedoms of individuals.
- Does not include special category data or criminal convictions or offence data.

There is no definition of these individual exceptions in the GDPR so businesses are required to make a judgement based on their own circumstances. To help you with your assessment the following advice and case studies may be of assistance.

- Occasional is defined in most dictionaries as "something that is done infrequently or irregularly". Examples of this criteria are described in Cases 1 and 2 of Case Study 8.1.
- Judging whether something is likely to result in a risk to the right and freedoms of individuals will depend on the individuals and circumstances. Examples of this criteria are described in Cases 3 and 4 of Case Study 8.1.

- Organisations such as schools medical practices, health spas, dentists all process special category information. Many of these will employ fewer than 250 staff but because of the nature of the data they process they will be required to document their processing activities.

    o   You will find more information about Special Category data in Chapter 6, p. 117.

More details about this exemption for small businesses can be found in is in the Resources Section at the end of the book (Resource 8.1).

CASE STUDY 8.1   SME ORGANISATIONS' REQUIRE-MENT TO DOCUMENT PROCESSING ACTIVITIES

Case 1 – Example of non-occasional processing – an individual visits the same hairdresser once a month. The hairdresser has personal details about them as well as contact details and information about treatments they have. Even though the business employs fewer than 250 staff the requirements of document processing applies.

Case 2 – Example of occasional processing – an individual visits the hairdresser on one occasion. The hairdresser collects their personal details including their contact details as part of the booking. Because this is a one-off event for this type of customer it is not mandatory to document this processing.

Case 3 – Example of risk to rights and freedoms – a musician teaches an instrument to a high-profile public figure. Lessons occur once a week. If the details of the lessons became public it could impact on the rights and freedoms of the individual. Even though the teacher is a sole trader the requirement to document processing still applies.

Case 4 – Example of risk to rights and freedoms – a band is plays at a venue on an occasional basis. They collect personal information about attendees (ages, names, events) to compile their set list. Releasing this information would not impact on the rights and freedoms of the individuals. It is therefore not mandatory to document this processing.

One way to document your processing activities of your business is to work out how the data flows within your organisation. Once you understand the data flow you will be able to complete a Data Audit. Both of these activities will help you to fulfil the "accountability" and "record keeping" requirements of the GDPR legislation.

Even if it is not compulsory for you to document your processing activities it is considered good practice to do so.

The requirement to demonstrate compliance is defined in Article 5(2) of the GDPR (*Article 5(2), EU GDPR, "Principles relating to processing of personal data"*). The requirement to keep a record of processing activities is defined in Article 30 of GDPR (*Article 30, EU GDPR, "Records of processing activities"*). The exact text from the legislation is extracted in Quote 8.1.

QUOTE 8.1   ARTICLES 5 AND 30 OF GDPR – RECORD OF PROCESSING ACTIVITIES

"The controller shall be responsible for, and be able to demonstrate compliance with, paragraph 5(1) [the data protection principles]"	Article 5(2)
Each controller and, where applicable, the controller's representative, shall maintain a record of processing activities under its responsibility. That record shall contain all of the following information:	Article 30 (1)

- *the name and contact details of the controller and, where applicable, the joint controller, the controller's representative and the data protection officer;*
- *the purposes of the processing;*
- *a description of the categories of data subjects and of the categories of personal data;*
- *the categories of recipients to whom the personal data have been or will be disclosed including recipients in third countries or international organisations*
- *where applicable, transfers of personal data to a third country or an international organisation, including the identification of that third country or international organisation and, in the case of transfers referred to in the second subparagraph of Article 49(1), the documentation of suitable safeguards;*
- *where possible, the envisaged time limits for erasure of the different categories of data;*
- *where possible, a general description of the technical and organisational security measures referred to in Article 32(1).*

Each processor and, where applicable, the processor's representative shall maintain a record of all categories of processing activities carried out on behalf of a controller, containing:	Article 30(2)

- *the name and contact details of the processor or processors and of each controller on behalf of which the processor is acting, and, where applicable, of the controller's or the processor's representative, and the data protection officer;*

- the categories of processing carried out on behalf of each controller;
- where applicable, transfers of personal data to a third country or an international organisation, including the identification of that third country or international organisation and, in the case of transfers referred to in the second subparagraph of Article 49(1), the documentation of suitable safeguards;
- where possible, a general description of the technical and organisational security measures referred to in Article 32(1).

The records referred to in paragraphs 30(1) and 30(2) shall be in writing, including in electronic form.	Article 30(3)
The controller or the processor and, where applicable, the controller's or the processor's representative, shall make the record available to the supervisory authority on request.	Article 30(4)
The obligations referred to in paragraphs 1 and 2 shall not apply to an enterprise or an organisation employing fewer than 250 persons unless the processing it carries out is likely to result in a risk to the rights and freedoms of data subjects, the processing is not occasional, or the processing includes special categories of data as referred to in Article 9(1) or personal data relating to criminal convictions and offences referred to in Article 10.	Article 30(5)

This chapter is designed to help the reader with their analysis task. Showing why a data map is required and providing guidance on how to completing a simple Data Audit. There is also advice on how to prepare a more detailed data flow diagram once the information has been collected.

On the book's companion website (www.pppmanagement.co.uk/resources) there are blank editions of the forms and guides contained in this chapter. These are free for the reader to download and complete themselves. More advice, bespoke consultancy and a "Data Protection Officer as a Service" can be obtained by emailing the author (enquiries@pppmanagement.co.uk) or completing the contact form at https://pppmanagement.co.uk/contact.

Why do I need to map the data?

In order to understand what data your organisation holds and the issues surrounding it you will need to create some form of document which captures these details. This will help to establish how large or how complex the data management and data protection task is within your organisation.

Data flow diagrams, maps and audits are mechanisms by which you can provide a clear (documented) picture of how your organisation processes personal data. You will be able to show:

- The type of information held.
- Where it is held.
- How it is held.
- How long it is held.
- Who has access to it and for what purpose.
- What your lawful basis is to have the information.
- How and when it is disposed of.
- Who you share data with.

Other than writing a long-winded report there is no other way to easily demonstrate that you have considered all these factors.

Is a Data Flow Analysis or Data Audit compulsory?

It is not compulsory to complete a Data Flow Analysis or a Data Audit. They are however considered examples of best practice.

How long will it take?

For a small organisation, the very the idea of completing a data map or Data Audit is quite daunting. Especially as it will have to take place while you are busy with your core business.

By following the advice in this chapter, you will find that it is not as bad as it first appears. To quote the EU Data Protection Working Party *"for many micro, small and medium-sized organisations, maintaining a record of processing activities is unlikely to constitute a particularly heavy burden"* (Working Party 29 Position Paper).

Most SMEs should be able to complete both a data map and a Data Audit on their own as long as they keep things simple. The most important thing is to make sure that the process is documented in some way so that you have the "evidence" that you are working in compliance with Articles 5(2) and 30 of GDPR.

 A full-scale detailed data mapping exercise in a large or complex organisation will take considerable staff, effort and expertise. It may even require specialist IT and legal assistance.

To help larger organisations with this task there are a number of very good data mapping tools on the market. Smaller organisations can also download or purchase this type of data mapping tool if they so wish. However, they are likely to be too detailed for a small organisation's needs.

Understanding how data flows in an organisation

To explain how information moves within the business you can use a simple table or a flow chart (both are equally valid). The most important thing is to understand what information comes in, where and how it is processed or how and where it is stored and what happens to it when it is no longer needed.

All you really need is a sheet of paper, a whiteboard or a series of sticky notes on the wall and a bit of time.

Case study example of understanding the flow of data

The easiest way to describe the flow of data is to study it in context of a case study company Exemplar Holistics, first discussed in Chapter 4 (Case Study 4.1).

Categories of personal data

First, we establish what categories/types of personal data are being processed by the case study company. We did this by circling the relevant cells in the personal data "honeycomb" (see Figure 8.1).

From the analysis we recognise that the company processes special category information (health data and private/subjective data). So, we know that we are required to document our processing activities.

Map the flow of information

Now we know what data we process we need to understand how it flows into and around the business. We do this by answering the following questions:

1.   How is the information gathered?

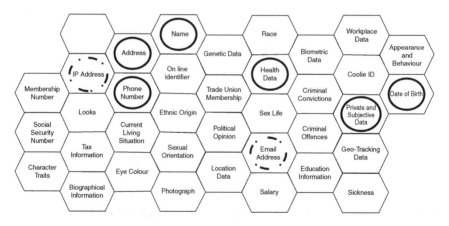

Figure 8.1 Exemplar Holistics Personal Data Analysis
Note: See Figure 6.2 on p. 131 for full page version of this figure.

Case Study 8.2
Exemplar Holistics Data Flow Questionnaire

Data Flow Questions	Exemplar Holistic Answers
How is the information gathered?	Paper Consultation Form
Where is the gathered information stored?	In paper filing system Certain patients data also on laptop (consent given – case studies for coursework)
Is it processed, updated any further or just filed?	Treatment details updated after each patient visit Patients asked to confirm medical details annually
Do other organisations provide personal information?	NHS
Is the information shared with other organisations?	Crime Prevention Course Tutor
Is there any standalone system that also contains personal information?	Facebook

Figure 8.2 Personal Data Flow Questionnaire for Exemplar Holistics

2. Where is the gathered information stored?
3. Is it processed (or updated) any further or just filed?
4. Do other organisations provide personal information?
5. Is the information shared with other organisations?
6. Are there any stand-alone systems that also contain personal information?

Our case study answers are in Figure 8.2.

Taking the answers from the questionnaire we can create a simple flow chart to illustrate this information (Figure 8.3).

The simple flow chart can then be further developed into a more complex flow map (Figure 8.4) which shows the process for each piece of information. This information could also be written in a document or procedure if preferred.

Once the organisation understands what data is held and has mapped the flow of data throughout the organisation it is time to start on a Data Audit.

Data Audit

Conducting a Data Audit will allow you to understand even more about the data you hold and who has access to it. It will help you to build up a clear picture of all the various types of data, their source, why you have them and how long you keep each for.

By completing a Data Audit, you will be able to demonstrate that you are processing personal information lawfully, fairly and in a transparent manner as required by GDPR. For each piece of data you must establish that you have a lawful basis (reason) to process the information. Without this legal reason

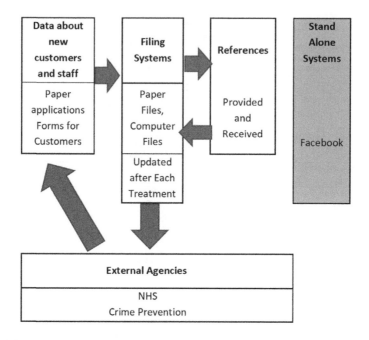

Figure 8.3 Exemplar Holistics Data Flow Chart

you are not permitted to carry on processing the data. More information on lawful bases can be found in Chapters 2 and 3.

The Data Audit will provide a clear picture of:

- How long you keep the information for.
- How the information is shared and with whom.
- How you dispose of the information.
- The type of information held.
- What your lawful basis is for holding the information.
- Where the information is held (server, cloud, hard copy etc.).
- Who has access to the information.
- Who the source for this information is.
- Any privacy risks.

From the Data Audit you will get a clear picture of how large and complex the data protection task is for your organisation. The audit can also identify areas where the data you hold is at risk or where you hold more information than you require or if you retain information for longer than necessary.

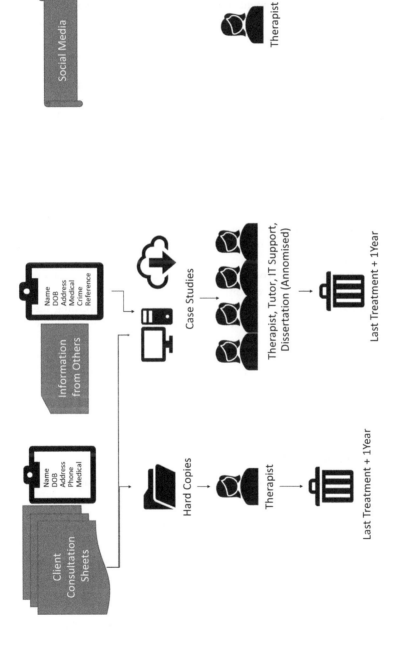

Figure 8.4 Detailed Data Flow – Exemplar Holistics

It is important that you give all the people who are responsible for data processing in your organisation the opportunity to interrogate your findings to confirm that you have covered every eventuality. During the audit process you should make sure that you consult with and take advice from your own staff, trade bodies, government departments (HMRC, DfE etc) and organisations such as the Information and Records Management Society (IRMS) where appropriate.

Who should do my Data Audit?

There are no perfect answers to the question "who should do my Data Audit?". You may decide to employ a consultant or third party to do this piece of work for you or you may do it "in house". Whatever you decide, it should be the business need that takes precedence. There will be a cost involved with both options and you should weigh these up against the need for you and your staff to conduct your day-to-day business.

If you decide to complete the audit "in house" there are several options of who can complete it and how they should go about it. These options are:

- **The single owner approach**. Where an individual "owns" the process. Conducting interviews with other staff and creating a database based on these interviews.
- **The questionnaire approach**. You could circulate a questionnaire to all staff and create a database from the information they provide.
- **The brainstorming approach**. You could hold a brainstorming session to agree the questions an populate the database together in one session.

Again, there is no right or wrong way to approach a Data Audit. You should select the method that works best in your particular circumstances.

 Any external auditor will still need to speak to you and your staff in order to understand your processes so even if you outsource the audit there will still be an impact on your day-to-day business.

Audit goals and boundaries

A Data Audit needs focus to be of value. It is therefore a necessary to set clear goals and boundaries for the audit. These should specify:

- Who is responsible and what their responsibilities are.
- The need for other staff to cooperate in the audit.
- What will happen if you identify potential issues, who will resolve them or find a way to resolve them.

The primary task is to identify how you manage all personal data. You need to make sure that this exercise is not be solely focussed on client's data because it should also include data that is collected on employees and business owners/investors as well as customers and suppliers.

The Data Audit process

You need to know as much as possible about the data for each group of Data Subjects and each type of data. Therefore, your Data Audit needs to capture all the relevant information about your data including who is accountable for the data, who has access to it as well as who is responsible for the data.

> If your audit is likely to be complex then there are a number of commercial data mapping tools available (these will cost in the region of €1,000). As with all commercial purchases you should investigate the alternatives and select the one that best fits your needs.

The easiest way to understand the Data Audit is to study it in context. Here we use a case study organisation "Kidz United Football Club" (Case Study 8.2).

CASE STUDY 8.2   KIDZ UNITED FOOTBALL CLUB DATA AUDIT

Kidz United is a small children's football club. The club is managed by a small administrative team which includes the owner. It employs a number of coaches. References are required for some coaching appointments. Because of the FA safeguarding rules all the coaches, volunteers and administrative staff require an up to date FA DBS (which includes safeguarding and First Aid training).

The information is collected in an Excel database such as the one in Table 8.1. A blank version of this database is available on the companion website (www.pppmanagement.co.uk/resources).

In the next sections we explain the information you should capture about the data that is collected and how you may collect the data.

What personal data is held?

For each Data Subject, you should consider first what data you hold and then what the source for that data is (as shown in Table 8.2). In many cases the information will come from the individual themselves (or in the case of a child the person with parental responsibility for them). You may also receive the information from a third party. Sometimes the source of the data

Table 8.1 Data Audit Database – Kidz United Football Club

		Parents		Coaches		Players	
What is held	**Type of information**						
	Source						
	Lawful basis						
Why is the information used							
Who has access to the information							
What role is being carried out							
When is it collected and updated	**Originally**						
	Updated						
Retention period	**Length of time**						
	Determined by						
Action at the end of the administrative life of the record							
Format held in							
Flagged as a risk to individual rights and freedoms							
Comments							

Table 8.2 Kidz United Football Club – Data Sources

		Coaches				
	Type of information	**Name**	**DBS/ Safeguarding**		**References**	**etc.**
What is held	**Source**	Individual	FA		Third party	
	Lawful basis					

will be someone within the organisation such as a supervisor writing a report on a member of staff.

Establish the lawful basis on which you hold this data

You should select the most appropriate lawful basis that suits your purpose from the lawful bases listed in Figure 8.5.

Figure 8.5 Lawful Basis for Processing

If you process special category data for example medical information you need both a lawful **and** an additional lawful basis to processing that data. These do not have to be linked but you must determine what they are before you begin processing. Remember to document this information.

In the case study, the lawful basis to process the name and a reference for a coach is "necessary for contract" (coaches are employed by the club and this forms part of their contractual obligations). The DBS/Safeguarding information is a legal obligation (i.e. a mandatory requirement from the FA).

As a further level of protection, the DBS information and references are flagged as a posing a potential risk to the individual's rights and freedoms (the information poses a greater risk if it were to be included in a Data Breach). We used a simple yes/no box. Table 8.3 shows the lawful basis for processing coaches' information in the case study company.

Identify the function/reason for processing every piece of data collected

Consider if you have a business need or reason to hold the information that you process. This will help to fill out the columns "Why is the information

Table 8.3 Lawful Basis for Processing – Kidz United Football Club

		Coaches			
What is held	**Type of information**	**Name**	**DBS/ Safeguarding**	**References**	**etc.**
	Source	Individual	FA	Third party	
	Lawful basis	Contract	Legal Requirement	Contract	
Flagged as a risk to individual rights and freedoms		N	Y	Y	

Table 8.4 Reason for Processing – Kidz United Football Club

		Coaches			
What is held	**Type of information**	**Name**	**DBS/ Safeguarding**	**References**	**etc.**
	Source	Individual	FA	Third Party	
	Lawful basis	Contract	Legal requirement	Contract	
Why is the information used		Identification	Safeguarding	Safeguarding and suitability	

used" and "What role is being carried out" (Table 8.4). It is particularly important if you process sensitive data such as religion, race or health information.

You may find that there are some types of personal data that you have traditionally gathered but don't actually have a business need for. This is the time to stop gathering that information. Change your data capture forms and delete that field from your processing tools.

Establish who in the organisation has access to the data

This is the time to consider who has access to systems that process particular elements of personal data and how this access is managed. Not everyone in your organisation will need access to every item of data. While information such as the names of the coaches for each team is available for everyone to view and published on the website other information is only required by a small number of individuals (such as team managers). There will also be information that only one member of staff requires access to, such as the payroll or the person who checks DBS information.

Table 8.5 Access to Personal Data – Kidz United Football Club

What is held		Coaches			
	Type of information	**Name**	**DBS/Safeguarding**	**References**	**etc.**
	Source	Individual	FA	Third party	
	Lawful basis	Contract	Legal requirement	Contract	
Why is the information used		Identification	Safeguarding	Safeguarding and suitability	
Who has access to the information		Available to all and on website	DBS Checker(named member of staff)	Appointments panel	
Flagged as a risk to individual rights and freedoms		N	Y	Y	

Table 8.5 shows the individuals who may have access to data in a Kidz United Football Club.

Establish what role the organisation has in relation to the data

Are you the Controller of this information or the Processor, or are you both? Do you have a sub-Processor and if so, who is it? Table 8.6 shows if the club is a Processor or Controller of information about their Coaches.

Table 8.6 Role in relation to Personal Data – Kidz United Football Club

What is held		Coaches			
	Type of information	**Name**	**DBS/Safeguarding**	**References**	**etc.**
	Source	Individual	FA	Third party	
	Lawful basis	Contract	Legal requirement	Contract	
Why is the information used		Identification	Safeguarding	Safeguarding and suitability	
Who has access to the information		Available to all and on website	DBS Checker(named member of staff)	Appointments panel	
What role is being carried out		Controller	Processor	Controller	

How the data comes into the organisation?

The next stage is to determine how the information comes into your organisation. There are many ways you will receive personal information, for example:

- Online forms.
- Paper "client" forms which are filled in on or off site.
- Telephone contact forms filled in by staff.
- Information received from third parties (e.g. references or medical or school data received electronically).
- Information provided in a letter by a parent or relative of the subject.
- Photographs (including your CCTV or dashcam).
- Information on a national database (e.g. DBS).

Whatever way you gather the information you will need to make sure that you have mechanism to keep the information contained in these "source documents" secure. Once the data is no longer required (for example if it has been put into a database) then the original document should be securely disposed of.

Make a note of the first time data is collected and if it is updated

If the data is part of a joining application or consultation form this will be the date of the first appointment. On other occasions it may be as a result of an annual report or non-routine occurrence. Table 8.7 shows when and how often the data is updated in the case study club.

Updating data and keeping it accurate are requirements of GDPR.

With some data there is no need for it to be updated (a date of birth does not change) however, for the majority of personal data as life changes so does the data about an individual (e.g. house moves, new contact details etc.). It is the Data Controller's responsibility to make sure the information is kept up to date.

You could do this is by asking the subject to update their details on an annual basis or providing them access to their own data via an online portal.

Identify where each type of data is stored and in what format

Consider where you store data. You may have a combination of manual and electronic records (as shown in Table 8.8). Information may also be on servers, in the "cloud" storage, on a stand-alone computer or on the website. Once you understand where the data is stored you also need to consider how it is kept secure, for example, do you have encrypted files, firewalls, role specific log ins etc. Some questions to ask are:

Table 8.7 Collection and Update of Data – Kidz United Football Club

		Coaches			
	Type of information	**Name**	**DBS/ Safeguarding**	**References**	**etc.**
What Is held	**Source**	Individual	FA	Third party	
	Lawful basis	Contract	Legal Requirement	Contract	
Why is the information used		Identification	Safeguarding	Safeguarding and suitability	
Who has access to the information		Available to all and on website	DBS checker (named member of staff)	Appointments panel	
What role is being carried out		Controller	Processor	Controller	
When is it collected and updated	**Originally**	On appointment	Before appointment	Before appointment	
	Updated	At request of Data Subject	Every 3 years	Never	
Flagged as a risk to individual rights and freedoms		N	Y	Y	

- If data is collected manually are there manual files, who has access to these files and how do you dispose of information that is out of date?
- If you store data electronically is it on a GDPR compliant computer database. How is it kept up to date or deleted?
- Do you have a person or organisation that processes the data for you? Do their systems comply with the GDPR legislation?
- How do you control access to the data?
- Do you have servers or is the information stored on the cloud and is the cloud based in the EU?
- What is stored on the website and is it secure?

How long should data be kept for and what determines this time?

Some data should be kept for as long as you have a contract with the individual while other information needs to be kept for a specific length of time (e.g. school records must be kept until the individual turns 24).

Table 8.8 Format and Storage of Data – Kidz United Football Club

		Coaches			
	Type of information	**Name**	**DBS/ Safeguarding**	**References**	**etc.**
What is held	**Source**	Individual	FA	Third party	
	Lawful basis	Contract	Legal requirement	Contract	
Why is the information used		Identification	Safeguarding	Safeguarding and suitability	
Who has access to the information		Available to all and on website	DBS Checker (named member of staff)	Appointments panel	
What role is being carried out		Controller	Processor	Controller	
When is it collected and updated	**Originally**	On appointment	Before appointment	Before appointment	
	Updated	At request of Data Subject	Every 3 years	Never	
Format held in		Hard and electronic	N/A	Hard and electronic	
Flagged as a risk to individual rights and freedoms		N	Y	Y	

For each item of data, you should identify how long you should keep it and what determines this time (see Table 8.9). For example, it may be as a result of legislation or because your own data retention policy says so.

The retention of data must always be lawful and fair and you should balance your needs against any impact that the retention will have on the individual and their privacy. At the end of any standard retention period you should review whether or not the personal data is still required. Where you no longer need the data, it should be erased or anonymised.

There are a number of legal requirements that require you to keep information for a certain period (e.g. for income tax/audit purposes, or to comply with health and safety requirements). Useful guides on retention periods are available from trade bodies, government departments (HMRC, DfE etc.) and organisations such as the Information and Records Management Society (IRMS). The National Archives (TNA) publishes practical guidance on a range of records management topics, including retention and disposal you can use this guidance to help to comply with the storage limitation principle. Links to these organisations are Resources 8.2, 8.3, 8.4 and 8.5 in the Resources Section of this book.

Table 8.9 Data Retention Database – Kidz United Football Club

		Coaches			
	Type of information	**Name**	**DBS/ Safeguarding**	**References**	**etc.**
What is held	**Source**	Individual	FA	Third party	
	Lawful basis	Contract	Legal requirement	Contract	
Why is the information used		Identification	Safeguarding	Safeguarding and suitability	
Who has access to the information		Available to all and on website	DBS checker (named member of staff)	Appointments panel	
What role is being carried out		Controller	Processor	Controller	
When is it collected and updated	**Originally**	On appointment	Before Appointment	Before Appointment	
	Updated	At request of Data Subject	Every 3 years	Never	
Retentionperiod	**Length of time**	End of contract + 7 years	Not retained	End of contract + 1 year	
	Determined by	HMRC rules	FA safeguarding rules	IRMS	
Format Held In		Hard and electronic	N/A	Hard and electronic	
Flagged as a risk to individual rights and freedoms		N	Y	Y	
Comments					

What happens at the end of the life of the data?

All data has a natural "lifespan" and at the end of this time it may either be archived (in the public interest) or disposed of. As shown in Table 8.10, you should clearly state what happens to your data at the end of its useful life. Where it is going to be retained you should consider anonymising the data if possible so that it can no longer be traced back to a "natural person".

Data security

As well as the physical security of your data, the mapping exercise can also help to identify any data protection issues such as the need for privacy filters

Table 8.10 Complete Data Audit – Kidz United Football Club

		Coaches			
	Type of information	**Name**	**DBS/ Safeguarding**	**References**	**etc.**
What is held	**Source**	Individual	FA	Third party	
	Lawful basis	Contract	Legal requirement	Contract	
Why is the information used		Identification	Safeguarding	Safeguarding and suitability	
Who has access to the information		Available to all and on website	DBS checker (named member of staff)	Appointments panel	
What role is being carried out		Controller	Processor	Controller	
When is it collected and updated	**Originally**	On appointment	Before Appointment	Before Appointment	
	Updated	At request of Data Subject	Every 3 years	Never	
Retention Period	**Length of time**	End of contract + 7 years	Not retained	End of contract + 1 year	
	Determined by	HMRC rules	FA safeguarding rules	IRMS	
Action at the end of the administrative life of the record		Secure disposal	N/A	Secure disposal	
Format held in		Hard and electronic	N/A	Hard and electronic	
Flagged as a risk to individual rights and freedoms		N	Y	Y	
Comments					

on computer screens etc. If you identify other data protection or security issues as part of the audit process these will need to be resolved.

Data security is covered in greater depth in Chapter 11, p. 193.

You should also consider how the data gets from one location to another whether this is by physical or electronic means (e.g. moving hard copy files to scan and email has security implications both in the physical move and the email scanning process as well as how information is transferred to memory devices). Other areas that could cause security issues include when data is transferred between organisations.

You may need to be more specific with degrees of security that you require for certain information. Certain records are only accessed by a small number of staff (e.g. senior management access to staff personal files) so these could be locked in secure cabinets and access to them monitored (by a log). Other matters such as historical records (e.g. records of school attendance/exam success) may need to be accessed by all administrative staff. It therefore may be more appropriate to consider the external security for the office where they are kept rather than any filing cabinets. By restricting access in some way to the office the whole room could be considered a "locked/secure" container. If you do this you should inform staff why you have taken this approach.

Data Protection Impact Assessment (DPIA)

A Data Protection Impact Assessment is a tool used to identify and analyse how data privacy might be affected by certain actions or activities within the business. GDPR introduces the requirement for DPIAs to be carried out in certain situations (e.g. when profiling activities are carried out).

The requirement for a DPIA is defined in Article 35 of the GDPR (*Article 35, EU GDPR, "Data protection impact assessment"*). The exact text from the legislation is extracted in Quote 8.2.

QUOTE 8.2   ARTICLE 35 OF GDPR – DPIA

Where a type of processing in particular using new technologies, and taking into account the nature, scope, context and purposes of the processing, is likely to result in a high risk to the rights and freedoms of natural persons, the controller shall, prior to the processing, carry out an assessment of the impact of the envisaged processing operations on the protection of personal data. A single assessment may address a set of similar processing operations that present similar high risks.   Article 35 (1)

The controller shall seek the advice of the data protection officer, where designated, when carrying out a data protection impact assessment.   Article 35 (2)

A data protection impact assessment referred to in paragraph 1 shall in particular be required in the case of: Article 35 (3)

- *a systematic and extensive evaluation of personal aspects relating to natural persons which is based on automated processing, including profiling, and on which decisions are based that produce legal effects concerning the natural person or similarly significantly affect the natural person;*
- *processing on a large scale of special categories of data referred to in Article 9(1), or of personal data relating to criminal convictions and offences referred to in Article 10; or*
- *a systematic monitoring of a publicly accessible area on a large scale.*

The supervisory authority shall establish and make public a list of the kind of processing operations which are subject to the requirement for a data protection impact assessment pursuant to paragraph 1. 2 The supervisory authority shall communicate those lists to the Board referred to in Article 68.

Article 35 (4)

The supervisory authority may also establish and make public a list of the kind of processing operations for which no data protection impact assessment is required. The supervisory authority shall communicate those lists to the Board.

Article 35 (5)

The supervisory authority may also establish and make public a list of the kind of processing operations for which no data protection impact assessment is required. 2 The supervisory authority shall communicate those lists to the Board.

Article 35 (6)

The assessment shall contain at least:

Article 35 (7)

- *a systematic description of the envisaged processing operations and the purposes of the processing, including, where applicable, the legitimate interest pursued by the controller;*
- *an assessment of the necessity and proportionality of the processing operations in relation to the purposes;*
- *an assessment of the risks to the rights and freedoms of data subjects referred to in paragraph 1; and*
- *the measures envisaged to address the risks, including safeguards, security measures and mechanisms to ensure the protection of personal data and to demonstrate compliance with this Regulation taking into account the rights and legitimate interests of data subjects and other persons concerned.*

Compliance with approved codes of conduct referred to in Article 40 by the relevant controllers or processors shall be taken into due account in assessing the impact of the processing operations performed by such controllers or processors, in particular for the purposes of a data protection impact assessment.

Article 35 (8)

Where appropriate, the controller shall seek the views of data subjects or their representatives on the intended processing, without prejudice to the protection of commercial or public interests or the security of processing operations.

Article 35 (9)

Where processing pursuant to point (c) or (e) of Article 6(1) has a legal basis in Union law or in the law of the Member State to which the controller is subject, that law regulates the specific processing operation or set of operations in question, and a data protection impact assessment has already been carried out as part of a general impact assessment in the context of the adoption of that legal basis, paragraphs 1 to 7 shall not apply unless Member States deem it to be necessary to carry out such an assessment prior to processing activities.

Article 35 (10)

Where necessary, the controller shall carry out a review to assess if processing is performed in accordance with the data protection impact assessment at least when there is a change of the risk represented by processing operations.

Article 35 (11)

The requirement to complete a DPIA is a new compulsory obligation under GDPR.

Data Subjects' rights

It is important that you are aware of what your Data Subjects' rights are in relation to the data you hold. You will need to have a process in place for Data Subjects to exercise their rights with respect to that data. Data Subjects' Rights of Access is covered in Chapter 13, p. 212.

Chapter 9

Sharing information electronically

Most organisations operate in a dynamic technological environment. This will include computers or devices on most desks, a company website, social media accounts, use of personal devices and apps as well as legacy platforms. Our staff learn to adapt to these changes in technology as they come along. However, some struggle to embrace the latest ideas and concepts especially if they bring with them new terminologies and processes as well as security protocols.

It is comparatively obvious that one should be careful with physical copies of sensitive documents. However, people tend to be less aware when it comes to handling information on their electronic devices (especially if they are using them away from the office environment).

This chapter discusses some of the common pitfalls of sharing information electronically and the potential changes that the new legislation have made to direct marketing. Basic guidance on cybersecurity and ideas on how to keep your data and the personal data of others safe together with an explanation of some of the terminology that abounds in the "technology environment" can be found in Chapter 11, p. 200.

In this "information age" everyone shares data all the time, whether this is photographs of friends and family or an informative email. The key is to make sure that organisations only share personal data in an appropriate manner with the intended audience.

 GDPR states that you may not share personal data without a lawful reason. This includes another person's email address or phone number.

To ensure that you comply with GDPR you should make sure that you understand the data environment, use safe procedures and "design in" privacy considerations. These should ensure that personal data is only stored and shared when it is needed.

As the Data Controller, you are responsible for the activities of your suppliers and Processors. You should take steps to:

- Understand where your information is hosted and stored
- Keep information safe on your:

  ○ Website.
  ○ Online file servers.
  ○ On site file servers.
  ○ Cloud storage.
  ○ Intranet.
  ○ Extranet.
  ○ Apps.
  ○ Social media accounts.
  ○ Internal and legacy systems.

- Have a policy on whether or not you will let staff use their own equipment (referred to as "Bring Your Own Devices" (BYOD)).
- Make sure emails are sent to the correct recipient.
- Encrypt any critical information that is sent by email.
- Protect the email addresses of the people you are sending information
- Do not use opt outs/automatic opt ins.
- Provide information about how personal data will be stored, deleted or used.
- Identify if your data needs to be stored within Europe and if so, make sure that it is.

If you have a mixture of technologies it is a good idea to review them from time to time to ensure everything is still GDPR complaint.

Email

This section is designed to highlight some of the most common pitfalls with email communication. Especially the unintentional sharing of personal details, following the GDPR "minimisation rule" and protecting individuals rights.

Email is a very useful tool but organisations need to make sure that staff take precautions with the information contained within it. Good email practice involves giving time to the email so that you make sure you understand its content and deal with it appropriately.

When you receive a message that you think you need to forward you should make a habit of checking the complete message trail and only share information with the intended recipient rather than a long mail list. It is important to make sure that no personal information (such as mobile numbers or personal information) is included in the shared message if it is going to an outside recipient. Case Study 9.1 is an example of good practice with a forwarded email.

Make sure that those who receive the message do not forward it on without permission. If you add recipients to a discussion make sure you check the email content beforehand so that they are not sent information they should not be party to.

CASE STUDY 9.1   EMAIL FORWARDING

A member of staff emailed their manager from their personal email account with a request for time off to attend a medical appointment and provided details of procedure they were to have. The manager forwarded the email to HR. Before they did so they removed/redacted the details of the medical procedure that the staff member had provided and also the staff member's personal email address.

Before sending the message consider what happens if an individual invokes their right to be forgotten. If you have sent their personal data to lots of people it will be very difficult to ensure that they all delete it.

 Be wary of the "reply to all" button and only use it if everyone needs to see your comments.

Using to and CC

When you address an email "To" someone (Figure 9.1) it is accepted that the email is for that person's attention or action. If this email is forwarded all the address details in both the "To" and "CC" boxes are automatically forwarded as part of the body of the text. Therefore, every person who receives the message will know the email address of everyone else who received the email. This is what happened in the Case Study 9.2.

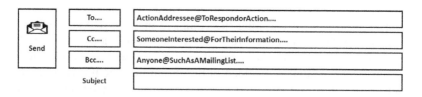

Figure 9.1 Email Addresses

CASE STUDY 9.2   SHARING INFORMATION INCORRECTLY

The Gloucestershire Police Force was fined £80,000 by the UK ICO in June 2018 after it sent out a bulk email that identified victims of non-recent child abuse. The force was investigating allegations of abuse relating to multiple victims when in December 2016, an Officer sent an update on the case to 56 recipients by email. The email addresses were entered in the "To" field and all concerned were able to see the names of the other potential victims.

It is important that you check that the person the email is being sent to is in fact the person you want to send it to and not someone with a similar name (Figure 9.2). This is particularly if the email contains personal data.

 It is no longer acceptable to have a footer on your email that says "if you are not the intended recipient . . . please delete". You have no way of proving that an individual actually deleted the email.

One uses the CC field to copy the email to a person for their information; they are not an action addressee (see Figure 9.3). If the email contains personal data then you should consider if every recipient really needs the information. If they do not really need the information or only need part of if you should not include them as a CC addressee but send them a separate message with just the information they require.

Blind carbon copy (BCC)

When an email address is in the BCC field of a message (see Figure 9.4) all the other BCC addresses are invisible to the recipient. For security and privacy reasons many companies use this feature when they send a message to a large number of people. Indeed, it is recommended by a number of Supervisory

ThePersonYouIntend@TheRightOrganisation....

SomeoneWithASimilarName@AnOrganisationWithaSimilarName

Send   To....   Cc....   Subject

Figure 9.2 Using "To" in Emails

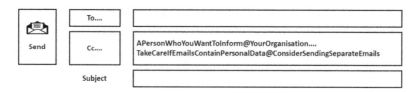

Figure 9.3 Using "CC" in Emails

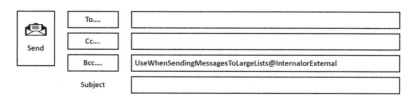

Figure 9.4 Using "BCC" in Emails

Authorities as the preferred way to send messages to multiple email addresses because it does not compromise the other BCC addressees' personal details.

Even if a BCC addressee uses the "Reply All" feature the replies are not shared with the whole address list but only with the sender and any To or CC addressee.

The drawback of BCC is that there is no way for you to personalise each email for every addressee. So, if your recipient favours a more personal approach this may not be the best system for you to use. In some organisations using a BCC field may trigger the spam filter and therefore your email could end up in the junk folder.

Sending multiple emails by mail merge

If you wish to send the same email to multiple recipients and feel BCC is not appropriate (e.g. because you wish to personalise the email in some way) then you should consider email merge tools or an email broadcast platform. This way you can then write one email, personalise the salutation and send it "To" each recipient separately.

If you have software such as MS Office then you can prepare the database in Excel, the letter in word and then select E-Mail Messages in the Mailings ribbon. Word will send individual personalised messages to each email address.

There are many email broadcast systems available and choosing the best solution for your organisation will depend a number of things; what you want to achieve, how many contacts you have and most importantly your budget. More advice and guidance can be found on line an internet search using terms such as "Best Email Marketing Software" or "Automation Tools" or you may wish to download one of the user guides or videos which you find online.

 You cannot use CC, BCC or send attachments in some mail merge email systems.

Email encryption or password protection

Antivirus software and firewalls will not protect an email in transit. Therefore, if you plan to send personal data to an external email address you will need to protect the information and email using some form of encryption. Otherwise you will not be complying with the GDPR.

By making sure any sensitive information is encrypted before you send it by email you ensure that the sensitive data cannot be accessed even if it is intercepted by malicious or accidental means. Encryption can be done easily and without fuss. There are a number of solutions available depending on your organisation size, technology in use and the level of encryption you require. These are discussed in Chapter 11.

Password protecting Word and Office files

Most word processing or office software allow you to protect a document with a password. This means that you can be sure that only your intended recipients are able to access it. In order to maintain security, you need to share the document and the password separately and to make sure that the recipient has the same software as you. Figure 9.5 shows the simple document protection such as that which can be found in the "Info" tab of a software tool such as MS Word.

In order to open an attachment that has been password protected the recipient will need to know what that password is. Without this password it would take even a "brute force attacker" a long time to get access to the document.

 You should give the recipient the password over a different "communication channel" to the document (e.g. by telling them the password over the telephone or face to face).

Protecting large files

Personal data comes in all shapes and sizes. Emails that contain CCTV, pictures or PDFs are notoriously large in size. A common restriction in data transfer is the limit that the mail server imposes on attachment sizes. Any encrypted attachment that exceeds the mail server limit would not be sent.

Figure 9.5 Simple Document Protection

One way to send larger files is to create a ZIP file which can then be protected with a password. There are a number of tools such as MAPILab, which will automatically compress files attached in the email using ZIP.

Software such as My Protected Mail encrypts the file to make sure that it can't be sent on to someone other than the intended recipient.

Alternatively, you could use a cloud based collaborative working mechanism such as GoogleDrive or OneNote to share and work on documents without the need to send them to everyone.

Encrypted email – when the information in the email body is sensitive

Sometimes it is necessary to send sensitive information in the body of the email e.g. sending payroll information to an external payroll company. Here the email itself needs to be encrypted as well as the attachments. Sending and receiving this type of email will require compatible email client software at both ends and this should be configured in advance. It also requires the generation of key pairs, one public and one private which also need careful management. The loss of a private key would mean that received emails cannot be decrypted.

There are a number of free and proprietary products available for desktop, laptop and mobile operating systems. There are also specialist webmail providers who support encrypted email. Should you require an encrypted email system you should consider the risks and investment required and whether there are alternative solutions for encrypted transfer of data which would work in your situation. It is also recommended that you seek expert advice.

Configuring encrypted email within a corporate environment may also cause complications for server-based malware scanning products because the encrypted mail and attachments could potentially be blocked by the scanning software.

Email tracking

A number of email systems use simple email tracking to check if emails are delivered. Some go much further, not only confirming delivery and when an item is read but also show who the email was forwarded to and even whether that person opened it or not. Figure 9.6 shows the email tracking options similar to those found in MS Outlook.

It is acceptable to ask for a standard read receipt as long as the recipient can choose to respond to or not. However, "hidden" data gathering such as the tracking options in Figure 9.6, this is not acceptable unless you have consent from both the original recipient and everyone they forward it on to.

Email retention and archiving

One of the key themes from GDPR that relate to emails are "the maintenance of orderliness and transparency" and "data minimisation". This means everything from data collection to storage, access, and processing to deletion/erasure of the data needs to be open, transparent and accurate.

New provisions in GDPR mean that you are required to have a Privacy Policy that sets how long you keep information. You are also required to ensure that personal data is either erased or anonymised when you no longer

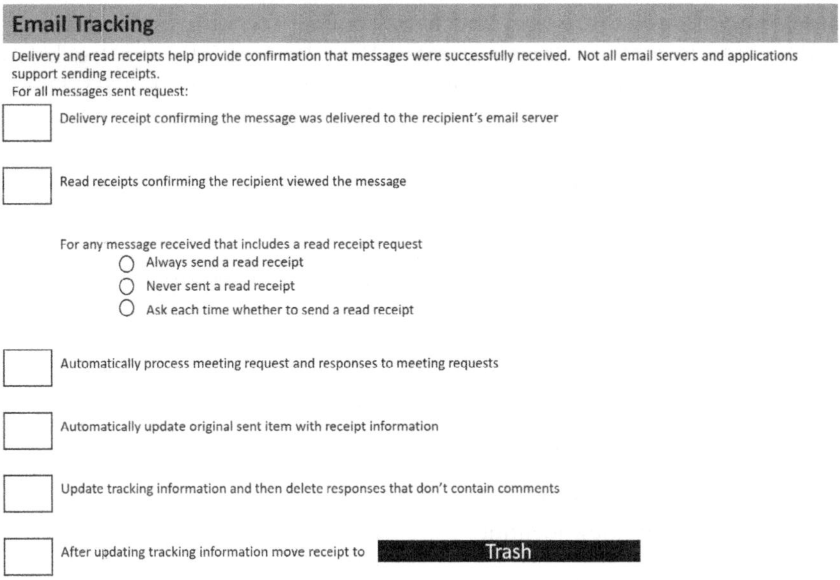

Email Tracking

Delivery and read receipts help provide confirmation that messages were successfully received. Not all email servers and applications support sending receipts.
For all messages sent request:

☐ Delivery receipt confirming the message was delivered to the recipient's email server

☐ Read receipts confirming the recipient viewed the message

For any message received that includes a read receipt request
○ Always send a read receipt
○ Never sent a read receipt
○ Ask each time whether to send a read receipt

☐ Automatically process meeting request and responses to meeting requests

☐ Automatically update original sent item with receipt information

☐ Update tracking information and then delete responses that don't contain comments

☐ After updating tracking information move receipt to ▐ Trash ▐

Figure 9.6 Email Tracking

need it. A critical part of any retention system will be Email archiving. Without a suitable archiving solution, many organisations have little control of where and how email is used and accessed.

Direct marketing

Direct marketing is an area where it is particularly easy to fall foul of the GDPR and the Privacy and Electronic Communications Regulations (PECR). Both of these regulations have completely changed the focus and imposed much stricter rules on marketeers.

Direct marketing is "the targeted promotion of information about your organisation or product which may be of interest to a consumer who you have decided is likely to buy/use your services".

Businesses who engage in direct marketing are likely to have to make changes to their working practices to make sure they are compliant (the alternative is a fine, being forced to change or needing to pay compensation). The anticipated effect that GDPR would have on marketing was one of the greatest sources of concern for many businesses in the run up to May 2018. There were many myths circulated and several articles asking "is this the end of email marketing as we know it". It has been clear since May 2018 that the situation is not as gloom laden as predicted. However, organisations will need to take some simple steps to ensure that their marketing campaigns are compliant with GDPR.

If you are planning a marketing campaign then make sure that you are aware of the new regulations. You need to pay particularly attention to unsolicited electronic messages sent by telephone, fax, email or text as well as those which relate to marketing material sent by post. The new legislation also deals with consent and bought-in marketing lists. A detailed Direct Marketing document for the UK can be found in the Resources section of the book (Resource 9.1).

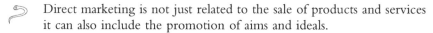 Direct marketing is not just related to the sale of products and services it can also include the promotion of aims and ideals.

In order to comply with the Regulation, you will need to:

1. Compile any marketing lists fairly and lawfully (e.g. make sure they accurately reflect people's wishes).
2. Define and allocate responsibility for compliance with the legislation in your direct marketing activities.
3. Devise and publish a direct marketing policy/procedure (which includes data protection and PECR guidance).
4. Ensure the business identifies itself when:

   • making live marketing calls.
   • making automated marketing calls.

- sending marketing faxes.
- sending electronic marketing messages.

5. Ensure you have the initial and ongoing permission from recipients.
6. Ensure you only send marketing mails to named individuals who have not objected to receiving such mailings.
7. Obtain assurances about the origins/accuracy of bought-in lists.
8. Obtained consent from individuals for marketing.
9. Provide marketing specific data protection training to all staff with direct marketing responsibilities.
10. Provide mechanisms for individuals to opt out of marketing.
11. Put a data retention policy and procedure in place.
12. Send marketing material only in accordance with the express wishes of recipients (both corporate and individuals).

If you wish to check if you are compliant in the UK then the ICO offers a "Direct marketing self-assessment checklist". A link to this (Resource 9.2) is in the Resources section of the book.

If you send out an email to a group of recipients, then depending on the content it could be considered email marketing – even if you're sending it from your own personal Outlook account.

According to a recent study by Return Path, 53% of the 269 billion emails sent every day are promotional emails.

Previous customers

If you consider that previous customers are interested in your products and therefore believe it is acceptable to send marketing emails or texts to someone you have dealt with in the past then you may do so (this is sometimes referred to as a "soft opt in"). If you intend to contact previous customers (or B2B email addressees) in this way you should make sure this is explicitly stated in your Privacy Notice.

Business to business (B2B) emails

If a B2B email address has a person's name on it then it is categorised as personal data and you will require consent for marketing unless you have another legal basis to contact that person. Some B2B emails addresses ("info@" or "operations@") could be considered to fall under "legitimate interest" because they are to do with the business rather than a named individual.

Positive marketing consent

You should have positive consent from an individual before you send them marketing material. The consent can be given using a website or online form with an "opt in" button or a specific paper form that individuals fill out.

Consent that has been given for another purpose may not be used as consent for marketing.

 Offer an "opt out"

If your email is purely for marketing purposes you **must** give customers (even B2B ones) an easy way to opt out or to review their preferences. The easiest way to do this is to provide a simple unsubscribe link at the bottom of every email.

> Make sure you keep a list of people and businesses who have given consent for marketing emails which shows when and what they have signed up to.

Where you have used "consent" as your lawful basis and a recipient asks for their email address to be removed from a mailing list or for the data that you have stored about them to be deleted you are legally bound to do so immediately. This is because under GDPR individuals are given the new right "to erasure"

 Make sure you create a "do not contact" list because if you continue to contact someone who has opted out, they can report you to the ICO.

"Opt in" and "opt out" boxes

You are no longer permitted to use an automatic "opt in" for marketing communications. This means that you can no longer automatically put a tick in an "opt in" as shown in Figure 9.7. The individual should have an equal choice of whether or not to accept the contact offered.

Unless they have "opted in", you are no longer permitted to contact people (business or consumer) with a newsletter, promotions or any other type of marketing email. Inaction by the recipient is not accepted as consent.

When you request an individual's contact details you need to tell them how their data will be stored, shared and deleted. Every different marketing use will need separate specific consent (see Figure 9.8) and if you wish you can ask subscribers to check another box to confirm they understand and acknowledge this.

Shopping Cart

Company Logo

Enter your e-mail [＿＿＿＿＿＿＿＿＿＿]

If you already have an account click here

Your first name [＿＿＿＿＿＿＿＿＿＿]

Your Surname [＿＿＿＿＿＿＿＿＿＿]

Please confirm your email [＿＿＿＿＿＿＿＿＿＿]

☑ I would like to subscribe to the "Company" newsletter to receive the latest news. "Company" does not share or sell your personal information

Confirm

Figure 9.7 Pre-Filled "Opt In"

My Charity

Charity Logo

☐ Keep me informed about "My Charity's" work in the field through email.

☐ I would like to receive text messages from "My Charity" to this number.

May we share your information?

☐ Yes you may share my name and mailing address with other charities.

Donate

"My Charity" explain that giving your details to third parties and other charities helps keep their costs down so is a good thing for people donating

Figure 9.8 Informed and Specific "Opt In"

Designing your "opt in" forms

There are some straightforward things you can do to make sure your "opt in" forms are compliant:

- Ensure you do not have a pre-checked box for "sign me up".
- Introduce a "double opt in". Send a follow-up email asking the user to confirm their subscription. This way you obtain positive consent. Ensure that if they do not confirm the email that they are not added to your list.
- If you are offering a downloadable PDF do not make subscription a requirement. You may offer an option to subscribe but this should not prevent users from downloading what you have offered.
- Consider if it is appropriate to ask your subscribers to re-opt in to your pre GDPR marketing list it. This will ensure that you have a record of their specific consent.
- Make sure every marketing email you send makes it clear that it is as easy for someone to unsubscribe from your list as it was to subscribe.

If you use a third-party solution such as MailChimp, the software will record the date and time of the opt in as well as where it originated from.

"Re-permissioning" emails

If you decide to send a "re-permissioning" email because you do not think you have all the necessary consents in place you should make sure it contains:

- A description of what your marketing emails include.
- Confirmation that recipients will be able to "opt out" on every marketing email you send.
- A link to your privacy statement.
- Confirmation that transactional/servicing emails will be unaffected.
- Confirmation that the subject can withdraw consent at any time.
- Confirmation that recipients will be "opted out" if they do not respond.
- Two clear and equal-sized buttons one to "opt in" or and one to "opt out".

An example of a clear "re-permissioning" email is in Figure 9.9.

Do not give up on marketing

A well organised marketing campaign can yield extraordinary results.

By increasing "buy in" from your supporters (e.g. sending a "re-permissioning email") you will be able to focus your attention on just keeping in contact with individuals who are actually interested in your organisation.

Please confirm that you are still happy to hear from us

The company is strongly committed to protecting the privacy of personal data that we maintain about clients, employees and other individuals. As part of our GDPR compliance we would like to verify that you are happy to continue to receive marketing material from us. More details of the company and our marketing materials click here.
By giving your consent, you will continue to receive the relevant publications, newsletters, offers and invitations to our events.

You will have the opportunity to opt out of receiving communications from us every time we contact you. You may also wish to read out privacy statement which provides further information about how we use personal data.

If you decide you don't want to receive marketing content from us any longer, please note that we may still be required to send you emails about a factual transactional and or service matter in connection with products or services that we are providing to you or the organisation for whom you work.

Please click one of the buttons below. A page will open in your browser confirming your choice with no further action required by you.

You have the right to withdraw your consent at any time.

If we have not heard from you we will send you a remainder email. If we do not hear from you after this, and in line with the new regulation, we will not send you further marketing unless you request it.

If you have any questions please contact us at Consent@mycompany.org.uk.

Figure 9.9 Example of a Clear Re-Permissioning Email

By targeting these individuals effectively, it is likely that you will increase revenue (whether this is sales, donations or increasing your organisation's standing in the community).

Physical security

Emails containing personal data can also be at risk if an individual gains unauthorised access to the email server or to an online account. Making sure that server rooms and password stores are physically secure should be part of the security precautions for your organisation.

Similarly, individuals should be instructed to be aware of their surroundings when opening emails containing personal information or talking about personal data on the phone. They should be particularly wary of using public Wi-Fi for work matters.

Ask your staff to consider who can see over your shoulder and what can they read?

WhatsApp and Messenger

If you use a platform such as WhatsApp or Messenger to send something to a list of contacts then every person in the group will be able to see the contact details of all the other group members and can contact them at will. If you use these platforms for work then you are likely to be in breach of GDPR unless you have the permission of each party to contact them in this way.

To stay on the safe side of the legislation you should either get consent from each party or stop using these platforms altogether for business. If you rely on a Messenger app to help in your daily work, then you should look for GDPR compliant alternatives.

You can continue to use WhatsApp solely for private purposes. Article 2 of the GDPR says that it "*does not apply to the processing of personal data by a natural person in the course of a purely personal or household activity*".

Email security and the data governance policy

Every organisation should have an email security policy that will form part of their data governance policy. This should be regularly reviewed and kept up to date. This policy is where you can set out the rules you wish the organisation to follow with regard to email, the privacy expectations you wish staff to bear in mind when they respond to or forward mail and where you detail any documents and emails that require encryption. All staff should read this policy and sign to acknowledge they have read and understood their responsibilities. The policy should also be clear on data management responsibilities including retention, archiving and destruction. More information on data security can be found in Chapter 11.

Chapter 10

Data Breaches

A Data Breach occurs when data, computer systems or networks are accessed or affected in an unauthorised manner.

One in every four organisations will experience a Data Breach of some sort. It is therefore sensible to make sure your organisation has a system in place to deal with a Data Breach should one occur.

This chapter will explain what Data Breaches are, and provide some examples of breaches. As well as discussing the fines and sanctions that organisations have been subject to as a result of breaches. The chapter will also describe how to recognise a breach and what to do in the event that your organisation experiences a breach.

What is a Data Breach?

A personal Data Breach is an occasion when personal data is:

- Accessed or passed it on without proper authorisation.
- Destroyed, corrupted or disclosed.
- Made unavailable, for example, when it has been encrypted by ransomware, or accidentally lost or destroyed.

A personal Data Breach is a breach of security and can be either accidental or deliberate. It is more than just being about losing personal data. Examples of Data Breaches are:

- Computing devices containing personal data being lost or stolen.
- Deliberate or accidental action (or inaction) by a Controller or Processor.
- Hacking of a computer system containing personal information.
- Loss of availability of personal data through ransomware etc.
- Personal data being altered without permission.
- Sending personal data to an incorrect recipient.
- Unauthorised access of personal data by a third party.

Examples of Data Breaches and penalties

There have been a number of recent high-profile examples of Data Breaches in the news; recent examples are shown in Table 10.1.

Breaches are not limited to household names and can happen to smaller organisations, individuals, councils and charities. Since GDPR came into effect in May 2018 the supervisory authorities have imposed monetary penalties and sanctions on numerous organisations or individuals. There are also a number of high-profile organisations whose data practices are under investigation. For those who wish to see a country by country summary Resource Link 10.1 contains a list of fines and penalties which have been applied throughout the EU for GDPR breaches. A summary of some of these can be found in Table 10.2.

Reporting a Data Breach

GDPR requires all organisations to report certain types of personal Data Breach to the supervisory authority within 72 hours of becoming aware of the breach. The organisation is also obliged to inform the individuals concerned without undue delay if they think it is likely that there is a high risk that breach will adversely affect the individual's rights and freedoms.

Because of this duty, businesses will need to put in place a procedure to detect, investigate and report Data Breaches. This will facilitate decision-making about who you need to notify in relation to any Data Breach. Figure 10.1 shows a simple Data Breach reporting flow chart.

Do I need to report all breaches?

You do not need to report every breach to the Supervisory Authority. The first thing to consider is whether there is a likelihood that there will be a risk

Table 10.1 High-profile Data Breach Examples

BRITISH AIRWAYS	British Airways apologised after admitting that 380,000 customers' payment details were stolen over a period of 15 days in a massive Data Breach that involved payments on their website BA.com and the BA app between 21 August 2018 and 5 September 2018.
FACEBOOK	Facebook reported a security issue that allowed hackers to access information that could have let them take over about 50 million accounts. An engineering team identified the issue when they became aware of a potential attack following a spike in user activity and found that attackers had identified a weakness in their "View As" feature.
TALKTALK	Staff from an IT firm working with TalkTalk could access large amounts of customer data through an online company portal. These "rogue" staff (in India) used the portal to gain unauthorised access to names, addresses and phone numbers of up to 21,000 people.

Table 10.2 Supervisory Authority Fines and Sanctions Imposed

Date	Supervisory Authority	Organisation	Reason for Fine/Sanction	Amount
25/07/2019	France CNIL	Active Insurance	Poor security after an online check revealed that customer accounts could be accessed via hypertext links referenced on a search engine.	€180,000
16/07/2019 09/07/2019	Netherlands UK ICO	Haga Hospital Marriott International	Poor security of patient records. Data Breach involving 339 million guests (30 million related to residents of 31 countries within the EEA).	€460,000 £99 million
08/07/2019	UK ICO	British Airways	Poor security of personal data relating to 500,000 customers. Data was diverted to a fraudulent site where it was harvested by the attackers.	£183.39 million
04/07/2019	Romania	Unicredit Bank	Failure to apply appropriate technical and organisational measure to minimizing data and integrating the necessary safeguards in processing.	€130,000
14/06/2019	Ireland	Facebook	The Irish regulator conducting nearly one dozen investigations into Facebook.	Ongoing
12/06/2019	Spain AEPD	La Liga	Violating provacy – spy mode can use the microphone and GPS of	€250,000

(Continued)

Table 10.2 (Cont.)

Date	Supervisory Authority	Organisation	Reason for Fine/Sanction	Amount
			fans' phones to record their surroundings	
12/06/2019	Austria	Datenschutzbehörde	Facebook	A potential landmark case against Facebook for violating GDPR rights. Ongoing
04/06/2019	9 EU Countries	Google	Privacy complaints over the way Google deals with data in online advertising.	Ongoing
08/05/2019	Norway	Municipality of Bergen (Local Government)	Data Breach – a file with login credentials for 35,000 students and employees found in a public storage area.	€170,000
24/04/2019	Finland Data Protection Ombudsman	Svea Ekonomi	Non-compliance – the company's online credit decision service should be considered automatic decision-making.	Ordered to correct its practices in the processing of personal data related to assessment of creditworthiness
30/03/2019	Poland	Bisnode	Failure to inform the data subject that it has obtained their information by using a third party ("scraping" the internet) to obtain the details of 6 million people.	€220,000

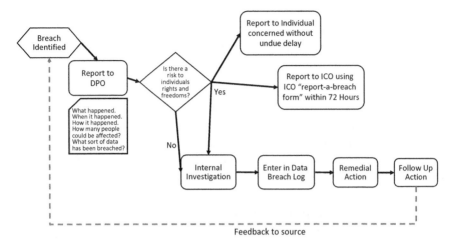

Figure 10.1 Simple Data Breach Reporting Flow Chart

to people's rights and freedoms as a result of the breach and then how severe that risk will be.

If it's likely there will be a risk to people's rights and freedoms following the breach, then you must notify the Supervisory Authority (you will need to complete their Personal Data Breach form, which will be on their website).

If it's unlikely there will be a risk to people's rights and freedoms following the breach then you don't have to report it but you must log it and deal with it appropriately.

Regardless of whether the breach needs to be reported to the Supervisory Authority, businesses are required to keep a record of any personal Data Breach.

Planning how to deal with a breach

The best thing to do is put a system in place so that you are ready to react to a breach. You can do this by adopting a proactive approach. If it is appropriate appoint, a Data Protection Officer to help you and to act as a focus for Data Protection issues. They will help you to identify your Data Breach risks and how a breach would impact your organisation.

Consider how long it will take to recover from each type of Data Breach and restore critical functions and then put a process in place to manage your response. Make sure that staff know how to escalate a security incident to the appropriate person(s) within your organisation.

You should then put measures in place to take action and address any Data Breaches that occur and have a mechanism to let Data Subjects and/or other organisations know you have suffered a breach.

You should also make sure that your information security programme and measures are in line with industry best practice.

Prevention is better than the cure, so you should deliver appropriate training to all staff who process personal data.

Your Data Audit will have helped you to identify and record the categories and number of individuals or data records involved.

It is particularly important that you make sure your system can report a breach and provide all necessary information within 72 hours of becoming aware of the breach

What do I need to tell the Supervisory Authority if I have a Data Breach?

You can report a Data Breach to the Supervisory Authority either by telephone or online. A list of Supervisory Authorities and their contact details can be found in Appendix 1 to Chapter 1, p. 13.

The Supervisory Authority will want to know the following information:

- What happened.
- When it happened.
- How it happened.
- How many people or records could be affected.
- The categories of data that have been breached.
- The categories of individuals involved.
- The DPO's name and contact details or other contact point.
- A description of the likely consequences of the breach.
- A description of the measures you have taken, or propose to take, to deal with the breach, including any measures taken to mitigate any possible adverse effects.

You should provide as much information as you can to the Supervisory Authority as soon as possible. It is not always possible to investigate a breach fully within 72 hours and therefore the Supervisory Authority will (under Article 34(4)) allow you to provide the information in phases as long as you warn them that you are not going to be able to provide the full information within 72-hour timeframe.

Supervisory Authorities often have a Data Breach Reporting form in MS Word, which you can download and complete as part of your preparation. You may wish to download one of these forms and keep it in your Data Protection Folders. Alternatively, you may develop an "in house" form to capture the relevant information and use this as a basis for your report.

Data Breach Register

Date Commenced:................ Compiled By:................

Brief Description:					Date:	Ser:
Reported to SA: Yes/No	SA Reference No (if reported)	SA Acknowledgement Email (Date and time)	SA Follow Up Comments:			Status Open/Closed
Description of how the breach came to light						
Areas where breach has an impact (one line for each)	What precautions were in place and/or what caused the breach	Who is affected by the breach?	Likelihood and severity of any risk to individual's rights and freedoms (Likely/Unlikely) (Low/Moderate/Severe)	What precautions are in place to eliminate or reduce the chance of this occurring again	What residual risk is there to rights and freedoms (Low/Moderate/Severe)	What further action is required as a result

Figure 10.2 Simple Example Data Breach Log Entry

Note: If the risk to rights and freedoms is Moderately Severe or Severe then the matter must be reported to the Superviory Authority

What will the Supervisory Authority do?

The Supervisory Authority will send you an acknowledgement to confirm they have received your report. They will contact you in due course depending on the severity of the Data Breach and may offer you some guidance or ask for more information. Sometimes a more serious breach will require a more in-depth investigation and they will ask the following questions:

- What did you have in place that could have stopped it?
- What have you done to help the people this affects?
- What have you learned?
- How can you stop similar breaches in future?

There are many online organisations such who offer a free assessment of how ready you are to deal with a Data Breach via a straightforward quiz.

What should I do next?

Whether you have informed the Supervisory Authority or not the first thing you will need to do is to make a record of the Data Breach. You will need some form of "log" that the DPO and Senior Management have access to.

Your log could be in a confidential hard copy folder or book or you could file it electronically with password protection, the choice is up to you. The aim should be to capture the details of the incident, what actions and decisions were taken and provide details of any precautions that have been put in place as a result, any residual risks and further actions to be taken. An example of a Data Breach register layout is in Figure 10.2.

You should then put in place measures to rectify the breach and take any remedial actions or follow up actions necessary to address any issues that remain. Finally, you should communicate information relating to Data Breaches to Data Subjects and/or other organisations and make sure you keep everyone involved in the breach up to date with what is happening.

Staff training

Best practice guidance states you should make sure that all staff involved in processing personal data receive appropriate training. This sort of training should take place every two years (at a minimum) and should include an overview of the Data Breach procedure in your organisation so that staff know how to escalate a security incident to the appropriate person(s) within your organisation.

Staff training is covered in detail in Chapter 14, p. 231.

Chapter 11

Keeping data safe

GDPR places an obligation on organisations to protect the information that they hold about individuals. This means that you should have an appropriate information security framework. Any "data" that is held should be protected in case of a breach, cyber attack or unauthorised access. Security was already one of the Data Controller's responsibilities under previous legislation but with GDPR it became a legal requirement.

The requirement for appropriate security measures to be put in place is defined in Article 5 of the GDPR (*Article 5(1)f, EU GDPR, "Principles relating to processing of personal data"*). The exact text is extracted in Quote 11.1.

QUOTE 11.1   ARTICLE 5(1) OF GDPR – PRINCIPLES RELATING TO PROCESSING OF PERSONAL DATA

Personal data shall be processed in a manner that ensures   Article 5(1)f
appropriate security of the personal data, including protection
against unauthorised or unlawful processing and against accidental
loss, destruction or damage, using appropriate technical or
organisational measures ("integrity and confidentiality").

GDPR provides specific guidance on what organisations should do to keep their processing secure, how they should assess risk, and the need to have appropriate systems in place. Information security supports good data governance and helps organisations demonstrate their compliance (the 7th principle of GDPR).

Keeping data safe (cybersecurity) is often overlooked by small organisations. Many believe that they are not big enough for the information they hold to be at risk. According to *Emma Bordessa in the IT Governance Blog (March 2018)* only 15% of the IT decision makers in small organisations think their employees have a good understanding about cybersecurity and yet only 26% of these organisations have introduced cybersecurity training for their staff. This is particularly worrying considering that 20% of the businesses believe their employees don't care about cybersecurity at all.

The risks to your data

Poor information security puts an organisation's services or systems at risk. Personal data is particularly at risk of loss or abuse and this can lead to harm, embarrassment, inconvenience or distress for the individuals about whom you process information. Such harm could include:

- Details of the activities of, or personal (e.g. medical) information about, high profile individuals being shared publicly.
- Exposure of contact details for at risk groups (e.g. domestic violence victims or crime witnesses).
- Fake applications for loans.
- Fake credit card transactions.
- Identity fraud.
- Mortgage fraud.
- Risk from vigilantes.

Many owners of small companies are concerned their company is vulnerable to cyber threats. It is however estimated that 75% of small businesses have not yet updated their cybersecurity protocols. Some of the headline Cybersecurity Statistics relating to Small Business are in Figure 11.1.

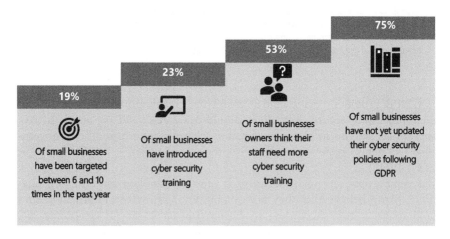

Figure 11.1 Small Business Cybersecurity Statistics

The GDPR data security requirement

The GDPR requires organisations to put in place appropriate security to prevent the personal data that the organisation processes being compromised. The level of security that each organisation requires should be decided on a risk-based approach. This means the level of security should be "appropriate" to the risks should the information be lost. This involves balancing the cost and difficulty of implementation against the reason why processing takes place and the sensitivity of the data involved.

What does data security mean?

Data security is an integral part of any organisation's business. It is the process by which the organisation protects the information it holds from unauthorised access, loss or corruption.

> Data security can also be known as information security or cybersecurity.

Data security can involve computers, databases and websites as well as physical security of items such as pen drives and mobile phones and filing systems. Areas to consider include:

- Authentication.
- Cloud computing.
- Data backup or masking.
- Data erasure.
- Encryption.
- IT asset disposal.
- Network access control.
- Physical security
- Security policy.
- Server and PC protection.
- Staff training.

Identify data security risks

By reviewing the personal data that your organisation holds and assessing the sources of this information you should be able to identify where your data risks are. How the data is used and how valuable, sensitive or confidential the material is will affect this decision.

Your review should address:

- How many individuals have access to personal data.
- If third parties or Data Processors act on your behalf.

- The company computer infrastructure (age, level of protection, software/hardware).
- The physical security systems in place (both on site, in transit and off site).

Put in place data security measures

Data Controllers are responsible for data security irrespective of who does the processing of that data. Controllers should therefore put the security of personal data at the heart of what they do. Security measures should ensure that the "confidentiality, integrity and availability" of the data is maintained. This means keeping complete and accurate data which can only be accessed by authorised individuals. If the worst happens and data is lost or altered you should have a mechanism to recover it.

Organisations who operate in sectors which have additional security requirements should apply these in addition to GDPR.

***

CASE STUDY 11.1   DATA SECURITY OF REFERENCES

A school provides university references for students. While these documents are in draft format, they are saved on staff personal pen drives so that they can be worked on at home and school. The data protection policy requires that the pen drive is password protected and that the references do not contain special category information while they are in draft state. Staff are required to delete or anonymise their draft copy once the final version is uploaded to the school servers.

***

"Confidentiality, integrity and availability" are collectively known as the "CIA triad". They are the three key information security measures which you should seek to guarantee both for systems and the data they process.

Because GDPR requires you to have an appropriate level of security based on your circumstances, the type of processing and the risks to your Data Subjects some smaller companies may not find it necessary to put in place a "formal" data security policy. However, at the very least you should be security aware.

Even if you do not require a dedicated DPO or data security policy it is prudent to nominate a member of staff with have responsibility for the security of your data. This person should coordinate requirements for IT (commissioning and decommissioning of equipment), and undertake periodic checks of the company's security measures as well as advising on business continuity planning and discussions over access by external agencies such as software developers, contractors or other organisations who process personal data on your behalf.

 The Payment Card Industry Data Security Standard applies to companies who process payment card data.

Physical security measures

You should address the physical security of the data that your organisation holds. This will include the disposal of confidential waste, keeping IT equipment secure as well as issues such as controlling access (especially to server rooms), doors, locks, alarms, security lighting and CCTV.

Cybersecurity measures

The measures that you need to implement will depend on a number of issues such as the sophistication of your systems and your staff. You may need to seek specialist advice to make sure your cybersecurity measures are appropriate for your business. You should consider the following four types of security in equal detail:

- Data security.
- Device security.
- Online security.
- System security.

 Not only do scammers impersonate organisations, but they can also pretend to be a colleague boss, supplier or customer. Five per cent of victims are said to be so ashamed that they didn't tell their team about their mistake. **Make sure your staff know what to look out for**.

Cyber essentials

Police forces throughout Europe have cybercrime teams who offer training packages, presentations and guidance. In the UK there is a government scheme Cyber Essentials which introduces a set of basic technical controls that can put in place relatively easily. More information on the scheme can be found on the National Cyber Security Centre website a link to which is Resource 11.1 in the Resources section at the end of the book.

The scheme indicates five key areas that businesses should concentrate on. These are:

- Access control.
- Boundary firewalls and gateways.

- Malware protection.
- Patch management.
- Secure network configuration.

It is estimated that 80% of cyber attacks would be prevented if organisations had implemented controls in these areas.

Pseudonymisation and encryption?

Pseudonymisation and encryption are specified in the GDPR as two measures that can be used to protect the data you hold. Whether you are just storing personal data, or transmitting it over the internet the use of pseudonymisation or encryption may be the most appropriate way of protecting the personal data you process.

Organisations should take this into account during the risk assessment stage and have include it in their selection of security measures.

Backups

By ensuring that you have an appropriate backup process in place you will have some level of assurance that if your systems do suffer a physical or technical incident you can restore them, and therefore the personal data they hold, as soon as reasonably possible.

Bring Your Own Device

Many organisations these days allow their staff to use their own devices for work. This is referred to as Bring Your Own Device (BYOD). You will need to consider the risks vs convenience of this when you develop a strategy for your organisation. Even though the processing is done on someone else's device the Data Controller is the one who is responsible for protecting personal information and not the device owner.

Organisations need an effective BYOD policy. Decide what information and services you want staff to access on their own devices. Prevent unauthorised devices getting access and make sure that authorised devices can only access what you want them to see. Other steps that organisations can take to limit the information that can be shared by devices are:

- Anticipate that these devices may require support which is different to the support you have on site.
- Consider alternative ownership models such as "Choose your own device" or "Corporately owned, personally enabled".
- Disable automated backups on BYOD devices.
- Engage with staff through an effective policy.

- Plan for security incidents.
- Protect against data loss by only "presenting" information rather than storing it locally on the device.
- Understand how devices and users share information.
- Use an effective authentication system.
- Use technical controls like Mobile Device Management (MDM).

    Check if there are any commercial agreements between your organisation and others that restrict the running of business software on personally owned devices.

Testing your security measures

GDPR specifically requires organisations to have a process to regularly test, assess and evaluate the effectiveness of any security measures that they have in place. What exactly you test and how often you do it depend on the individual circumstances.

Vulnerability scanning and penetration testing

Techniques like vulnerability scanning and penetration testing are essentially "stress tests" of your network and information systems. You do this in order to reveal areas of potential risk and things that you can improve.

Whether your testing is done internally or externally (or both) will depend on the individual circumstances. But you should document the results and make sure that you act upon any recommendations.

    These tests do not test your defences they merely identify areas of your network that can be exploited

ISO 27001/2:2013

You may wish to seek certification or to work in compliance with the International Standard ISO 27001 (an information security management system). ISO 27001 is designed as a formal, management-driven risk management system. Organisations apply information security control objectives and security controls in line with the specific risks that their business faces. It requires cooperation from the whole organisation and provides a checklist of the controls that should be considered. The standard is made up of 12 main sections:

- Access control.
- Asset management.
- Business continuity management.
- Communications and operations management.

- Compliance.
- Human resources security.
- Information security incident management.
- Information systems acquisition, development and maintenance.
- Organization of information security.
- Physical and environmental security.
- Risk assessment.
- Security policy.

Adopting the ISO 27001 standard will take time (a minimum of 6 months) and money. Organisations will require external and internal auditors if they choose to go down the certification route. Even if you decide to work in compliance with the standard then training your staff could cost approximately €3,000.

Data security terms

There are a number of terms used in the data security world, with which the small business owner may not be familiar. Some of the most common of these terms are included in Table 11.1.

Keeping yourself "cyber safe"

There are several things even the sole trader should do to protect themselves in the cyber environment.

Back up your data

Make sure you keep your important data safe. Back them up to an external hard drive or a cloud-based storage system on a regular basis.

Keep your apps and software up to date

The updates for software and apps are designed to provide vital security updates which will help protect your devices.

Lock the screens on your smart devices

Using the screen lock will provide an extra layer of security.

Table 11.1 Common Cybersecurity Terms

Term	Explanation
Antivirus	Software to detect, stop and remove viruses or malicious software.
Attacker	Someone who exploits computer systems in a malicious way.
Botnet	A network of infected devices which are connected to the internet to commit coordinated cyber attacks without their owner's knowledge.
Brute force attack	When computer power is used to automatically send a vast number of requests or input a series of numbers in order to discover passwords and gain access to a system. (A dictionary attack is a brute force attack using known words, phrases or passwords).
Click Farm	A large group of low paid workers who are employed to click on paid advertising links and liking them in order to generate better results for the organisation being reviewed.
Cyber attack	A malicious attempt to damage, disrupt or gain unauthorised access to computer systems, networks or devices, using cyber means.
Cyber incident	A breach of cybersecurity rules.
Digital footprint	A "footprint" of digital information that a user's online activity leaves behind.
Denial of service (DoS)	When legitimate users are denied access to computer services (or resources), usually by overloading the service with requests.
Download attack	The unintentional installation of malicious software or virus onto a device without the user's knowledge or consent.
Firewall	Hardware or software that uses a defined rule set to constrain network traffic to prevent unauthorised access to or from a network.
Hacker	Someone with some computer skills who uses them to break into computers, systems and networks.
Honeypot	A decoy system to attract potential attackers that helps limit access to actual systems.
Internet of things (IoT)	Everyday objects such as televisions (not computers and devices) that connect to the internet.
Keylogger	Sofware that tracks keyboard inputs – used to monitor the user.
Malvertising	Using online advertising to deliver malware.
Malware	Malicious software (viruses, trojans, worms or any code) that could have an adverse impact on organisations or individuals.
Man-in-the-middle Attack	Computer Evesdropping – an attacker secretly relays computer communication through themselves to compromise the integrity and confidentiality of messages.
Patching	Updates for firmware or software to improve security and/or enhance functionality.

(Continued)

Table 11.1 (Cont.)

Term	Explanation
Pentest	An authorised test of a computer network or system designed to look for security weaknesses so that they can be fixed
Pharming	An attack on a network that results in a user being redirected to an illegitimate website even though they entered the correct address.
Phishing	Untargeted, mass emails asking for sensitive information (such as bank details) or directing them to a fake website.
Pwned	Your account's defences have been compromised.
Ransomware	Malicious software that makes data or systems unusable until the victim makes a payment.
Sanitisation	Electronic or physical destruction methods to securely erase or remove data from memory.
Software as a service (SaaS)	A business model where consumers access centrally-hosted software applications over the internet.
Smishing	Phishing via SMS text.
Spear-phishing	A targeted form of phishing, where the email is designed to look like it's from a person the recipient knows and/or trusts.
Spoofing	Faking (or imitating) a sending address to get access to a system.
Trojan	A malware or virus that is disguised as legitimate software and used to hack into the victim's computer.
Two-factor authentication	The use of two different components to verify a user's claimed identity. Also known as multi-factor authentication.
Water-holing	A fake website (or compromising a real one) in order to exploit visiting users.
Whaling	Highly targeted phishing attacks (masquerading as a legitimate emails) aimed at or purporting to come from senior executives.
Whitelisting	A list of approved applications or addressees in an organisation which protects systems from potentially harmful applications.

Use a strong password

You should protect yourself by using a strong and separate password for each account or application. The recommended standard is three random words. If you wish you could use a password manager to create and remember passwords.

Use two-factor authentication

Wherever possible you should use two-factor authentication to make sure your data is secure.

Chapter 12

Retaining and deleting data

One of the key tenants of GDPR is the minimisation of data. This means that organisations are no longer allowed to keep records indefinitely and they must tell individuals at the point of collection how long the information will be kept for. Some organisations are permitted to retain information for longer periods if they have a good reason such as if they are part of an archive in the public interest or scientific or historical research.

This chapter discusses the best way to manage how long you keep data. It discusses the individual's rights of erasure and provides advice on how to delete various types of data.

Figure 12.1 shows the five key actions to take in regard to data retention.

 The right to be forgotten is not the only way that you are obliged under GDPR to consider whether to delete personal data.

Retaining data

It is important that an organisation's data retention policy is fair and lawful. This means it should strike a balance so that both the needs of the Data Subject and the business are taken into account.

There are a number of legal requirements that regulate how long certain records are retained. Particularly those that relate to tax, audit, health, education and the rehabilitation of offenders. Where it is available industry specific guidance and standards should be followed.

Guidance on records management topics, including retention and disposal, is available from both the National Archives (TNA) and the International Records Management Society (IRMS). This guidance can help organisations to comply with the regulation and is commended to all organisations even though it is primarily aimed at public authorities.

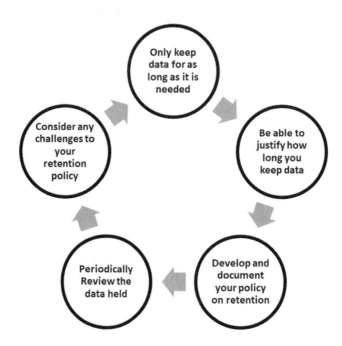

Figure 12.1 Retaining Data in an Organisation

Documentation

All organisations should make a record of their decision on why they have selected a particular retention period. This decision needs to be reviewed on a regular basis and amended in accordance with changes to legislation or use of the data.

Standard retention periods

Where organisations adopt a standard retention period (e.g. 6 months after last contact) they should review the data at that point and decide if the information is still required.

If the information is still required but the personal details are not then they should take steps to anonymise or pseudonymise the data.

If the data is still required the retention period should be amended, privacy documentation updated and the Data Subject should be informed.

> There are a number of automated systems that can be used to flag records for review.

Reviewing retention periods

It is not compulsory to define a set retention period for personal data. However, if you do not have a defined retention period it is imperative that you regularly review whether you still need the data.

Where your retention period is lengthy you should review your retention periods at regular intervals to minimise any impact on individuals.

If a Data Subject asks you to review whether you still need their personal data, you should comply with their request.

What to do with personal data once it has been reviewed

When you no longer require data, you should either anonymise or erase it. Hard copies should be disposed of securely.

Archiving, research and statistical retention

You are not permitted to hold personal data indefinitely "just in case" it might be useful in future. However, it is possible to keep personal data indefinitely if it is for:

- Archiving purposes in the public interest.
- Scientific or historical research purposes.
- Statistical purposes.

Where this exemption applies this should be the only purpose for which you use the data and you must put in place appropriate safeguards to protect the rights and freedoms of the Data Subjects.

Anonymisation

If it is possible to anonymise the data by removing any personally identifiable information so that the individual can no longer be identified then this should be done as soon as possible/practical. Thereafter you can keep anonymised data for as long as you wish.

If records are kept for public interest, archiving, scientific or historical research, or statistical purposes (and there are appropriate safeguards in place) the record does not need to be anonymised.

Pseudonymisation

Pseudonymisation is where personally identifiable information is replaced by a different piece of information or pseudonym. This will make the personal data element less identifiable but the remainder of the record can be used for data analysis.

Pseudonymisation can be a useful tool in order to comply with the principles of data minimisation and security. It cannot be used as a tool to anonymise data this is because it is still possible to identify personal data that has been pseudonymised if one has the "key".

Deletion

With physical (paper) records data deletion is achieved by "destruction". This may be by means of shredding or burning or through some outsourced secure document disposal service.

When used in context of electronic data disposal, the term deletion means removing as much of the data (including any backups) and putting any data that remains beyond use. This includes deleting the file and removing it from the "waste folder on the computer".

Under certain circumstances it may not be possible to remove every trace of the data but you should make an effort to remove as much as you can (taking into account technology and cost). Organisations may require assistance from a computer expert to make sure that the information can no longer be accessed.

If you plan to sell on IT that confidential data has been processed on, it may be appropriate to remove and destroy the hard drive.

Taking data "offline"

Taking data "offline" is not the same as permanently deleting data. Where data is stored off line you are still considered to be processing it. You should therefore only store data "offline" if you can justify retaining it. You will still be required to respond to any Subject Access Requests for data stored "offline".

Do not just delete everything

GDPR **does not require** all records to be destroyed in order to achieve compliance with the regulation. If records have a continuing value they should be retained.

The right of erasure

When does the right to erasure apply?

Individuals were given greater rights to their personal data with GDPR. These rights can be exercised using verbal or written forms.

In addition to knowing how and why the information is collected and who it is shared with, individuals have the right to ask organisations to erase the data that is held about them. This also known as the right to be forgotten.

The right to erasure (the right to be forgotten) apply where:

- Data has been obtained through "consent".
- Data is being processed for direct marketing.
- Data is being processed to offer information society services to a child.
- Data is being processed unlawfully.
- Data is no longer required for the original purpose.
- Where the individual objects to you processing data using "legitimate" interests.
- You have been legally obliged to delete the data.

The right to be forgotten/the right to deletion is not absolute. Neither is it the only way that you are obliged under GDPR to consider whether or not to delete personal data.

Children's rights of erasure

Children's information is an area where GDPR has created enhanced protection. Any request to erase data should be carefully considered if the data relates to a child (even if the subject is no longer a child).

Where the processing relates to the internet or other online environments this right for children is absolute.

When does the right to erasure not apply?

The right to be forgotten (erasure) does not apply where:

- Data is processed for archiving purposes.
- Data is processed in order to comply with a legal obligation.
- Data is processed in order to exercise the right of freedom of expression and information.
- Data is processed in order to perform a task carried out in the public interest or in the exercise of official authority.
- Data is processed for the establishment, exercise or defence of legal claims.
- The data is "Special Category Data" and is being processed for:
  - public health purposes in the public interest.
  - the purpose of preventative or occupational medicine.

There are some other exemptions from the right to erasure which are contained within the relevant national data protection legislation.

CASE STUDY 12.1   INDIVIDUAL EXERCISING THE RIGHT TO BE FORGOTTEN

A secondary school receives a request from an old pupil to delete all of their school records from 20 years ago. The school has a public duty to keep pupils' educational records until the pupil is 24, thereafter, they are destroyed. However, as a public body the school also keeps a copy of all public exam results in their archive because they are a public record.

Decision: The school determines that it holds no records other than the public examination records for the pupil and his cohort. It determines in this case no information will be deleted. The school informs the individual that it will not delete the information as it is serving both for "archiving" and "public interest".

Receiving a request for erasure

The legislation is not specific on how a request for erasure may be made. There is no requirement for the request to include the words "request for erasure/to be forgotten" nor does the particular article (Article 17) of the GDPR legislation need to be quoted.

Requests may be made either verbally or in writing and the accepted norm is to reply to the individual using the same medium that they made the request by.

The request must be dealt with within a 1-month timescale. This can be problematic as individuals may approach anyone in your organisation with their request. It is therefore important that everyone in the organisation can recognise when they have received a request for erasure and deal with it appropriately.

Larger or more complex organisations will need to have a mechanism in place to log all the requests that they receive (this should cover both verbal and written requests).

Organisations need to develop appropriate methods to delete the information and to ensure that all data has been removed. This includes from back up folders and archives. Figure 12.2 is a checklist for organisations to follow in the event of a request for erasure.

How long do I have in order to comply?

You must comply with the request within 1 calendar month from the day on which you receive the request (you may reply sooner if you wish).

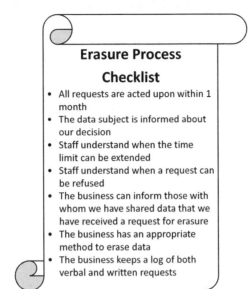

Erasure Process Checklist

- All requests are acted upon within 1 month
- The data subject is informed about our decision
- Staff understand when the time limit can be extended
- Staff understand when a request can be refused
- The business can inform those with whom we have shared data that we have received a request for erasure
- The business has an appropriate method to erase data
- The business keeps a log of both verbal and written requests

Figure 12.2 Request for Erasure Checklist

This period may be extended if you have a reasonable reason for the delay such as the issue is complex or there are a number of requests involved. Whatever your reason, you will need to inform the person making the request of the reason behind any delay.

You may ask for additional information to clarify with the individual that you have understood their request.

Checking that the request is bona fide

You may ask for additional information to identify the individual making the request. Particularly if you doubt that they are the Data Subject. You should only request sufficient information to confirm that they are the person about whom you have the records.

You must ask for this identification information from the individual within one month of receipt of the request.

If you ask for additional information to identify the individual the time limit commences when the additional information is received.

Erasing data that has been shared with other organisations

Where data has been shared with another organisation or person you will need to inform them that the data needs to be deleted. This applies equally to data that has been shared directly with a recipient as well as where it has been shared online (e.g. on a website).

Each recipient of the data should be informed that the data has been erased. If this is not possible (e.g. if it involves disproportionate effort) then you should inform the Data Subject who the recipients of their data were so that they can make a choice whether or not to contact them.

If personal data has been made public online, then other Controllers should be advised to erase links to it or to cease taking copies of this data.

Where data has been shared with another organisation you should agree between you what happens when the data is no longer required or if you no longer wish to share it. In some instances, all organisations should delete their copies but in others the shared data should be returned to the original Controller (without a copy being retained in the other organisation).

Erasure from backup systems

Organisations must be clear with the individual making the request just how the request for erasure will be fulfilled. The key issue is to remove the data so that it is no longer available. In practice this may require a 2-phase approach:

- With a live system it should be possible to instantly fulfil the request for erasure.
- Any data in a backup system may remain there until it is overwritten. This will be considered acceptable as long as the data within the backup is not used for any other purpose.

Refusing a request for erasure

Where you receive a request for erasure that you consider is repetitive or "manifestly unfounded or excessive" you are permitted to refuse to deal with the request.

You should inform the individual of your decision within one month of the request being received giving the reasons why you are not acting on their request. Your response should also remind the individual that they have the right to seek a court order (judicial remedy) to enforce their request or may complain to the supervisory authority about the way you dealt with the case.

Charging to erase data

In most circumstances you are not permitted to charge a fee when an individual has exercised their "right to be forgotten".

However, you may charge a "reasonable fee" (e.g. to cover the administrative costs of complying with the request) if you consider that the request is repetitive or "manifestly unfounded or excessive". There is no need to comply with the request until you have received this fee.

Should you decide to make a charge you should inform the individual of the reasons why you have made this decision. Your response should also include advice to the individual that they can make a complaint to the Supervising Authority about your decision or to seek a judicial remedy in order to force you to comply.

Retaining data from dashcams/helmet cams/CCTV

Dashcams/helmet cams and CCTV take images of other people and their cars in public areas. The legislation does not prescribe any specific minimum or maximum retention periods for these systems.

Retention of data from dashcams/helmet cams/CCTV should therefore reflect the organisation's purposes for recording. The details of this purpose and the retention period should be included in the privacy documentation.

If someone requests that you delete dashcams/helmet cams/CCTV footage that shows them you should comply with their request.

An individual who publishes dashcam footage on a social media platform will have infringed the privacy rights of the individuals in the recording and could be subject to a fine or prosecution.

Chapter 13

An individual's rights under GDPR

Individuals rights as Data Subjects are much improved by GDPR. Organisations are now obliged to tell Data Subjects how their data is going to be used and who it will be shared. They must do this at the time the individual provides the data or the first time that the organisation starts to use it.

The "biggest" new right that individuals have under the legislation is the right to obtain a copy of all the personal data that a particular organisation collects about them. This is called a Subject Access Request. In some cases, individuals can also ask for their data to be erased, made more accurate or even to stop the data being processed at all.

Because the individual's rights is such a complex area, many of the Supervisory Authorities have produced detailed guidance about it on their websites.

GDPR applies to any personal information that relates to an "identifiable person". ALL companies and organisations who process the personal data of people based in the EU, regardless of where the company is located, are covered by the legislation as are any organisation within the EU who process personal data of individuals outside the EU.

Providing information to individuals

GDPR requires organisations to provide clear information about how they will process, share and dispose of an individual's information. They are also required to inform the individual why the information is required, what their rights are in respect of the data being processed and provide information on how individuals can request access to their personal data.

Organisations are obliged to make it clear if individuals are under a statutory or contractual obligation to provide the personal data and provide details of what will happen if they don't provide that data.

Data Subjects' rights

GDPR gives individuals 12 rights:

- **Right of Access** – Individuals have the right to ask for access to their personal data (Subject Access Request), whether this is verbally or in writing. The organisation has one month to respond to the request.
- **Right to Data Portability** – individuals have the right to obtain and reuse any personal data that they provided a Controller.
- **Right of Erasure** – individuals have the right to ask for their personal data to be erased. This is also known as the Right to be Forgotten. In some circumstance's organisations do not have to comply with this request.
- **Right to Object** – in certain circumstances individuals the right to object to their data being processed. This is particularly used for direct marketing or where the processing is likely to cause, or is causing, damage or distress.
- **Rights to Object to Automated Decision Making and Profiling** – individuals are able to object to decisions being taken by automated means (where a computer makes the decision without any human involvement). Article 22 of GDPR imposes additional rules to protect individuals which include restrictions on the use of automated decision making unless it is:
  - ◦ necessary for a contract.
  - ◦ authorised by Union or Member state law.
  - ◦ based on the individual's explicit consent.

- **Right to be Informed** – Individuals have the right to be informed when their personal data is collected and what it will be used for. This is a key transparency requirement under the GDPR. The information provided should include the purposes for processing, retention periods and details of who it will be shared with. This is known as "privacy information".
- **Right of Rectification** – In certain circumstances, individuals can ask for inaccurate personal data to be rectified, blocked, erased, destroyed or completed if it is incomplete.
- **Right to Refuse Cookies** – individuals have the right to refuse to allow cookies to be placed on their device.
- **Right to Restrict Processing** – individuals have the right to request that the processing of their personal data is supressed or restricted. In particular they may use this right to stop direct marketing.
- **Right to Request Access to a Specific Record** – where specific records are kept individuals may request access to these records (e.g. when an individual wants to see their medical/school record).
- **Right to Seek Redress** – individuals have the right to seek redress, either through the Supervisory Authority or the courts.

- **Right to Withdraw Consent** – if consent was used as the legal basis for processing the subject can withdraw consent at any time (consent must be as easy to withdraw as it is to give).

Individual's data access options

There are three ways in that data can be accessed by an individual (see Figure 13.1). The most appropriate route will depend on what information they want. The three types of request are:

A Subject Access Request (SAR). This is where an individual about whom you hold personal data asks to see some, or all, of the information that you have about them. This can include internal reports, emails and comments as well as paper files and meeting minutes. They don't have to give you a reason and can make this request as often as they wish (you can only refuse on grounds that it is manifestly unfounded or excessive). A SAR must be answered within one month of the request being made.

Figure 13.1 Individual Data Access Options

A SAR can only be made by the subject (or someone representing them).

A Freedom of Information Request (FOI). The Freedom of Information Act is used to get specific information from a public body about their general business. Generally, a FOI request is made by someone who is conducting research and it must be answered within 20 working days.

A FOI request may not include personal information about individuals.

A request for a specific type of record. An individual about whom data is processed by a medical practice or school, may ask to see what has been written them on that record. If this applies then the individual may make a request for this specific record. The organisation should respond in line with industry guidelines.

Subject Access Request

Individuals have the right to receive a copy of any personal data and other supplementary information that an organisation has on them. It will help the individual to understand the legal basis on which the data is being processed and how and why the data is being used.

A link to the UK ICO Subject Access Request Code of Practice is Resource 13.1 in the Resource section of this book.

Format of a Subject Access Request

A Subject Access Request can only come from the Data Subject or the person with parental responsibility for the subject if they under 16. It does not need to contain the words "Subject Access Request" and it should be clear to individuals that they may make their request in **any** format they wish as long as their wish to receive their personal information is clear.

A SAR can be made verbally, by letter, email or even on social media to any member of an organisation.

Recital 59 of the GDPR recommends that organisations "*provide means for requests to be made electronically*". In practical terms this means you can design an electronic form and ask the subject to complete it and return to a specific person in the organisation. However, even if you have a form you must still respond within the 30-day time limit.

Can I charge for a SAR?

The organisation should provide the information requested in a SAR free of charge. Under certain circumstances a charge can be made to cover the printing of a large volume of information.

However, if the organisation believes that the request is manifestly unfounded or excessive you may charge a "reasonable fee" for the administrative costs of complying with the request.

You can also charge a reasonable fee if an individual requests further copies of their data following a request. You must base the fee on the administrative costs of providing further copies. The individual should be informed that a fee is due without delay. They should be informed that they have a right to complain to the Supervisory Authority or to seek a judicial remedy.

Can we refuse to comply with a request?

You can refuse to comply with a SAR if you believe it is manifestly unfounded or excessive or repetitive in nature. If you consider that a request is manifestly unfounded or excessive you can either request a "reasonable fee" to deal with the request or refuse to deal with the request. In either case you need to justify your decision.

Any fee you charge should be based on the administrative costs of complying with the request. If you decide to charge a fee you should contact the individual promptly and inform them. You do not need to comply with the request until you have received the fee.

What should we do if we refuse to comply with a request?

You must inform the individual without undue delay (within one month maximum) of:

- The reasons you are not taking action.
- Their right to make a complaint to the Supervisory Authority.
- Their ability to seek to enforce this right through a judicial remedy.

Data that includes information about other people?

Responding to a SAR may involve providing information that relates both to the individual making the request and to another individual. You do not have to comply with the request if it would mean disclosing information about another individual who can be identified from that information, except if the other individual has consented to the disclosure or it is reasonable to comply with the request without that individual's consent.

When determining whether it is reasonable to disclose the information, you must take into account all of the relevant circumstances, including:

- The type of information being disclosed.
- Any duty of confidentiality to the other individual.
- Steps you have taken to seek consent from the other individual.
- Whether the other individual is capable of giving consent.
- Any express refusal of consent by the other individual.

You may sometimes be able to disclose information that relates to a third party but you need to decide whether it is appropriate to do so in each case. This decision will involve balancing the Data Subject's right of access against the other individual's rights. If the other person has consented to you disclosing the information about them, then it would be unreasonable not to do so. But where there is no such consent, you must decide whether to disclose the information anyway.

You cannot refuse to provide access to personal data about an individual simply because you obtained that data from a third party. The rules about third party data apply only to personal data which includes both information about the Data Subject and a third party.

Exemptions

In addition to the manifestly unfounded or excessive exemption there are several statutory exemptions contained in the DPA18.

The majority of these exemptions relate to the detection and prevention of crime, national security and public functions such as immigration control.

There are also exemptions which relate to a commercial context including if the information:

- Is subject to legal or litigation privilege.
- Is purely personal or for household use.
- Is a reference for employment, training or educational purposes.
- Is processed for management forecasting or planning in a business activity which could be prejudiced if it were to be disclosed.
- Consists of records of intentions and relate to negotiations between the employer and employee and compliance with the request would prejudice the negotiations.
- Contains a third party's personal data.
- Is of the type which would be likely to prejudice crime prevention/detection or the prosecution of offenders if disclosed.

Further advice on these exemptions is being worked on by the Supervisory Authorities and can be expected in due course.

Information about a third party may only be disclosed where that person has consented to the disclosure or where it is reasonable to disclose the information without their consent. Therefore, the Data Controller should balance the rights of all the individuals involved but taking into account:

• The type of information you would disclose.
• Any duty of confidentiality you owe to the other individual.
• Any steps you have taken to seek consent from the other individual.
• Whether the other individual is capable of giving consent.
• Any express refusal of consent by the other individual.

In a "tie-breaker" situation, the presumption will fall in favour of non-disclosure. This view is not yet replicated in the guidance.

How long do I have to respond to a Subject Access Request?

You should act on a SAR request without undue delay and at the latest within one month of receipt. The time limit is calculated from the day you receive the request until the corresponding calendar date in the next month.

This time limit may be increased by up to two months in special circumstances but only if the request is complex or you have received a number of requests from the individual. The individual must be informed that there will be a delay and the reason for the delay within one month of the request being received.

How to identify a Subject Access Request

It is important that the organisation can recognise a SAR so that you can respond appropriately and in time. You should have a process in place to swiftly recognise and act on SARs whatever source they come from. Because any of your employees you should make sure everyone in the organisation knows how to handled them appropriately.

Ideas for training staff who regularly interact with individuals are included in Chapter 14, p. 231. A flow chart for dealing with a SAR is in Figure 13.2.

Recording SAR requests

It is considered good practice to make a record of the details of any SAR you receive, particularly those that are made verbally. This will help to confirm that you have understood the request correctly and you can use the notes to

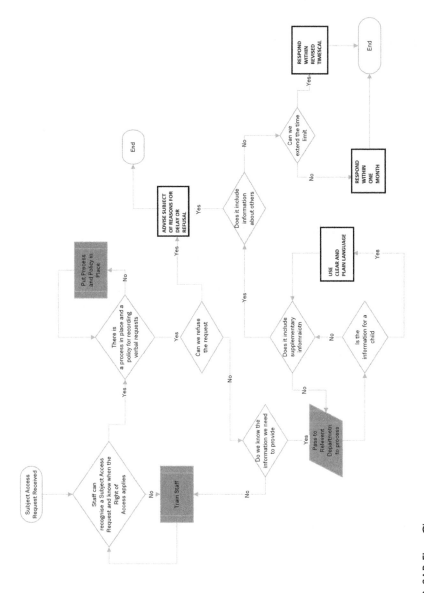

Figure 13.2 SAR Flow Chart

contact the subject and to confirm your understanding of their request. If you keep a log of SAR requests you will be able to understand how you interpreted a request and how long you took to respond. This is useful in case of disputes at a later stage.

Requests for large amounts of personal data

If you process a large amount of information about an individual you can ask them to clarify their request. But you may only ask for information that you need to in order to find the requested data.

If you need more information before responding to a request then you should let the individual know as soon as possible. The timescale for responding to the request begins when you receive the additional information.

If an individual refuses to provide any additional information, you must still endeavour to comply with their original request.

Requests made on behalf of others

The GDPR does not prevent an individual making a SAR via a third party such as a solicitor. In these cases, you need to be satisfied that the third party making the request is entitled to act on behalf of the individual. The third party should provide you with evidence of this entitlement (either written authority or a more general power of attorney).

Requests for information about children

Young children are likely to exercise their rights through those who have parental responsibility for them. But, even if a child is too young to understand the implications of SAR, it is still their right of access rather than their parent or guardian's that is being exercised.

Before responding to a SAR for information held about a child, you should consider whether the child is mature enough to understand their rights. If you are confident that the child can understand their rights, then you should usually respond directly to the child. You may, however, allow the parent to exercise the child's rights on their behalf if the child authorises this, or if it is evident that this is in the best interests of the child.

What matters most is that the child is able to understand (in broad terms) what it means to make a SAR and how to interpret the information they receive as a result of doing so. When considering borderline cases, you should take into account, among other things:

- The child's level of maturity and their ability to make decisions.
- The nature of the personal data.

- Any court orders relating to parental access/responsibility.
- Any duty of confidence that you owe to the individual.
- Any possible consequences providing access to the information to those with parental responsibility will have (e.g. safeguarding).
- Any detrimental effect it will have on the individual if the person with parental responsibility cannot access this information.
- Any views the individual has on the matter.

Although the GDPR states that the age of maturity is 16, a number of Member States have chosen to lower this age threshold to 15, 14 or 13. For more information of the age in each European state, see the national data protection law. In Scotland, a person aged 12 years or over is presumed to be of sufficient age and maturity to be able to exercise their right of access, unless the contrary is shown. In England and Wales, or in Northern Ireland, competence is assessed depending upon the level of understanding of the individual.

More information on situations where the request has been made by a child, can be found in Resource Link 13.2 in the Resources section of this book.

Can I confirm the identity of the requestor?

The organisation must verify that that the person requesting the information is entitled to receive it. If the identity of the person making the request is in doubt proof of identity (such as photographic ID) can be requested. Case Studies 13.1 and 13.2 explain this issue.

CASE STUDY 13.1A   IDENTIFYING THE INDIVIDUAL MAKING A SAR

A former member of staff who has recently left your organisation asks for all their personal data including their personnel file. They do this from an email address you know to be theirs. In this case there is no need to confirm their identity.

CASE STUDY 13.1B   IDENTIFYING THE INDIVIDUAL MAKING A SAR

A former student request for a copy of their exam results. No one in the school can remember the individual. In this case ID is required

The Data Controller should let the individual know as soon as possible if more information is required. They should make it clear that without this confirmation of identity a response will not be given. You should also inform them of their right to make a complaint to the Supervisory Authority and their ability to seek to enforce their rights right through a judicial remedy.

> If you have asked for proof of identity, the period in which you must respond to the request begins when you receive this additional information.

What to include in a Subject Access Request response

In simple terms when making a SAR the individual is entitled to see everything about them.

Your SAR response should include:

- Confirmation that the organisation is processing their personal data.
- A copy of all their personal data.
- Any other supplementary information about your data processing activities (ordinarily contained in your Privacy Notice), which includes:
  - your purpose for processing.
  - the categories of data you process.
  - who you share/disclose the data with.
  - how long you store the data or, how you determine how long to store it.
  - confirmation of their right of rectification, erasure or to restrict processing relevant to the situation (depending on your legal basis for processing).
  - confirmation that they have a right to complain to the Supervisory Authority.
  - information about the data source (if it is not themselves).
  - information if automated decision-making takes place (including profiling).
  - details of the safeguards you provide if you transfer personal data to a third country or international organisation.

What is **NOT** included in a Subject Access Request response?

An individual is **not** entitled to receive any information that relates to another person in a SAR response (unless they are acting on behalf of someone e.g. a Lawyer or Parent). It is the organisation's responsibility to remove or redact any data which relates to other individuals.

It is up to the organisation to decide if the information requested falls within the definition of personal data or not.

Responding to a SAR

It is generally accepted that the best way to respond to a request is to use the same format that the request was made in. Unless the person making the request says otherwise. GDPR requires that the information you provide to an individual is in a concise, transparent, intelligible and easily accessible form, using clear and plain language. This is particularly important where the information is for a child. If you use an internal code in the source document you should explain the meaning of any coded information.

> You are not required to decipher poorly written notes or to ensure that that the information is provided in a form that can be understood by the individual making the request.

If data is regularly updated or altered it is reasonable for an organisation to supply only the information that is held at the time of sending out a response, even if this is different to information which was held when the request was received. Be very careful here because it is an offence to make an amendment simply to prevent disclosure.

> It is not acceptable to amend or delete data if you would not otherwise have done so.

It may be possible or appropriate to provide Data Subjects with remote access to a secure self-service system so that they can see all the personal information that you hold on them (as long as this does not adversely affect the rights and freedoms of others). While this is not appropriate for all organisations there are some situations such as employee payroll management and sectors such as clubs and societies where this may work well.

Should our Processor deal with Subject Access Requests we receive?

The Data Controller is responsible for complying with a SAR. Controllers therefore, need to make sure that they have contractual arrangements in place to guarantee that SARs are dealt with properly, irrespective of who they are sent to.

The one month time limit may not be extended simply on the basis that a Processor has not provided the information that you need to respond.

Data held by credit reference agencies

There are special provisions about how to access to personal data held by credit reference agencies. Unless otherwise specified, a SAR to a credit reference agency only applies to information about an individual's financial standing. In the UK credit reference agencies must also inform individuals of their rights under s.159 of the Consumer Credit Act.

Freedom of Information Act

The aim of the Freedom of Information Act (FOIA) is to provide the public with open and transparent access to official information. It gives legal rights for members of the public to view information that a public authority holds.

The FOIA applies to anyone of any age, nationality, group, organisation or place of residence. Public sector organisations include government departments, local authorities and other public bodies (e.g. the Parole Board) as well as schools, colleges and universities and some private entities if they are wholly owned by a public authority.

The FOI is designed to increase transparency in public organisations. It therefore falls to these organisations to publish info in a proactive manner and to respond to requests for information in a timely way.

An organisation may only refuse a FOI request in certain circumstances such as if the information is sensitive or the costs are too high.

If the FOI response contains personal data from a third party this may be omitted or redacted or the request refused.

Some organisations such as GPs and the BBC only have to provide information about some of the services they provide, such as their work within the public realm.

More information for the application of the FOI in UK is available in the "Freedom of Information Code of Practice" on the gov.uk website, which can be found in the Resources section of this book (Resource 13.3).

An individual's rights under FOI

The individual making the request has both the right to be informed whether the public authority holds the information as described in the request **and** the right to receive the information the holds.

The individual making the request can ask for any recorded information that they think the authority may hold (including information on computers, in emails and in printed or handwritten documents as well as images, video and audio recordings). The individual does not have to specify whether the information requested the Freedom of Information Act, Environmental Information Regulations or the INSPIRE Regulations (it is up to the authority to decide which law should be followed).

It should be clear what information an individual is requesting. The request can be phrased as a question or as a request for specific documents. The authority does not have to answer a question posed in this way if this would mean giving an opinion or judgment or requires new information to be created.

Response limit for a FOI request

The public authority must answer a FOI request within 20 working days. The record will be produced as it is on the day of submission.

Under FOI the public authority will confirm in writing from whether it holds information that has been requested. It will then provide the information that was requested.

> Organisations who receive a request under FOIA or EIR may in certain circumstances give a "neither confirm nor deny" response where the disclosure would breach data protection principals or involve giving personal data away. This is quite a complicated area and it is recommended that you seek guidance from the ICO or in this case.

Public sector publication schemes

The FOI act only applies to information that is not already in the public domain. Where a public authority publishes its information in an openly available "publication scheme" then the person making the request should first be guided by staff to check if the information is available through this scheme.

Legislation linked to FOI requests

In addition to the Freedom of Information act there are three regulations in UK that also apply to FOI Requests. The appropriate legislation in each individual case will depend of the type of information being asked for. These regulations are the:

*   Data Protection Act 2018 (and GDPR 2018) – provides access to information an organisation holds about an individual (a SAR).
*   Environmental Information Regulations 2004 – provides public access to environmental information held by public authorities.
*   INSPIRE Regulations 2009 – require public authorities to make any spatial or geographic information that they hold available to the public.

Charges for requests

Organisations may charge a fee for the cost of "disbursements" such photo-copying and postage. A public authority can charge for the time taken by its staff to answer the request using a flat rate of £25 per hour, irrespective of the salary of the member of staff. They may also charge for the time it takes a member of staff to actually redact the exempt information. If complying with a request would cost more than the £450 or £600 limit, the request can wither be refused outright or an extra charge made. If an organisation chooses to comply with a request costing over £450 or £600, they should only do so with written agreement from the requester that they will pay the extra costs.

If a fee is appropriate then the requester should be sent a fee notice. The organisation does not have to send the information until the fee has been received. The time limit for complying with the request excludes the time spent waiting for the fee to be paid.

Refusing a FOI request

If the authority decides that the information cannot be released it must tell the individual and explain why. FOI requests can only be refused on the following grounds:

- If the request is vexatious or repeated.
- If the cost of responding exceeds an appropriate limit (£450 or £600).
- If its release would prejudice national security.
- If its release would prejudice commercial interests.
- If the public interest in withholding the information outweighs the public interest in releasing it.
- If the request is for personal information (in which case a SAR would be appropriate).

Refusing a request for environmental information

The Regulation requires public organisations to have a publication scheme whereby they proactively publish environmental information (policies, plans and procedures relating to the environment, reports on the state of the environment, environmental impact studies and data from monitoring activities and risk assessments that affect or are likely to affect the environment).

EIR requests can only be refused on the following grounds

- If the request is for environmental data and the organisation does not hold the information.
- The information is archived and it is difficult to access.
- It is personal information and subject to Regulation 13.
- Part of the document is exempt from disclosure and publishing the redacted document would be impractical.

When a decision is taken not to publish information the reasons for this decision should be noted for future reference.

Format of a FOI response

It is commonly accepted practice to respond to a FOI request in the same format that the requester used. However, the requester has the right to ask for a preferred means of communication, in their request. Under equality law the organisation has a duty to make sure that its services are accessible to all service users. Therefore, request could be made for a particular format such as Braille, large print, email or audio format as well as email, as a printed copy, on a disk, or by viewing the information on site.

 Beware of forwarding electronic documents as these often contain extra hidden information or "metadata" in addition to the visible text of the document (this might include the name of the author, or details of earlier draft versions).

Further guidance

Further guidance on responding to a FOI request can be found on the Supervisory Authorities website. Those making a request should be aware that it will be much more effective if it is clear, specific, focused and unthreatening.

A flow chart for responding to FOI request is in Figure 13.3.

Accessing educational and medical records

If a request is made for information containing, in whole or in part, a pupil's "educational record" or a patient's "medical record" then industry specific constraints may be in place.

Access to medical and dental records

Certain practices in England offer a self-service portal where patients can view their medical/dental record. Where this is not available individuals may request access to their own records. The process is generally to make a verbal/written request for access to the record with the practitioner concerned. You would then be able to view the record on site. Should you require copies of the information you will need to make a subsequent request.

There is normally a £10 charge to see your records if they are in computerised format, if there are also manual records the fee could be up to £50. Charges for making copies of the information are decided by the practice.

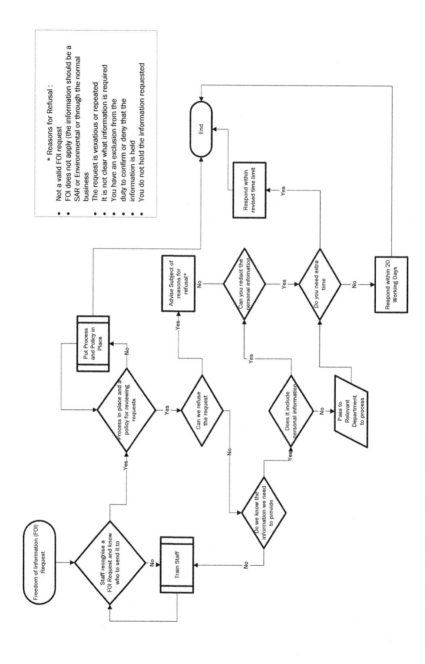

* Reasons for Refusal :

• Not a valid FOI request
• FOI does not apply (the information should be a SAR or Environmental or through the normal business
• The request is vexatious or repeated
• It is not clear what information is required
• You have an exclusion from the duty to confirm or deny that the information is held
• You do not hold the information requested

Figure 13.3 Flow Chart for Responding to a FOI Request

Educational records

Students (and their parents) who attend or attended a maintained educational establishment have the right to access their educational record. There is currently no such right of access to students attending free schools, academies or independent schools.

Where a request for educational record is made, a response must be provided within 15 school days.

The educational establishment may charge for answering the request (the amount will depend upon the number of pages of information which are to be supplied).

If a child is under 12 the person with parental authority may access their educational record (details of what you will be provided are listed by the school). If the child is over 12 the child's permission is required to provide a parent with access to the record. Should the pupil ask for their own educational record they may be charged for copying e.g. 1 to 19 pages will cost £1.20 up to a maximum of 500+ pages at a cost of £50.

The record will be produced as it is on the day of submission. Where possible it should be as up to date as possible. Schools may stipulate that requests should be made via by email to a specific mailbox.

 Different Member States have chosen to lower this age threshold to 15, 14 or 13. For more information of the age in each European state. See Resource Link 13.4.

Individuals' rights – exemptions

The right to be informed

When personal data was collected from the individual, you do not need to provide them with any information that they already have. When you have obtained personal data from other sources, you do not need to provide individuals with the information if:

- The individual already has the information.
- Providing the information would be impossible.
- Providing the information would involve a disproportionate effort.
- Providing the information would render impossible or impair the achievement of the objective of the processing.
- You are required by law to obtain or disclose the personal data.
- You are subject to an obligation of professional secrecy regulated by law that covers the personal data.

The right of access, rectification, erasure

You can refuse to comply with these requests only if they are manifestly unfounded or excessive, taking into account whether the request is repetitive in nature.

The right to restrict processing

The right to restrict processing applies when the subject has requested a rectification.

The right to data portability

The right to data portability only applies when the lawful basis for processing this information is consent or for the performance of a contract; and processing is by automated means (i.e. excluding paper files).

Can I require an individual to make a Subject Access Request?

In the UK it is a criminal offence, in certain circumstances and in relation to certain information, to require an individual to make a SAR.

> Supervisory Authorities are expected to provide further guidance on this offence in due course.

Chapter 14

GDPR training

GDPR requires organisations to make sure that anyone acting on their behalf who has access to personal data does not process that data unless they have been instructed to do so. It is therefore vital that everyone involved in processing the data understands the importance of protecting personal data and are familiar with the policies and procedures in place.

Every business will therefore need some type of GDPR awareness training. This way the organisation can ensure that everyone is aware of what the legislation is, how and why they need to comply with it and what they must do if a Data Subject contacts them to exercise their rights.

This chapter discusses the reason why staff training is required and the key points that should be covered as part of this training. To assist those who wish to conduct their own training there are a series of PowerPoint slide packs and a Game of "GDPR" Snakes and Ladders available on the companion website (www.pppmanagement.co.uk/resources).

Larger organisations or those with the time and funds to devote to classroom training courses may choose to obtain detailed practitioner training for DPOs, Risk and Compliance staff and senior management. There are a number of providers of these courses, which are offered both as classroom or online training. These courses are quite expensive and time consuming.

Other training is available via self-service style courses or companies who offer "in house" training solutions. National Supervisory Authorities also offer videos on their websites or YouTube channels. A simple internet search for "GDPR Training Videos" will bring up a selection of suitable presentations. Examples of companies offering GDPR foundation and practitioner training are included in the resources pack (Resource 14.1).

The requirement

GDPR explicitly states that **all** organisations develop some form of in-house GDPR awareness training for all their staff. This requirement for training is defined in Articles 39 and 47 of the GDPR (Article 39, EU GDPR, "Tasks of the data protection officer") and (Article 47, EU GDPR, "Binding corporate rules"). The exact text from the legislation is extracted in Quote 14.1.

QUOTE 14.1   ARTICLES 39(1) AND 47(2) OF GDPR – GDPR AWARENESS TRAINING

[The data protection officer shall] monitor compliance with this Regulation, with other Union or Member State data protection provisions and with the policies of the controller or processor in relation to the protection of personal data, including the assignment of responsibilities, awareness-raising and training of staff involved in processing operations, and the related audits;   Article 39 (1)b

[The binding corporate rules shall specify] the appropriate data protection training to personnel having permanent or regular access to personal data.   Article 47(2)n

The purpose of such training is to clearly explain the legislation and how it applies to your business. It will include information on what rights individuals have in relation to information you process and what you expect staff in your organisation to do when dealing with personal data.

Where possible some industry specific examples of Data Breaches should be included as well as guidance on the policies and processes that you have in place for data protection and security.

What should the training include?

On the companion website you will find slide decks to support this section. Appropriate initial and refresher training should include:

- The organisation's responsibilities as a Data Controller.
- Staff responsibilities for protecting personal data.
- Restrictions you have placed on the personal use of your systems by staff.
- Procedures used to identify callers.
- The dangers of people trying to obtain personal data by deception (e.g. "phishing" attacks).

Initial training key training points

The initial training of your staff on GDPR will depend on their level of knowledge. It should however cover elements of the following:

- What is GDPR, what has changed.
- What is meant by Processing Data.

  - Key terms.
  - Types of personal data your organisation processes and the lawful basis on which it is processed.
  - Data Controllers/Processors and the DPO.
  - Outline of the organisation's Privacy Policy (Policies).
  - Explanation of how data flows within the organisation.

- Data Security – Guidance for staff on handling, retaining, sharing and deleting data and the penalties for non-compliance.
- Individuals' Rights.

  - What rights individuals have.
  - Recognising, responding to and dealing with individuals exercising their data protection rights.
  - Marketing – what constitutes marketing and (terminology and rationale within the organisation).

- Where relevant discussion of International data transfers and third-party agreements and any related compliance areas such as Safe Harbour, PCI DSS, Cyber Essentials/Plus, ISO27001.

What is GDPR and what has changed from the previous legislation

GDPR is a European Union Regulation on data protection that came into effect on 25 May 2018. It protects the privacy of individuals living and working in the EU as well as those outside the EU whose data is processed in the EU.

GDPR is based on the principles of **lawfulness, fairness and transparency**. It centres on the simple concept that individuals have a right to privacy and a right to decide what happens to their personal data.

You should discuss the links between GDPR, national data protection legislation PECR and any other legislation such as the FOI that are relevant to your organisation.

What is meant by processing data?

GDPR defines processing in Article 4 (Article 4(2), EU GDPR, "Definitions"). The exact text from the legislation is extractedin Quote 14.2.

QUOTE 14.2   ARTICLE 4(2) OF GDPR – PROCESSING DATA

Any operation or set of operations which is performed on   Article 4(2)
personal data or on sets of personal data, whether or not by
automated means, such as collection, recording, organisation,
structuring, storage, adaptation or alteration, retrieval,
consultation, use, disclosure by transmission, dissemination or
otherwise making available, alignment or combination,
restriction, erasure or destruction.

Key terms

The key terms used in GDPR and data security should be understood by all. Table 14.1 shows the terminology that all staff should be familiar with.

To make the training more interesting you could devise your own "GDPR Bingo", which you use to reinforce the most important training points. The companion website has a series of GDPR Bingo Game Cards (www.pppmanagement.co.uk/resources).

Types of data that the organisation processes

Training should include a discussion of the types of data that the organisation holds and processes. This will ensure that every member of staff can identify who the Data Subjects are and what their (the staff member) role is in processing the data.

Table 14.1 GDPR Key Terms

Accountability	Consent	Data
Data Breach	Data Controller	Data Processor
Data Protection Authority	Data Protection Officer	Data Minimisation
Data Subject	Data Protection Impact Assessment	Information Society Service
Legal Person		Natural Person
Personally, identifiable Information	Privacy Impact Assessment	Privacy Notice
Profiling	Purpose Limitation	Recipient
Subject Access	Supervisory Authority	Third Party

Where appropriate you could include a review of the organisation's Privacy Policy (policies) or the latest Data Audit to develop understanding within the organisation (and to check for any errors).

If you collect a lot of personal data, you may choose to include a task for staff to complete. See Figure 14.1 "Our Organisation's Personal Data Honeycomb".

The organisation's lawful basis for processing

In particular it is important that the information is:

- Processed lawfully, fairly and in a transparent manner.
- Collected for specified, explicit and legitimate purposes and not further processed in a manner that is incompatible with those purposes.
- Adequate, relevant and limited to what is necessary in relation to the purposes for which they are processed.
- Accurate and, where necessary, kept up to date.
- Kept in a form that permits identification of Data Subjects for no longer than is necessary for the purposes for which the personal data are processed.

The lawful basis that your organisation has selected on which to process each element of personal information should be agreed. Staff should have a basic understanding of which of the following six lawful basis' for processing are relevant in their setting:

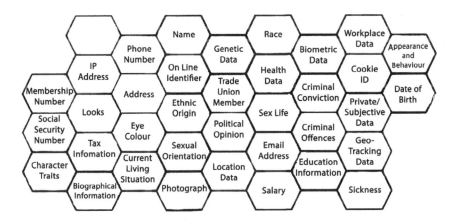

Figure 14.1 Our Organisation's Personal Data Honeycomb

- Consent.
- Contract.
- Legal obligation.
- Legitimate interests.
- Public task.
- Vital interests.

If you use consent then the Data Subject must understand completely what they are providing their data for, how it will be processed, who will process it and how long it will be stored. Your process for gaining consent must be clear and unambiguous and staff need to make this clear when gaining consent.

Accountability

Organisations are responsible for demonstrating that they comply with GDPR. Providing appropriate training for staff can be useful way of demonstrating compliance.

Data Controllers/Processors and the DPO

Staff should be clear what their role is in relation to the data they process. Who are the Controllers and Processors in their organisation? Where there are sub-Processors involved, staff in both organisations should understand the role of the other individuals.

Definitions of Controllers and Processors should be provided:

- A "Data Controller" is the person or organisation who (alone/jointly) determines why the data is going to be processed, what data should be processed and how it is processed.
- A "Data Processor" is any person (other than an employee of the Data Controller) who processes the data on behalf of the Data Controller. The Processor can decide the means and methods used to process the data and details of security and storage.

Where an organisation has a Data Protection Officer (DPO), the role of the DPO should be clearly explained to staff during training.

Privacy notices and policies

All organisations who process personal data will have a need for some form of Privacy Notice or Policy. It is good practice to ensure that your staff are aware of the Privacy Policies and notices that apply to the organisation and what impact this will have on their day to day work.

There should be a discussion of the way this information is provided (Signage, electronically, in writing, or in meetings/face to face).

Data flows

The way data flows into and out of the organisation will have been mapped as part of the Data Audit. Part of staff training should include an explanation of these data flows.

Guidance on handling, retaining, sharing and deleting data

Data must be processed in a manner that ensures appropriate security and staff should be aware of the need to protect against unauthorised or unlawful processing and against accidental loss, destruction or damage

Up-to-date tailored information on how you expect them to handle, share and delete data should be provided. Including their legal duty to keep customer information secure. Further help on this can be found in Chapters 9 to 13 and the accompanying Slide Decks.

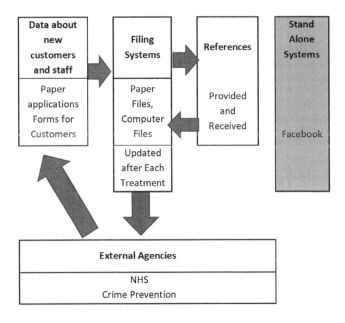

Figure 14.2 Data Flows

The UK ICO also have a video on Data Protection a link to which is Resource 14.2 in the Resources section.

Staff need to be aware of the fines the organisation could face and their role in making sure that breaches do not occur. It is recommended that staff are provided information on fines similar businesses have received to reinforce the need for them to take care in their data processing role.

Details of how the organisation uses marketing including direct under GDPR

Marketing became subject to more stringent constraints under GDPR and the Privacy and Electronic Communications Regulations 2003, the concept being that you cannot assume just because someone has asked for information from you in the past, that they are happy for you to contact them in the future.

Organisations are required to actively obtain explicit permission to contact individuals for marketing reasons in the future. Customers should specifically be given the option to opt in to newsletters and marketing material.

Staff training should be used as an opportunity to discuss with your staff how you do this in your organisation.

 Pre-ticked boxes that automatically opts them in aren't acceptable anymore.

Individuals have a right to ask you to remove them from marketing lists (if you are using consent as your legal basis). It is recommended that staff are aware of why you include an unsubscribe link as part of marketing emails.

Data minimisation

Train staff to only collect the information that they need. If the information is no longer required it should not be collected. Information that is no longer required should be disposed of it securely.

Individuals' rights

You should make sure that your staff understand that GDPR provides the following rights for individuals and what this means for the organisation:

- The right of access.
- Right of erasure.
- Right to be informed.
- Right of rectification.
- Right to restrict processing.

- The right to data portability.
- The right to object.
- Rights in relation to automated decision making and profiling.

You should provide guidance on how to recognise, respond to and deal with individuals exercising their data protection rights, such as:

- Subject Access Requests.
- Freedom of Information requests.
- Where appropriate access to their "personal record" (e.g. in a medical or educational setting).

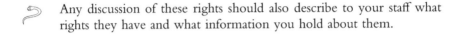 Any discussion of these rights should also describe to your staff what rights they have and what information you hold about them.

GDPR resource links

The resources and websites referred to in the book are listed here for easy reference.

Companion website

The book is supported by a companion website, which can be found at www.pppmanagement.co.uk/resources.

Websites

Authority	Country	Website
European Data Protection Authority		www.edps.europa.eu
National Supervisory Authorities	Austria	www.dsb.gv.at
	Belgium	www.privacycommission.be
	Bulgaria	www.cpdp.bg
	Croatia	www.azop.hr
	Cyprus	www.dataprotection.gov.cy
	Czech Republic	www.uoou.cz
	Denmark	www.datatilsynet.dk
	Estonia	www.aki.ee/en
	Finland	www.tietosuoja.fi/en/
	France	www.cnil.fr
	Germany*	www.bfdi.bund.de
	Greece	www.dpa.gr
	Hungary	www.naih.hu
	Iceland	postur@personuvernd.is
	Ireland	www.dataprotection.ie

Authority	Country	Website
	Italy	www.garanteprivacy.it
	Latvia	www.dvi.gov.lv
	Liechtenstein	info.dss@llv.li
	Lithuania	www.ada.lt
	Luxembourg	www.cnpd.lu
	Netherlands	https://autoriteitpersoonsgegevens.nl
	Malta	www.dataprotection.gov.mt
	Norway	postkasse@datatilsynet.no
	Poland	www.giodo.gov.pl/
	Portugal	www.cnpd.pt
	Romania	www.dataprotection.ro
	Slovakia	www.dataprotection.gov.sk
	Slovenia	www.ip-rs.si
	Spain	www.agpd.es
	Switzerland	contact20@edoeb.admin.ch
	Sweden	www.datainspektionen.se
	United Kingdom	https://ico.org.uk
European Commission Guidance	EU	https://ec.europa.eu/newsroom/article29/news.cfm?item_type=1360
UK National Cyber Security Centre	NCSC	https://ncsc.gov.uk

* Germany splits complaints among a number of different agencies, to understand which one applies: see www.bfdi.bund.de/bfdi_wiki/index.php/Aufsichtsbeh%C3%B6rden_und_Landesdatenschutzbe auftragte

Resources Referred to in the Text

Resource Link Number	Description	Link
Resource Link 1.1	UK ICO online questionnaire for businesses to assess their compliance with GDPR	https://ico.org.uk/for-organisations/resources-and-support/data-protection-self-assessment
Resource Link 1.2	List of EU supervising authorities	https://ec.europa.eu/justice/article-29/structure/data-protection-authorities
Resource Link 4.1	ICO tools and resources to help businesses	https://ico.org.uk/for-organisations/business

(Continued)

Resource Link Number	Description	Link
Resource Link 4.2	UK ICO Data Protection Registration tool and fee self-assessment tool	https://ico.org.uk/registration/new https://ico.org.uk/registration/payment https://ico.org.uk/for-organisations/data-protection-fee/self-assessment/
Resource Link 4.3	UK ICO online self-assessment checklist to improve understanding of data protection	https://ico.org.uk/for-organisations/making-data-protection-your-business/
Resource 5.1	UK and French SA tools	https://ico.org.uk/for-organisations/gdpr-resources/ https://www.cnil.fr/en/search/tools
Resource Link 5.2	Register of UK businesses who have registered with the UK ICO	https://ico.org.uk/about-the-ico/what-we-do/register-of-fee-payers/
Resource Link 6.1	UK ICO guide on what is and what is not personal data	https://ico.org.uk/for-organisations/guide-to-data-protection/guide-to-the-general-data-protection-regulation-gdpr/what-is-personal-data/
Resource Link 7.1	The UK ICO one-page privacy notice checklist	https://ico.org.uk/media/for-organisations/documents/1625126/privacy-notice-checklist.pdf
Resource Link 8.1	The EDPB description of where a SME is exempt from the need to document their processing	https://ec.europa.eu/newsroom/article29/item-detail.cfm?item_id=624045
Resource Link 8.2	The UK Information and Records Management Society guidance on records management including retention and disposal	https://irms.org.uk/page/RetentionWiki
Resource Link 8.3	The UK National Archives (TNA) guidance on records management including retention and disposal	www.nationalarchives.gov.uk/information-management/manage-information/policy-process/disposal/advice-on-retention/

Resource Link Number	Description	Link
Resource Link 8.4	The French CNIL ROPA tool	www.cnil.fr/en/record-processing-activities
Resource Link 8.5	The UK Documentation of Processing Activities tool	https://ico.org.uk/for-organisations/guide-to-data-protection/guide-to-the-general-data-protection-regulation-gdpr/documentation/how-do-we-document-our-processing-activities/
Resource Link 9.1	UK ICO direct marketing self-assessment checklist	https://ico.org.uk/for-organisations/data-protection-self-assessment/direct-marketing-checklist/
Resource Link 9.2	The UK ICO Direct Marketing document Guidance	https://ico.org.uk/media/for-organisations/documents/1555/direct-marketing-guidance.pdf
Resource Link 10.1	List of fines and penalties throughout EU for GDPR breaches	https://edpb.europa.eu/news/national-news/2019_en
Resource Link 11.1	The UK National Cyber Security Centre Cyber Essentials scheme	www.cyberessentials.ncsc.gov.uk/
Resource Link 13.1	The UK ICO Subject Access Request Code of Practice	https://ico.org.uk/media/2259722/subject-access-code-of-practice.pdf
Resource Link 13.2	The UK ICO guidance on children and the GDPR	https://ico.org.uk/for-organisations/guide-to-data-protection/key-data-protection-themes/children/
Resource Link 13.3	The UK "Freedom of Information Code of Practice"	www.gov.uk/government/publications/freedom-of-information-code-of-practice
Resource Link 13.4	Age thresholds for EU Member states;	www.betterinternetforkids.eu/web/portal/practice/awareness/detail?articleId=3017751
Resource Link 14.1	Companies offering GDPR foundation and practitioner training	www.itgovernance.co.uk www.focus-on-training.co.uk/data-protection-gdpr-training/ www.highspeedtraining.

(Continued)

Resource Link Number	Description	Link
		co.uk/business-skills/ gdpr-training.aspx
Resource Link 14.2	UK ICO Video about data protection	www.youtube.com/watch? v=7w9MQzwN4bQ
Resource Link 14.3	Game GDPR Jeopardy	https://www.mediapro. com/this-is-gdpr-jeopardy/
Resource Link 14.4	Link to Companion Website Training	www.pppmanagement.co. uk/resources

Index

A–Z of terminology 26
ability 26, 236
accuracy 3, 4, 7, 8, 23, 35, 93–94, 99, 102, 120, 162, 177, 196, 212
adequacy 2, 40, 41, 62–63, 136
adequate 3, 4, 10, 23, 35, 62, 105, 235
anonymised/anonymisation 7, 10, 119, 127, 129, 164, 177, 205
antivirus 175, 201
applying GDPR to your organisation 83–100
archive/archiving 26, 203, 205, 208, 242
Articles of GDPR: Article 1 28, 34; Article 2 34, 184; Article 3 34; Article 4 16, 20, 22, 34, 87, 103, 110, 117, 121, 126, 143, 233, 234; Article 5 3, 4, 16, 35, 149, 193; Article 6 16, 35, 121, 122, 135, 136, 168; Article 7 36, 144; Article 8 36; Article 9 16, 37, 114, 121, 123, 124, 125; Article 10 38, 123, 126; Article 11–12 38; Article 13 39; Article 14 41; Article 15 42; Article 16 43; Article 17 43, 208; Article 18 45; Article 19–21 46; Article 22 25, 47, 213; Article 23 48, 122; Article 24 16, 49, 104; Article 25 49; Article 26–27, 50; Article 28 16, 50, 111, 112; Article 29 52; Article 30, 52, 89, 107, 149; Article 31 53; Article 32 53, 106, 112, 149; Article 33 53; Article 34 19, 54; Article 35 16, 55, 167, 168; Article 36 56; Article 37 16, 56, 114; Article 38–39 57; Article 40 58, 106; Article 41 59; Article 42 60; Article 43 61; Article 44–45 62; Article 46 63; Article 47 64; Article 48 66; Article 49 66; Article 50–53 67; Article 54–57 68; Article 58–60 70; Article 61–62 72; Article 63–65 73; Article 66–70 74; Article 71–75 75; Article 76–80 76; Article 81–83 77; Article 84–88 79; Article 89 80; Article 90–94 81; Article 95–99 82
Articles/recitals cross reference 31
attack 201
attacker 201
Austria 13, 188
automated decision making 25, 43, 47–48, 138, 213, 222; right to object 46, 213

backup 198, 210
backup systems: erasure from 210
Belgium 13, 240
binding corporate rules 26 63–65, 73, 232
biometric data 20, 26, 125
Bisnode 10, 188
botnet 201
Brexit 1, 2
Bring Your Own Device 198
British Airways 10, 186–187
Bulgaria 13, 240

CCTV 2, 94, 101, 108, 128, 134, 197, 211
certification 60; bodies 61
changing behaviour 5
children: consent 36; requests 220; rights 207
churches and religious associations 36, 81; rules for 36, 81
click farm 201
code of conduct 49, 51, 53, 58–59, 64, 69, 73, 104–106, 113, 168; monitoring 59
common identifiers 121
communication 98; of data breach 54

competence 68
complaint 17, 41, 59, 61, 65, 68, 69,
    70–71, 76, 140, 171, 188, 216, 241; to
    Supervisory Authority 39, 40, 41, 76
compliance 9; as an ongoing journey 11;
    demonstrating 3, 4, 8, 23, 26, 35, 36,
    38, 39, 47, 50, 51, 53, 55, 60, 104–105,
    112, 125, 140, 147, 149, 151, 153, 168,
    193; improving 6; proportionate 11,
    38, 42, 46, 48–49, 54, 77, 104, 122,
    124, 210, 229; timescales 208, 218;
    who has to comply 6
confidentiality 28; European Data
    Protection Board 76
confirming identity 209, 221
consent 8, 10, 12, 16, 19, 20, 22–23, 25,
    26, 29, 35, 36–37, 40, 41, 44, 45, 46,
    47, 48, 58, 66, 78, 93, 95, 106,
    121–123, 125, 136, 138, 141–145, 153,
    177–184, 201, 207, 213–218, 236, 238;
    children 36; cookies; definition 22;
    withdrawing 136, 138, 214
consistency 33, 70, 73
cookies 127, 144, 145, 213; consent 145
cooperation and consistency 33, 53, 70;
    international 67
Crown Prosecution Service 10
Croatia 13, 240
cross-border processing 22
customers, previous 179
cyber: essentials 197; incident 201;
    security measures 9, 197
Cyprus 13, 241
Czech Republic 13, 240

dashcams 162, 211
data access 24, 42, 80, 213, 217, 220, 221,
    229, 230, 238; by individuals 214;
    establishing who has access 93, 84, 94,
    151, 153, 154, 157, 160–166, 231;
    public access to official documents 26,
    79, 225; individual's rights 142; requests
    24, 30, 103, 223, 234
data audit 11, 14, 19, 58, 84, 91, 94–95,
    132, 133, 148, 150–167, 190, 235, 237;
    goals 156; time to complete 151
Data Breach 8, 9, 10, 26, 28, 51, 53–54,
    58, 87, 96, 105, 106, 108, 111, 140,
    159, 185–192, 232, 234;
    communication 54; cost of recovery
    9,196; fines 10, 77, 78, 187; log 20;
    notification 58, 71, 72, 75, 79, 105,

111, 186, 189; planning for 18;
    reducing risk 9; reporting 108,
    186–192; responding 96
data collection information 142
Data Controller 18–19, 26–27, 30, 38–39,
    43–44, 47–50, 53–54, 70, 76–77,
    86–87, 101–110, 111, 162, 170, 193,
    198, 218, 222–223, 232, 234, 236;
    decisions 103; registering as 12, 109;
    representative 29, 41, 50, 52, 104, 107,
    113, 136, 138, 149; responsibilities 18,
    104; training 236
data flow: diagram 90; understanding 152
data governance policy 184
data handling 237
data minimisation 4, 7, 26, 49, 93, 97,
    102, 105, 177, 203, 206, 234
Data Processors 2, 8, 18, 19, 26–30, 32,
    34, 37, 49–53, 54, 56, 57–58, 60–61,
    63–64, 65, 68–69, 70–72, 76–78, 79,
    81, 86, 87, 90–91, 93, 101–116, 129,
    140, 149–150, 161, 164–166, 168, 170,
    185, 195, 223, 232–234; decisions 111;
    main establishment 28, 71, 73;
    representative 29, 41, 50, 52, 104, 107,
    113, 136, 138, 149; responsibilities 110,
    112; training 236
data protection: by design and default 27,
    49, 60, 97, 105, 167; certification 60;
    policies 49, 58, 84, 104, 197; training
    65, 97, 179, 232
Data Protection Acts 1, 5: 1998 Act 85;
    2018 Act 1, 5, 225
Data Protection Authority 13, 14, 16, 27,
    143, 234, 240
Data Protection Impact Assessment 27,
    55–56, 58, 104, 167, 169
Data Protection Officer 1, 8, 17–19, 27,
    39, 41, 52, 54, 56–58, 65, 70, 84, 93,
    101–113, 114–116, 105, 113–115, 136,
    138, 143, 149–150, 189, 190, 192, 196,
    231, 232, 233, 234, 236; appointment
    115; impartiality 115; position 57;
    responsibilities 114;
    tasks 57, 116; training 236;
    who needs one 115
data retention 97, 135, 164–165, 179,
    203; how long to keep data 8, 22, 86,
    98, 100, 105, 133, 135, 138, 142, 151,
    154, 163–164, 177, 189, 203, 218, 220,
    222, 236; reviewing retention periods
    205; standard retention period 164, 204

data security 165–166, 184, 195–197, 233, 234; identification of risks 195; terms 200–201; what it means 195

data sharing 142; guidance 237

Data Subject 3, 4, 7, 8, 10, 12, 18, 19, 22, 23, 26, 27, 29, 30, 34, 35–38, 38–49, 50, 51, 53, 54, 55, 56, 57, 58, 59, 60, 61, 63–64, 64–65, 66, 69–70, 72, 76, 78, 79, 80, 83–84, 87, 89, 93, 98, 105, 106, 107, 112, 113, 114, 115, 116, 117, 121–124, 125, 127, 130, 135–136, 140, 142, 143, 144, 150, 157, 164–166, 168, 169, 188, 190, 192, 196, 203, 204, 205, 209, 210, 212, 215, 217, 223, 231, 234, 235, 236; information required by 39, 41, 135–137; representation 76; rights and freedoms 4, 7, 18, 43, 46, 48, 49, 53, 54, 68, 79, 93, 96, 104, 105, 107, 108, 113, 122, 124, 148, 150, 158, 159, 161–166, 168, 186, 189, 191, 205, 223

data transfer 9, 26, 27, 30, 40, 41, 43, 49, 62, 63, 66, 73, 79, 82, 87, 106, 107, 111, 135, 136, 144, 175, 176

deceased persons 127

definitions 22, 34, 87, 102, 103, 110, 117, 126, 143, 234; consent 22; controller 103; occasional 147; personal data 87, 117; processor 110; processing 126, 233

delegation 81

deletion 7, 8, 10, 51, 87, 94, 96, 97, 98, 111, 112, 160, 163, 171, 172, 173, 177, 180, 196, 203, 206, 207, 208, 210, 211, 223, 237

denial of service 201

Denmark 14, 240

derogations 36, 66, 80

digital footprint 201

direct identification 128, 129, 130

direct marketing 7, 47, 142–143, 170, 178–179, 207, 213, 243

documenting decisions 12, 125, 204, 243

document protection, simple 175–176

DPA *see* Data Protection Act 1998

educational records 22, 98, 120, 203, 208, 214, 217, 227, 229, 239

email 8, 11, 88–99, 119, 129, 131, 142–143, 150, 166, 170–180, 183, 184, 202, 214, 215, 221, 224, 238; blind carbon copy (BCC) 173; business to business (B2B) 179; encryption 176–177; forwarding 172; security 184;

sending multiple emails 174; tracking 177–178; using "to" and "cc" 172

encrypted data 10, 27, 96, 162, 175, 176, 185

end of the life of the data 165

erasure and rectification 8, 25, 38, 40, 41, 43, 46, 80, 135, 213, 222, 230, 238; receiving a request 208; request check list 13, 209; shared data 210; when the right to erasure does not apply 207

Estonia 14, 240

ethnicity 84, 125, 129

European Data Protection Board 5, 58–61, 69, 71, 73–76, 81, 113, 242, 243; chair 75; committee procedure 81; confidentiality 76; dispute resolution 73; opinion 73; procedure 75; reports 75; secretariat 75; tasks of the board 74; tasks of the chair 75

European Data Protection Supervisor 6, 75

EU-US Privacy Shield 27

exceptions 1, 125, 147

exemptions 109, 208, 217, 229; organisations 85, 109

Facebook 9, 90, 92, 153, 155, 186–188

fairness principle 3, 4, 11, 23, 27, 35, 58, 102, 106, 122, 164, 203, 233, 235

filing system 27, 90, 153

fines: for data breaches 10, 77, 78, 187; general conditions 77; higher maximum amount 9; standard maximum amount 9; substantial 4; tiers 9

Finland 14, 188, 240

firewall 201

France 6, 10, 14, 84, 187, 240

freedom of expression 36 44, 45, 73, 79, 207

Freedom of Information 6, 14, 214, 215, 224 227, 239; act 224; charges 225; format for response 227; guidance 227, 239; individual rights 224; legislation 225; refusal 226; request 98, 214, 215; time limit 225

GDPR: application 19, 30, 65, 67–68, 82–83; Article 31–33, 34–82, 106, 112, 151, 232; awareness 24, 83, 87–88, 231–232; basic concept 3; building

blocks 83; consent 143; controller and processor 49; cooperation and consistency 33, 70; delegated acts and implementing acts 33, 81; entry into force 82; final provisions 33, 81; general provisions 31, 34; introduction to 1; principles 1, 3, 35; simple concept 1, 18, 233; Supervisory Authorities 67; training 88, 231; what it is 1–12, 233
general obligations 49
general provisions 31, 34
genetic data 20, 21, 28, 30, 37, 87, 117, 123, 124, 125, 128, 131
Germany 6, 9, 10, 14, 17, 67, 84, 241
Greece 14, 143, 240

hacker 201
Haga hospital 10, 187
health data 10, 20, 26, 28–30, 37–38, 44, 48, 56, 80, 84, 89, 95, 101, 123–126, 129, 131, 142, 148, 152, 160, 164, 203, 207
health spa 148
honeypot 201
Hungary 14, 240

Iceland 17 30, 240
ICO see UK ICO
indirect identification 2, 19, 28, 87, 101, 117, 126, 128, 129
individual rights 7, 8, 34, 135, 138, 212, 213: access 24, 42, 80, 142, 213, 217, 220, 221, 229, 230, 238; compensation 77; complaint to Supervisory Authority 39, 40, 41, 76; exercising rights 98; exemptions 22; of erasure (also known as right to be forgotten) 24, 43, 80, 97, 206, 207, 208, 211, 213, 238; requesting access 213; to their data 24, 98; to data portability 25, 40, 41, 46, 80, 213, 230, 239; to information 24, 43, 213, 224, 229; to judicial remedy 39, 76; to object 25, 40, 41, 46, 47, 80, 135, 142, 213, 239; to object to automated decision-making 46, 213; to rectification 43, 80; to redress 142, 213; to restrict processing 25, 45, 80, 213, 230, 238; to withdraw consent 36, 138, 214
individuals: content about 120; data access 214; identification by name 127; identification in order to respond 127, 129, 130, 209, 221; methods of identification 128; relating data to 119; responsibilities 97
information: about children 220; collection 142; exchange 74, 75; individuals' rights to 24, 43, 213, 224, 229; including details about others 216; layered approach 12, 134, 140; personally identifiable information (pii) 28; presenting 137; providing 212; required by data subjects 39, 41, 135–137; selling on 7; Information Society Services 28, 36–37, 44, 207, 234; sharing electronically 96, 97, 170–184; sources 88; storage 142; understanding 11
Information Commissioner see UK ICO
internet of things 201
Ireland 6, 9, 15, 84, 187, 221, 241
ISO 27001/2:2013 199, 200
Italy 6, 10, 15, 241

Joint Controller 50, 52, 107, 108, 149

keeping data safe 94, 193–202
key terms 18–30, 234
keylogger 201

La Liga 10, 187
Latvia 15, 241
lawful basis (for processing) 3, 7, 12, 22–24, 93, 121, 132, 135, 138, 141, 143, 151, 153–154, 158–161, 164–166, 180, 230, 233, 235
legal person 19, 26–29, 45, 66, 103, 110, 118, 234
legitimate interests 28, 35, 40–42, 58, 106, 121, 125, 136–138, 168, 179, 236
Liechtenstein 17, 241
list of registered organisations 109
Lithuania 15, 241
living human 19, 117
Luxembourg 15, 241

main establishment 28, 71, 73
Malta 15, 241
malvertising 201
malware 201
Marriott 10, 187
material scope 34
medical practices 148, 215
medical records 227

messenger 184
monitoring bodies 59–60
mutual assistance 67, 70, 72

National Supervisory Authorities 21, 5,
    13, 240–241; Austria 13; Belgium 13;
    Bulgaria 13; Croatia 13; Cyprus 13;
    Czech Republic 13; Denmark 14;
    Estonia 14; Finland 14; France 14;
    Germany 14; Greece 14; Hungary 14;
    Iceland 17; Ireland 15; Italy 15; Latvia
    15; Liechtenstein 17; Lithuania 15;
    Luxembourg 15; Malta 15; Netherlands
    15; Norway 17; Poland 16; Portugal
    16; Romania 16; Slovakia 16; Slovenia
    16; Spain 16; Switzerland 17; United
    Kingdom 14
natural person 19, 26, 28, 29, 35, 62,
    87, 104, 117, 121, 123, 165, 167, 184,
    234
Netherlands 6, 10, 15, 187, 241
Norway 17, 30, 188, 241

obligation of secrecy 81, 124
office CCTV 108
online help and guidance 99, 250
online identifiers 127, 128
opinion 59, 69, 73, 74, 120, 225, 221
opt in 180
opt out 180
organisation tiers: tier 1 85;
    tier 2 86; tier 3 86

password protection 96, 175, 176, 183,
    192, 196, 201, 202; strength 202
patching 201
penalties 8, 33, 34, 48, 76, 79, 107, 186,
    233, 243
penetration testing 199
pentest 202
people or entities, definition 18
personal data 1–10, 13–30, 32, 34–51
    53–59, 62, 63–67, 70, 78, 198–236;
    analysis 117; definition 87, 117;
    examples 89; movement 90; types of
    19, 20, 21, 88, 117, 118, 136, 152, 160,
    186, 233; what is held 157
pharming 202
phishing 202
physical security measures 165, 183,
    195–197; testing 199
point of contact 501, 143

Poland 16, 241
political opinions 20, 37, 123, 125
Portugal 16, 241
powers 2, 67, 70, 72, 74
previous legislation 233
principles 1, 3–5, 9, 23, 27, 31,
    35, 49, 102, 104, 137, 149,
    193, 206, 233
prior consultation 55, 56
privacy impact assessment 26, 29, 234
privacy notices and privacy policies 8, 12,
    26, 29, 83, 84, 93, 99, 134, 135, 137,
    140–141, 177, 179, 222, 233–236
processing 1, 3, 4, 7, 12, 18–30; by
    a Controller/Processor 52, 110;
    cross-border 22; definition 102; for
    employment 37, 125, 217; lawful basis
    3, 7; national identification numbers
    36, 79; non-occasional 17, 148, 150;
    objections 29, 47, 71, 73, 81, 135;
    occasional 50, 107, 118, 147, 148;
    purpose 19, 42, 43, 52, 93, 120; reason
    for 38, 159, 160; Record of Processing
    Activities 52, 107, 113, 147, 149, 151,
    242; restriction of 25, 45, 80, 213, 230,
    238; security 53, 58, 105, 106, 113,
    168; under the authority of
    a controller/processor 52, 110
profiling 47
protecting large files 175
pseudonymisation 22, 29, 53, 58,
    105–106, 114, 123, 127, 198, 204–206
public sector publication schemes 225
purpose limitation 4, 29, 122, 234
purpose and means 26, 50, 51, 56,
    103, 108, 110
pwned 202

race 21, 84, 125, 129, 131, 160
ransomware 202
recitals 31–33
recipient 19, 28, 29, 41, 42., 46, 64, 136,
    138, 171, 173–177, 180, 185, 202, 210,
    234
Record of Processing Activities 52, 107,
    113, 147, 149, 151, 242
references 90, 157, 159, 162, 166, 196
refusing a request 210, 216, 226
registers of fee payers 5, 109, 242
registration: under previous legislation
    84; tiers 85
relating data to the individual 119

relationship with other matters: directive
    2002/58/EC 82; previously concluded
    agreements 82
religious or philosophical beliefs 20, 30,
    37, 84, 123, 125, 142
remedies, liability and penalties 33, 63, 76
repeal of directive 95/46/EC 81
re-permissioning 182, 183
reports: activity reports 70; commission
    reports 82; European Data Protection
    Board 75; data breach 108, 186–192
representative 29, 41, 50, 52, 104, 107,
    113, 136, 138, 149
resource links 240
requests: charging for 211, 216, 225;
    checklist 209; information about
    children 220; large amounts of data 220;
    on behalf of others 220
responsibility: Controller 49, 60, 104,
    106, 108, 149, 162; enforcement 5;
    Processor 51, 60; organisation 220;
    parental 37, 58, 98, 106, 157,
    215, 220, 221
restrictions 25, 48, 213, 232
retaining data 10, 97–98, 177, 203–206,
    211, 237
review of other union acts 82
risks: analysis 94; to data 55, 127,
    194–195; to rights and freedoms 936,
    148, 191; reduction 9;
    understanding 94
Romania 16, 241

safeguards and derogations:
    archiving 36, 80
sanitisation 202
schools 148, 224, 229
sensitive data 20, 89, 102, 160, 175
sex life/sexual orientation 37, 123,
    125, 131
Slovakia 16, 241
Slovenia 16, 241
small businesses 102, 107, 147, 151, 186;
    SME 148, 242; statistics 194
software as a service 202
Spain 6, 16, 187, 241
spear-phishing 202
special categories of data 20, 27,
    30, 50, 53, 55, 56, 78, 84,
    88, 107, 113, 114, 121, 123–125, 133,
    137, 141, 150, 207

spoofing 202
staff training see training
subject access 24, 30, 103, 223, 234
Subject Access Request 7, 8, 39, 98,
    212, 213, 214, 215, 218, 222,
    230; charging for 216; format of 215,
    218; identification of requestor 218;
    process (flow chart 218); response
    216, 220, 222–223, 227, 228, 233;
    UK ICO Code of Practice 243;
    what to include in a response
    222
subject matter 34, 59, 78, 102
sub-processor 51, 90, 111, 161, 236
substantial fine 4
Supervisory Authority 6, 12, 13–17, 19,
    23, 25, 30, 40, 41, 43, 45, 52–65,
    67–78, 81, 83–85, 96, 105, 107–109,
    113, 115–116, 135, 138, 142,
    150, 168, 186, 187–192, 210,
    213, 216, 222, 234; advisory powers
    70; complaints to 39, 40, 41, 76;
    independence 67; lead 68, 70;
    registering with 12, 84
suspension of proceedings 77
Switzerland 17, 241

taking data "offline" 206
TalkTalk 186
Taxa 4x35 10
terminology 18–30
territorial scope 30, 34, 63
third countries 9, 32, 40–43, 52, 59, 60,
    62–64, 66–67, 73, 79, 82, 105–107,
    112, 136, 138, 149, 150, 222; transfers
    to 62
third party 19, 30, 156, 157, 166, 182,
    185, 188, 217, 218, 220, 224
time to respond 38, 72, 225, 229
trade bodies or associations 105,
    156, 164
Trade Union membership 20, 21, 30, 37,
    123, 125, 131
training 9, 57, 58, 65, 75, 88, 97,
    99, 116, 157, 179, 190, 192,
    193, 195, 197, 200, 217, 218, 222,
    231–239, 243
transparency 3, 4, 8, 10, 23, 24, 27, 35,
    38, 39, 58, 60, 61, 67, 98, 102, 106,
    134, 137, 153, 177, 213, 223, 224,
    233, 235

Trojan 202
two-factor authentication 202

UK Data Protection Act 1
UK ICO 5, 6, 7, 17, 21, 84, 85,
    86, 94, 96, 97, 105, 108, 109, 111, 113,
    121, 135, 137, 140, 173, 179, 180, 187,
    189, 215, 225, 238, 241–244; self-
    assessment
    checklist 99
unambiguous 22, 26, 98, 143, 145, 236
understand the information held 11
understanding data 8, 88

United Kingdom 1, 2, 5, 6, 7, 9, 10, 17,
    37, 84, 85, 97, 99, 105, 107, 109, 121,
    135, 137, 173, 178, 179, 187, 197, 215,
    224, 225, 230, 238, 241–243
urgency procedure 72, 74

vigilance 9
vulnerability scanning 199

water-holing 202
whaling 202
WhatsApp 184
whitelisting 202

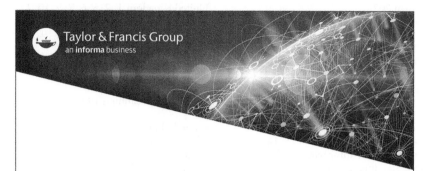

For Product Safety Concerns and Information please contact our EU
representative GPSR@taylorandfrancis.com Taylor & Francis Verlag GmbH,
Kaufingerstraße 24, 80331 München, Germany

Printed and bound by CPI Group (UK) Ltd, Croydon, CR0 4YY

01/05/2025

01858387-0003